How to Understand Israel In 60 Days or Less

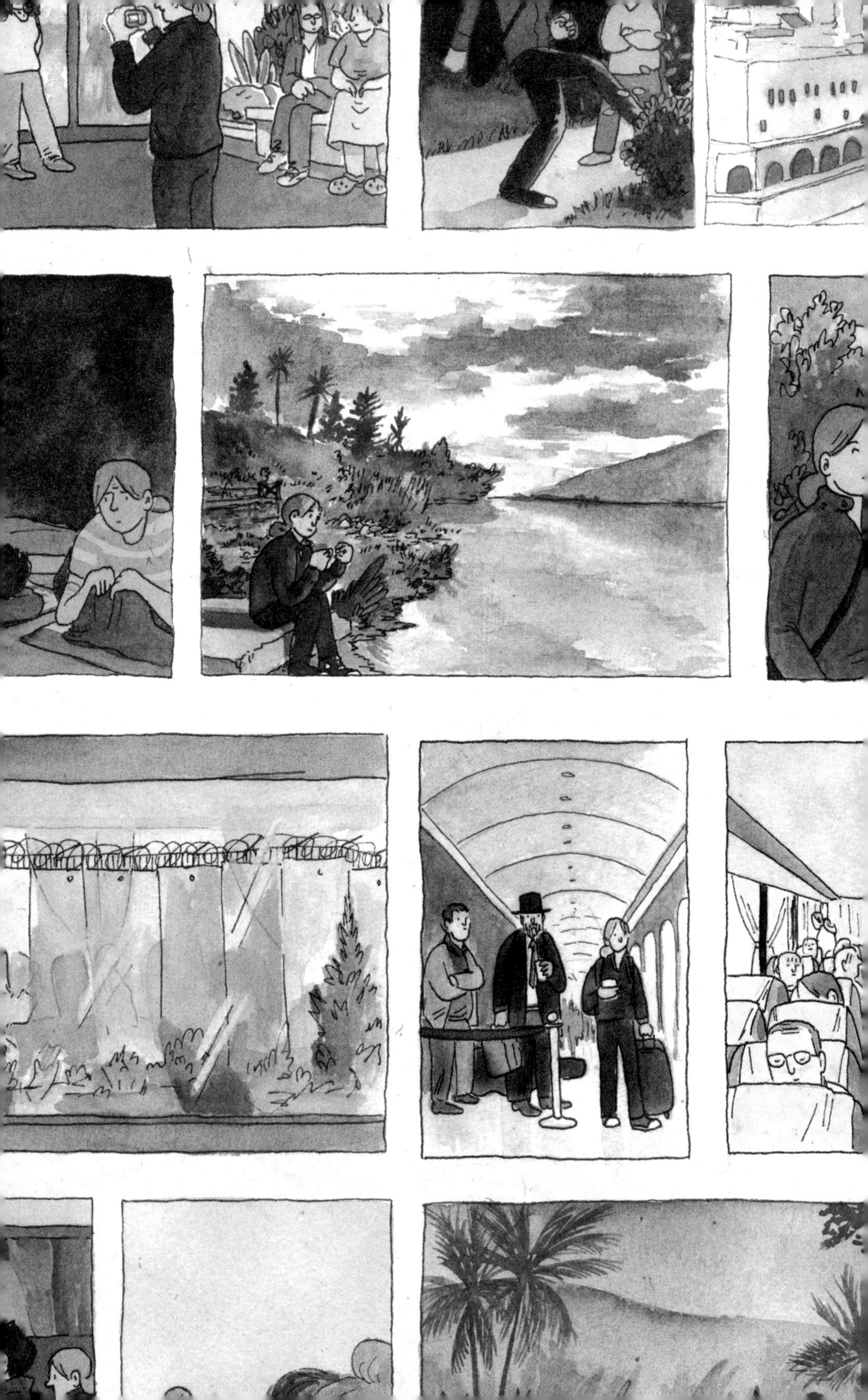

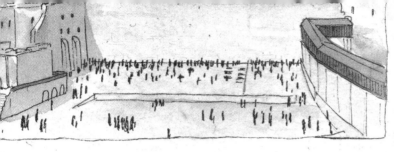

HOW TO UNDERSTAND ISRAEL
IN 60 DAYS OR LESS

Writer & Artist: Sarah Glidden
Letterer: Clem Robins

Photo by Clément Louis

Dedication: For Stephen

Thank-yous go out to Julia Wertz, Tom Hart, Tim Kreider, Jason Little, Nadan Feldman, Emily Brandt, Dylan Williams, Alec Longstreth, AWP, Chen Tamir, Bob Mecoy, Jonathan Vankin, Bill Frankel, L'Entreprise Culturelle, WOAH Gallery Berlin and my family.

And very special thanks to Jamil Zaki.

– Sarah Glidden

Sarah Glidden was born in Boston in 1980. Her comics have appeared in numerous anthologies and she has received an Ignatz Award and a Maisie Kukoc Award for her minicomics. *How to Understand Israel in 60 Days or Less* is her first book. Sarah lives and works in Brooklyn.

Author's Note:
The reader should be aware that this is a memoir. Certain conversations and timelines have been altered either due to the decay of memory or in order to suit the narrative but always in keeping with an earnest intent to honestly describe the author's experience of events as they occurred.

Karen Berger SVP-Executive Editor   **Jonathan Vankin** Editor   **Sarah Litt** Asst. Editor
Robbin Brosterman Design Director-Books   **Louis Prandi** Art Director

DC COMICS
Diane Nelson President   **Dan DiDio** and **Jim Lee** Co-Publishers   **Geoff Johns** Chief Creative Officer
John Rood Executive Vice President-Sales, Marketing and Business Development
Patrick Caldon Executive Vice President-Finance and Administration   **Amy Genkins** Senior VP-Business and Legal Affairs
Steve Rotterdam Senior VP-Sales and Marketing   **John Cunningham** VP-Marketing
Terri Cunningham VP-Managing Editor   **Alison Gill** VP-Manufacturing   **David Hyde** VP-Publicity
Sue Pohja VP-Book Trade Sales   **Alysse Soll** VP-Advertising and Custom Publishing
Bob Wayne VP-Sales   **Mark Chiarello** Art Director

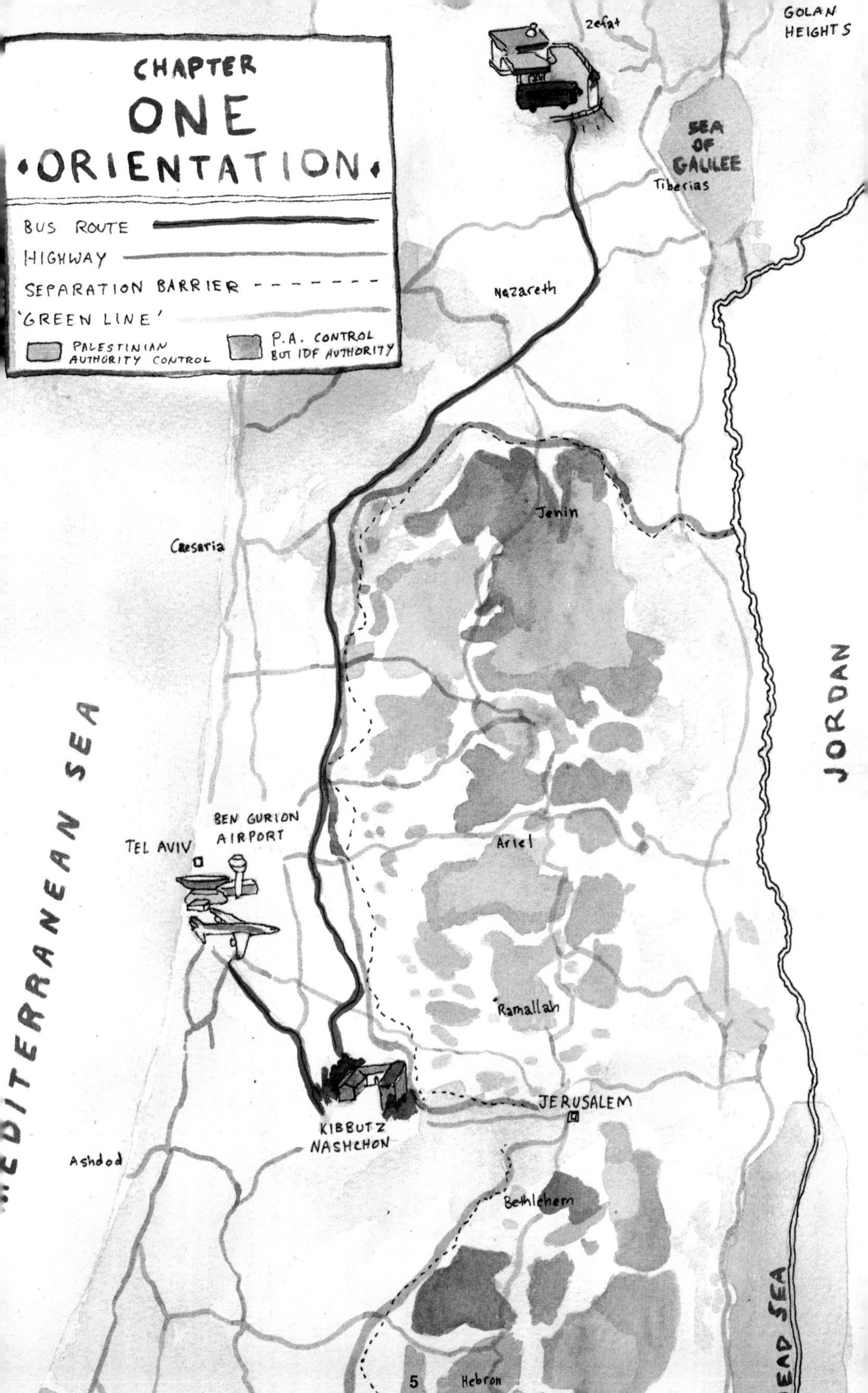
CHAPTER
ONE
•ORIENTATION•
BUS ROUTE
HIGHWAY
SEPARATION BARRIER
'GREEN LINE'
PALESTINIAN AUTHORITY CONTROL
P.A. CONTROL BUT IDF AUTHORITY
Zefat
GOLAN HEIGHTS
SEA OF GALILEE
Tiberias
Nazareth
Jenin
Caesaria
MEDITERRANEAN SEA
JORDAN
BEN GURION AIRPORT
TEL AVIV
Ariel
Ramallah
JERUSALEM
KIBBUTZ NASHCHON
Ashdod
Bethlehem
DEAD SEA
Hebron

HMMMM...

SHOULD I JUST LEAVE THESE BEHIND THEN?

A HISTORY OF THE ISRAELI-PALESTINIAN CONFLICT

WRESTLING WITH ZION

YEAH, GIVE IT A REST. YOU'LL BE TOO BUSY SEEING THE REAL THING TO HAVE TIME TO READ ABOUT IT.

YOU'RE RIGHT. I GUESS THAT'S IT, THEN.

OKAY, JAMIL, I'M READY TO GO THERE AND DISCOVER THE TRUTH BEHIND THIS WHOLE MESS ONCE AND FOR ALL. IT'LL ALL BE CRYSTAL CLEAR BY THE TIME I COME BACK!

WONDERFUL! THAT MEANS WE WON'T HAVE TO TALK ABOUT IT ANYMORE, RIGHT?

I KNOW I'VE BEEN A LITTLE FIXATED ON THIS STUFF FOR THE PAST MONTH--

MONTH AND A HALF.

--RIGHT. WELL, I HAD A LOT TO CATCH UP ON. AND I NEEDED TO BE PREPARED FOR WHATEVER PROPAGANDA THEY TRY AND THROW AT ME!

IF THAT'S WHAT IT TAKES TO GUARANTEE THAT YOU DON'T COME BACK A BRAINWASHED, RAGING ZIONIST, READY TO DUMP YOUR "GOY" BOYFRIEND, THEN IT WAS WORTH IT.

I DON'T THINK YOU HAVE TO WORRY ABOUT THAT.

NEWARK EXPRESS

AIRPORT EXPRESS

EXCUSE ME, IS THIS THE ISRAEL EXPERTS BIRTHRIGHT GROUP?

SURE IS! WHAT'S YOUR NAME?

SARAH.

HEY THERE! I'M SHARON AND I'LL BE YOUR GROUP LEADER.

SARAH...SARAH GLIDDEN? YEP, HERE YOU ARE. OKAY, WHY DON'T YOU GO AHEAD AND GET QUESTIONED SO YOU CAN CHECK IN?

QUESTIONED?

YEAH, EL AL HAS A REALLY RIGID SECURITY PROCEDURE. THEY PRETTY MUCH ASK YOU FOR YOUR WHOLE LIFE STORY AS A JEW. THEY EVEN ASKED ME WHAT MY FAVORITE HOLIDAY IS THE LAST TIME I WENT TO ISRAEL.

ALL RIGHT THEN. HEY, HAS MY FRIEND MELISSA CHECKED IN YET? MELISSA SHAW?

EL YYAL

MELISSA? YEAH, SHE'S HERE. SHE GOT RED-FLAGGED. SHE DIDN'T KNOW HER HEBREW NAME.

IS SHE DOING YOGA?

SO...READY TO GO TO ISRAEL, MISSY?

I'M REALLY TRYING VERY HARD TO MAINTAIN MY LOVE RIGHT NOW, FOCUSING ON IT AND TRYING NOT TO DISLIKE ISRAELIS. I'M. REALLY. TRYING.

NOBODY TOLD ME THEY WOULD BE ASKING ME THESE KINDS OF QUESTIONS! THEY SAID IT DIDN'T MATTER IF YOU DON'T COME FROM A RELIGIOUS BACKGROUND! AND NOW I HAVE TO GET STRIP-SEARCHED? THIS IS RIDICULOUS!

LOOK ON THE BRIGHT SIDE, AT LEAST NOW WE'LL KNOW FOR SURE THAT YOU'RE NOT A TERRORIST!

FUCKING GREAT!

NEXT! NEXT IN LINE, PLEASE!

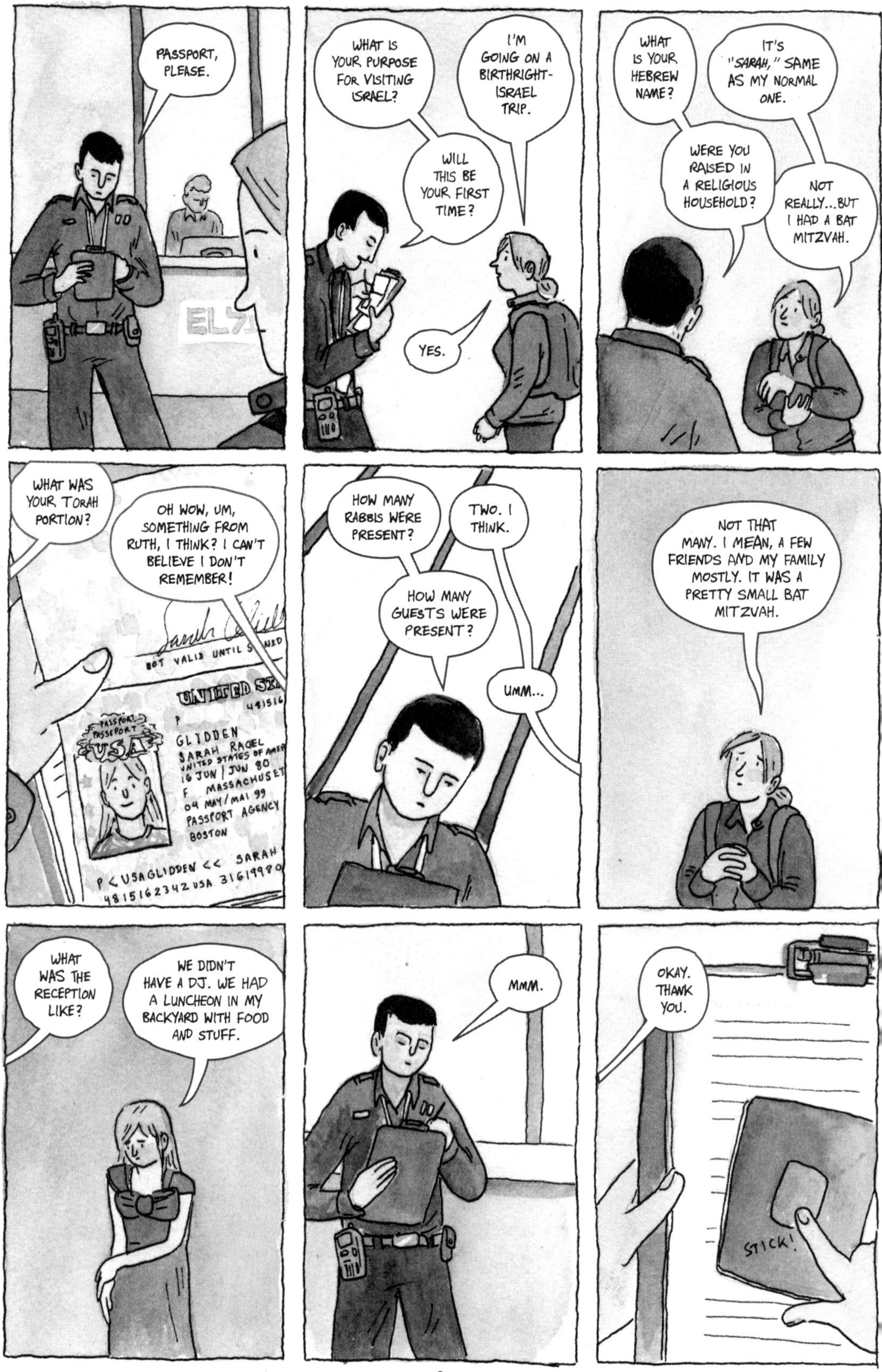
PASSPORT, PLEASE.
WHAT IS YOUR PURPOSE FOR VISITING ISRAEL?
I'M GOING ON A BIRTHRIGHT-ISRAEL TRIP.
WILL THIS BE YOUR FIRST TIME?
YES.
WHAT IS YOUR HEBREW NAME?
IT'S "SARAH," SAME AS MY NORMAL ONE.
WERE YOU RAISED IN A RELIGIOUS HOUSEHOLD?
NOT REALLY...BUT I HAD A BAT MITZVAH.
WHAT WAS YOUR TORAH PORTION?
OH WOW, UM, SOMETHING FROM RUTH, I THINK? I CAN'T BELIEVE I DON'T REMEMBER!
HOW MANY RABBIS WERE PRESENT?
TWO. I THINK.
HOW MANY GUESTS WERE PRESENT?
UMM...
NOT THAT MANY. I MEAN, A FEW FRIENDS AND MY FAMILY MOSTLY. IT WAS A PRETTY SMALL BAT MITZVAH.
WHAT WAS THE RECEPTION LIKE?
WE DIDN'T HAVE A DJ. WE HAD A LUNCHEON IN MY BACKYARD WITH FOOD AND STUFF.
MMM.
OKAY. THANK YOU.
STICK!

HOW'D IT GO?

WELL, I DIDN'T GET "FLAGGED." BUT HE DID MAKE ME THINK ABOUT JUNIOR HIGH SCHOOL. I THINK THAT MAY BE WORSE.

ARE ALL OF THESE PEOPLE IN OUR GROUP?

NOT ALL OF THEM...

THAT'S THE "ISRAEL OUTDOORS" BIRTHRIGHT GROUP. I TALKED TO SOME OF THEM; THEIR TRIP SOUNDS AWESOME!

THEY'RE GOING ROCK CLIMBING, HIKING, WHITEWATER RAFTING AND BIKING IN THE DESERT! *AND* THEY'RE MORE ATTRACTIVE THAN OUR GROUP FOR SOME REASON.

MAYBE WE SHOULD HAVE SIGNED UP FOR THAT BIRTHRIGHT TRIP INSTEAD. IT SOUNDS FUN.

NO WAY! OURS IS GONNA BE GREAT! WE DON'T NEED *RAFTING*.

"ON OUR TRIP WITH ISRAEL EXPERTS WE WILL BE EXPLORING THE HISTORY AND POLITICS OF ISRAEL IN AN OPEN-MINDED AND PLURALISTIC MANNER."

NOW *THAT'S* FUN.

RIGHT. I ALMOST FORGOT.

OKAY, SARAH, HERE'S YOUR TICKET. WHY DON'T YOU GO CHECK YOUR BAGS AND THEN MEET US AT THE GATE?

OKAY.

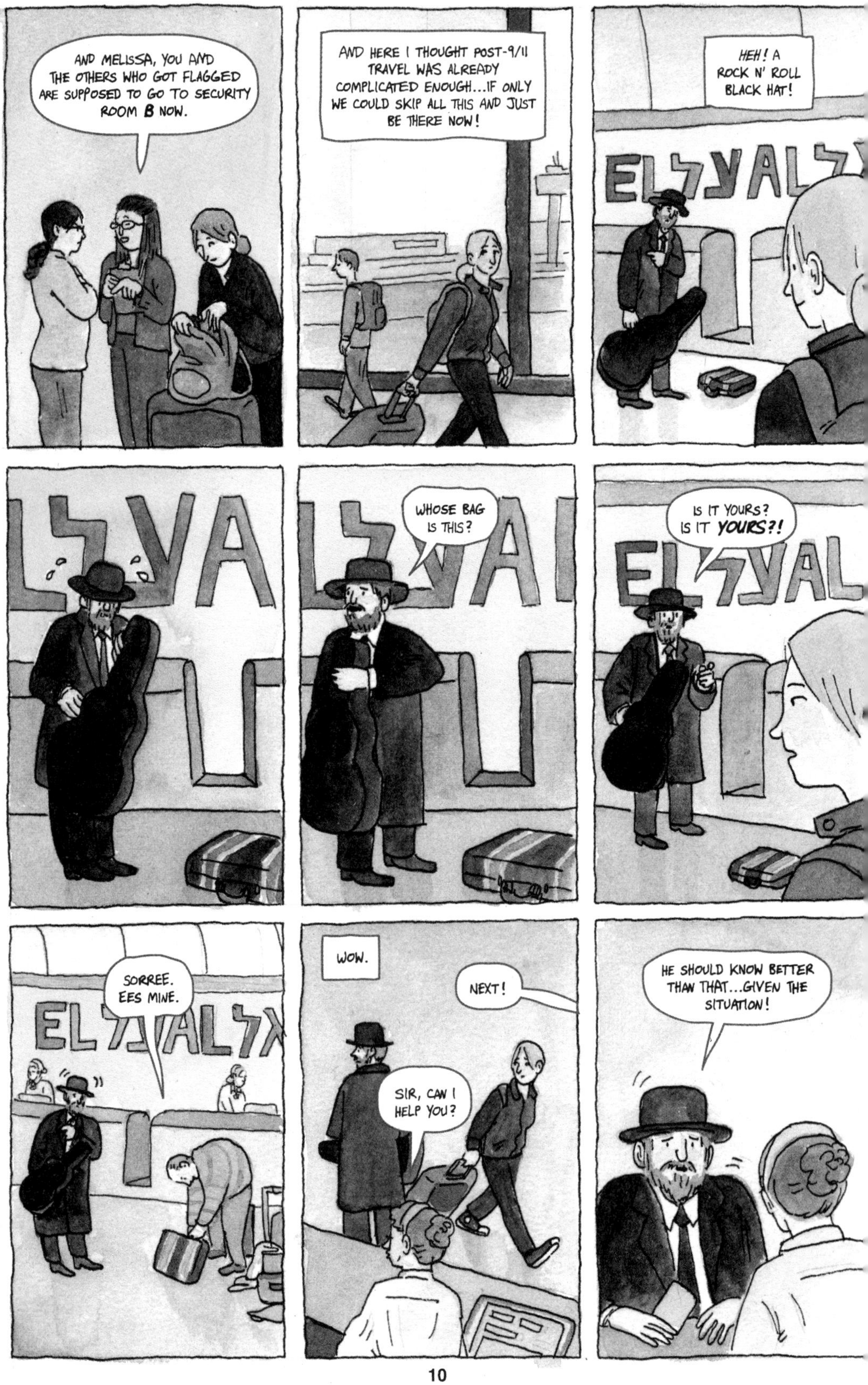
AND MELISSA, YOU AND THE OTHERS WHO GOT FLAGGED ARE SUPPOSED TO GO TO SECURITY ROOM B NOW.
AND HERE I THOUGHT POST-9/11 TRAVEL WAS ALREADY COMPLICATED ENOUGH...IF ONLY WE COULD SKIP ALL THIS AND JUST BE THERE NOW!
HEH! A ROCK N' ROLL BLACK HAT!
WHOSE BAG IS THIS?
IS IT YOURS? IS IT YOURS?!
SORREE. EES MINE.
WOW.
NEXT!
SIR, CAN I HELP YOU?
HE SHOULD KNOW BETTER THAN THAT...GIVEN THE SITUATION!

SO MAYBE EVEN THOUGH I'M TECHNICALLY STILL IN NEWARK, IT DOES FEEL LIKE WE ARE A LITTLE BIT "THERE" ALREADY.

NO ONE SHOULD EVER LEAVE A BAG UNATTENDED LIKE THAT...

BUT THEN AGAIN, I'VE BEEN A LITTLE BIT THERE FOR WEEKS NOW.

AFTER THE TWO OF US DECIDED TO GO ON THIS TRIP I SPENT EVERY SPARE MOMENT READING ABOUT ISRAEL, PALESTINE AND THE CONFLICT. I WANTED TO FILL IN THE GAPS BETWEEN WHAT I ALREADY KNEW, TRYING TO PREPARE MYSELF.

HA'ARETZ REPLACED THE NEW YORK TIMES AS MY DAILY LEFT-LEANING NEWS SOURCE.

I STARTED WITH THE BEGINNINGS OF RECORDED HISTORY AND WORKED MY WAY FORWARD, TRYING TO FIGURE OUT WHAT HAPPENED.

GATE 48

GATE 49

GATE 5

WHAT WENT WRONG OVER THERE? AND WHY AREN'T THERE ANY ANSWERS WITHOUT BIAS? OBJECTIVE SOURCES ARE VERY HARD TO FIND.

FLIGHT 17
TEL AVIV

EL YYALIN

HUNDREDS OF PAGES LATER, I HAD ALIENATED FRIENDS WITH MY OBSESSION...

IGNORED IMPORTANT THINGS IN MY LIFE...

AND SOMEHOW KNEW LESS THAN WHEN I STARTED.

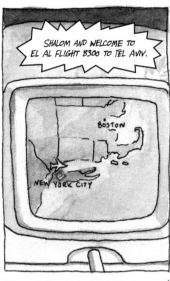

SHALOM AND WELCOME TO EL AL FLIGHT 8300 TO TEL AVIV.

BOSTON

NEW YORK CITY

SARAH! WE'RE REALLY GOING TO ISRAEL!

I CAN'T LOOK! I HATE TAKING OFF!

HOW WAS YOUR HOMELAND SECURITY SEARCH?

OH, IT WASN'T THAT BAD. THEY JUST ENDED UP SWABBING MY SHOES.

HALF OF THE PASSENGERS ON THIS FLIGHT ARE BOUND FOR BIRTHRIGHT, JUST LIKE US.

WHILE THE REST ARE PART OF A STORY I CAN'T EVEN GUESS AT.

THE HUM OF THE PLANE AND THEIR QUIET CONVERSATION LULLS ME TO SLEEP. HOURS LATER I WAKE UP TO THE INTERCOM ANNOUNCING OUR DESCENT.

PLEASE FASTEN YOUR SEATBELTS AND RETURN YOUR SEATS TO AN UPRIGHT POSITION...

חיפה

תל אביב-יפו

HEY, SARAH, LOOK!

IT'S TEL AVIV!

IT LOOKS LIKE LOS ANGELES FROM UP HERE.

WOULD YOU PLEASE SIT DOWN?

WE HOPE YOU ENJOY YOUR STAY IN ISRAEL. IF THIS IS YOUR RETURN FLIGHT, WELCOME HOME.

AH...WE ARE IN THE HOLY LAND! ISN'T IT MAGNIFICENT? DON'T YOU FEEL OVERCOME BY SOME KIND OF SPIRITUAL FEELING?

OVERCOME BY EXHAUSTION IS MORE LIKE IT. I SHOULD HAVE TAKEN A XANAX.

WOW, SO MANY HASIDIC JEWS! IT FEELS LIKE WE'RE IN SOUTH WILLIAMSBURG!

I'M NOT USED TO SEEING THEM DOING MUNDANE THINGS LIKE WAITING FOR LUGGAGE.

IN BROOKLYN THEY'RE GHOSTS TO THE REST OF US, TALKING TO NO ONE OUTSIDE OF THEIR COMMUNITY UNLESS ABSOLUTELY NECESSARY.

OH! MY SUITCASE!

C'MERE! OOOF!

HEH, UH... SORRY!

MY COUSIN MATT IS IN HIS FIRST YEAR OF MEDICAL SCHOOL AT TEL AVIV UNIVERSITY. HE MEETS ME AT THE AIRPORT TO WELCOME ME AND LEND ME A CELL PHONE.

SO ARE THEY THE SAME AS THE HASIDIM IN NEW YORK?

KIND OF. YOU'LL ONLY REALLY SEE THEM IN JERUSALEM. FOR THE MOST PART ISRAEL IS A PRETTY SECULAR STATE. THE ORTHODOX CAUSE A LOT OF CONTROVERSY THOUGH.

AS MATT TELLS ME ABOUT THE RIFT BETWEEN THE HASIDIC AND SECULAR JEWS IN ISRAEL, I CAN'T HELP BUT FEEL SATISFIED AS MY OWN PREJUDICES ARE VALIDATED. I HAVEN'T HAD GOOD EXPERIENCES WITH THE HASIDIC COMMUNITY...

FRESH OUT OF ART SCHOOL IN BOSTON, I CAME TO BROOKLYN TO LOOK FOR AN APARTMENT. I HAD HEARD A LOT ABOUT THE BOHEMIAN WILLIAMSBURG NEIGHBORHOOD, SO I STARTED THERE.

BUT I WANDERED SOUTH INSTEAD OF NORTH ON BEDFORD AVENUE, AND INSTEAD OF ULTRA-HIP I FOUND ULTRA-ORTHODOX.

HOW CAN HE WEAR THAT? IT'S NINETY DEGREES OUT!

EXCUSE ME!

HELLO!

CAN YOU TURN ON THE LIGHTS?

THE LIGHTS? OH, OF COURSE! IT'S SHABBAT.

I'M SUCH A GOOD SAMARITAN, HELPING OUT AN OLD MAN.

OH THANK YOU, THANK YOU.

OF COURSE!

I THOUGHT THEY WEREN'T SUPPOSED TO TOUCH WOMEN?

THANK YOU!

AUGH! GET OFF ME, YOU PERV!

I'M CALLING THE COPS, YOU PIG!

--BECAUSE NOT ONLY ARE THEY EXEMPT FROM ARMY SERVICE BUT THE GOVERNMENT ACTUALLY PAYS THEM TO STUDY TORAH! SO A LOT OF PEOPLE REALLY HATE THEM.

YOU DON'T SAY.

IS THAT YOUR GROUP?

YEAH. I'D BETTER GET GOING.

THANKS SO MUCH FOR MEETING ME HERE!

NO PROBLEM! CALL ME WHEN YOU GET BACK TO TEL AVIV!

WHAT'S GOING ON?

OH MAN, YOU TOTALLY MISSED THE DRAMA.

DRAMA? ALREADY?

APPARENTLY THAT GUY, FRANK, DOESN'T BELIEVE IN GAY PEOPLE.

WHO'S FRANK?

FRANK, THAT GUY WITH THE SUNGLASSES ON HIS HEAD.

OH. WHAT DO YOU MEAN, HE DOESN'T BELIEVE IN GAY PEOPLE?

WELL, HE AND THIS GIRL BECCA WERE TALKING AND IT CAME UP THAT HE'S A REPUBLICAN--

BLEH.

I KNOW, RIGHT? SO SHE ASKED HIM IF HE THINKS GAYS SHOULD BE LEGALLY ALLOWED TO MARRY.

AND HE SAID "NO", AND THAT HE "DOESN'T BELIEVE IN IT!"

WHOA.

IT'S NICE TO KNOW WE HAVE SUCH PROGRESSIVE THINKERS IN THIS GROUP.

RIGHT.

I NEED TO PICK UP MY RENTAL PHONE. WHY DON'T YOU GRAB US SOME SEATS?

I'M ON IT!

15

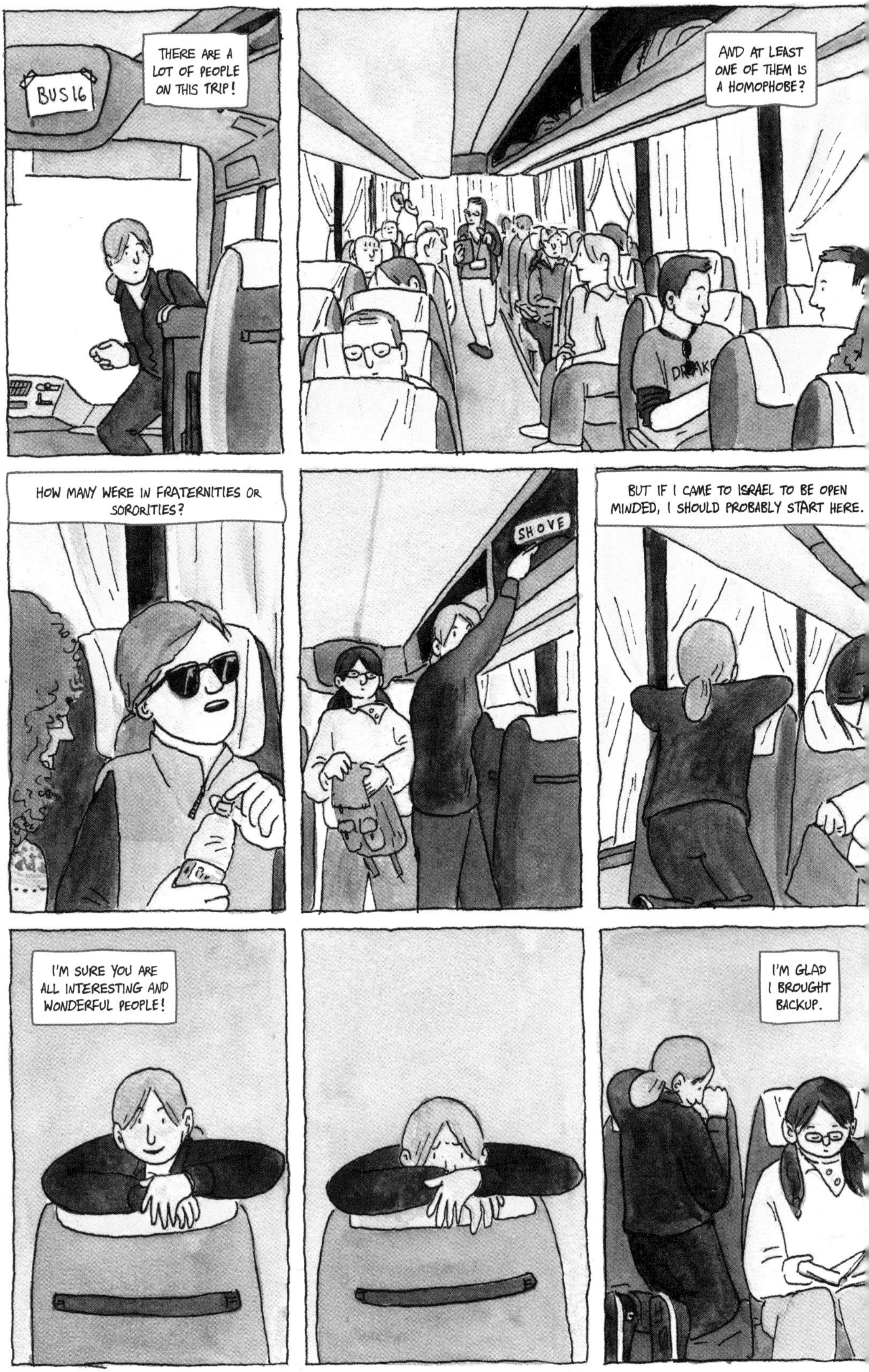
BUS 16
THERE ARE A LOT OF PEOPLE ON THIS TRIP!
AND AT LEAST ONE OF THEM IS A HOMOPHOBE?
HOW MANY WERE IN FRATERNITIES OR SORORITIES?
SHOVE
BUT IF I CAME TO ISRAEL TO BE OPEN MINDED, I SHOULD PROBABLY START HERE.
I'M SURE YOU ARE ALL INTERESTING AND WONDERFUL PEOPLE!
I'M GLAD I BROUGHT BACKUP.

MELISSA WAS THE FIRST PERSON I THOUGHT OF WHEN I HAD THE IDEA TO COME ON A BIRTHRIGHT TRIP.

MELISSA, WE'RE GOING TO ISRAEL! WE HAVE TO GO. WE WOULD BE FOOLS TO LET AN OPPORTUNITY LIKE THIS PASS US BY.

ANYWAY, CALL ME BACK WHEN YOU GET THIS MESSAGE AND I'LL EXPLAIN EVERYTHING.

NOT ONLY IS SHE ONE OF MY CLOSEST AND OLDEST FRIENDS, SHE'S ALSO ONE OF MY ONLY JEWISH FRIENDS.

SO WHAT DO YOU THINK? THE NEXT TRIP LEAVES IN A FEW MONTHS.

SARAH. I CAN'T GO TO ISRAEL. MY GRANDMOTHER WOULD KILL ME, I DON'T HAVE A PASSPORT, I HAVE NO MONEY...

YOU DON'T NEED ANY MONEY; IT'S FREE! AND YOU CAN GET YOUR PASSPORT RUSHED IF YOU HAVE TO.

I DON'T KNOW...*ISRAEL?* IT SOUNDS STRESSFUL.

BUT I ALREADY SIGNED US UP!

≥SIGH≤... I'LL THINK ABOUT IT.

SHE EVENTUALLY WARMED UP TO THE IDEA.

I CAN'T BELIEVE WE'RE ACTUALLY DOING THIS.

...AND WE CAN EXTEND OUR STAY TOO. I REALLY WANT TO GO TO THE WEST BANK.

IS THAT SAFE?

OH SURE, JESSICA AND ALEX HAVE BEEN THERE A BUNCH OF TIMES ON REPORTING TRIPS AND KNOW TONS OF PEOPLE. THEY PUT ME IN TOUCH WITH THIS GUY HUSSEIN WHO'S GONNA MEET ME IN JERUSALEM AND THEN TAKE ME INTO RAMALLAH.

I THINK IT'S OUR RESPONSIBILITY TO CHECK OUT THE REALITY ON THE OTHER SIDE OF THE GREEN LINE. WANNA COME?

MAYBE. I'M GOING TO TAKE THIS ONE STEP AT A TIME.

HERE YA GO, SUGAR. THAT'LL BE SIX BUCKS.

MELISSA STILL ISN'T CONVINCED ABOUT THE WEST BANK EXCURSION, BUT AT LEAST SHE'S HERE.

LOOK, THAT MUST BE OUR GUIDE.

AH, SHALOM EVERY-ONE! CAN YOU ALL HEAR ME IN THE BACK?

SO GOOD MORNING! MY NAME IS GIL AND I WILL BE YOUR GUIDE.

BEFORE WE START, CAN YOU TELL ME HOW MANY OF YOU ARE IN ISRAEL FOR THE FIRST TIME?

WOW, ALMOST ALL OF YOU! WHAT A BURDEN AND RESPONSIBILITY I HAVE TO SHOW THIS COUNTRY TO YOU!

GIL INTRODUCES US TO THE REST OF THE ISRAEL EXPERTS STAFF ON OUR TRIP. THERE IS NADAV, SHARON'S ISRAELI COUNTERPART.

AND BEN, OUR ARMED GUARD AND MEDIC.

SHAI IS OUR DRIVER, AND HE SEEMS TO ENJOY DRIVING THE BUS AS IF IT WERE A SMALL CAR WITH GREAT PICKUP.

IT'S HARD TO BELIEVE THERE'S A SOLDIER SOMEWHERE IN GIL.

I KNOW YOU MUST BE VERY TIRED, BUT IF WE PUSH THROUGH TODAY YOUR JETLAG WILL BE EASIER TO OVERCOME, BELIEVE ME.

HE MAY HAVE FOUGHT IN ONE OF THE WARS! AND NOW HE IS OUR TOUR GUIDE.

SO PLEASE RELAX AND WE WILL SOON STOP FOR BREAKFAST AND ORIENTATION.

SO...THIS IS IT? THIS IS THE LAND THAT ALL THE BLOODSHED AND CONFLICT IS ABOUT?

IT'S PROBABLY SO MUCH DEEPER THAT WE CAN EVEN IMAGINE.

YEAH, BUT YOU JUST CAN'T SEE ANY SIGNS OF THE TROUBLES AT ALL! I DON'T KNOW WHAT I WAS EXPECTING BUT...

...IT'S JUST SO *PLAIN.*

BUT WHAT'S FIRST ON OUR AGENDA? THE GOLAN HEIGHTS? I BET *THAT* DOESN'T LOOK LIKE A BUNCH OF FIELDS.

HEY, LOOK! THOSE SIGNS ARE IN HEBREW *AND* ARABIC! I'M SURPRISED THAT THE GOVERNMENT WOULD ALLOW THAT...

WELL, THEY HAVE TO. ARABIC IS THE OFFICIAL SECOND LANGUAGE IN ISRAEL. THEY'RE REQUIRED BY LAW TO HAVE IT ON ALL PUBLIC SIGNS.

EVEN THOUGH ARABIC WAS HERE FOR A LONG TIME BEFORE HEBREW CAME BACK...

SORRY! DOES IT ANNOY YOU THAT I KEEP TALKING ABOUT THE CONFLICT ALL THE TIME? I'LL STOP.

IT'S FINE, SARAH. MAYBE WAIT UNTIL I'VE HAD SOME COFFEE, OKAY?

I DON'T KNOW MUCH ABOUT ALL THAT STUFF, BUT THERE MUST BE TWO SIDES TO THE STORY, YOU KNOW? SOME KIND OF BALANCE.

MMM. DOESN'T SEEM BALANCED TO ME.

HONESTLY, I'M STILL JUST SO AMAZED THAT WE'RE EVEN HERE...I HAVEN'T GIVEN THE CONFLICT MUCH THOUGHT YET.

OH, YEAH! I KEEP FORGETTING THAT THIS IS YOUR FIRST TIME ABROAD! YEAH, THIS MUST BE TOTALLY CRAZY FOR YOU.

SLAP!

OUR FIRST STOP IS KIBBUTZ NACHSHON, SITUATED SOMEWHERE BETWEEN JERUSALEM AND TEL AVIV.

THIS ISN'T HOW I HAD IMAGINED A KIBBUTZ TO LOOK AT ALL.

IN THE PHOTOGRAPHS MY MOTHER TOOK OF HER STAY AT A KIBBUTZ NOT FAR FROM HERE, YOUNG INTERNATIONALS IN CUT-OFFS AND TEE SHIRTS BONDED IN THE BRIGHT SUN.

AT THE END OF A LONG DAY WORKING IN THE COTTON FIELDS, THEY SLUMPED EXHAUSTED IN THEIR SPARTAN WOOD CABINS AND EXCHANGED STORIES ABOUT TRAVEL AND POLITICAL PROTEST.

THAT WAS IN 1972. MY MOM DOESN'T EVEN KNOW IF KIBBUTZ EY AL STILL EXISTS.

AT KIBBUTZ NACHSHON THERE ARE CINDERBLOCK BUILDINGS INSTEAD OF WOODEN BARRACKS.

AND INSTEAD OF KHAKI CLAD KIBBUTZNIKS CARRYING BOXES OF GRAPES AND ORANGES, THE ONLY PEOPLE AROUND SEEM TO BE *US*...

A BUNCH OF AMERICAN JEWS IN THEIR TWENTIES, PALE AND JETLAGGED.

NO SOY MILK. GREAT.

WHERE IS EVERY-BODY? ISN'T THIS A WORKING KIBBUTZ?

DUNNO. MAYBE THEY'RE HIDING FROM US.

WELL, AT LEAST THEY LEFT US SANDWICHES. I'M STARVING!

HEY, EVERYONE! PLEASE TAKE A SEAT IF YOU'RE DONE EATING!

GROANNN...I HOPE THIS ISN'T GONNA BE SOME SORT OF NAME GAME.

HI, EVERYONE, MY NAME IS BILL AND I'M THE DIRECTOR OF ISRAEL EXPERTS. BEFORE I START, LET'S GO AROUND THE CIRCLE AND HEAR WHY EACH OF YOU CHOSE TO COME ON A BIRTHRIGHT-ISRAEL TRIP.

THIS IS MY OPPORTUNITY TO LEARN MORE ABOUT THE 39 OTHER PEOPLE IN MY GROUP, THE PEOPLE WITH WHOM, ACCORDING TO ALUMNI ACCOUNTS, I WILL MAKE "FRIENDSHIPS THAT WILL LAST A LIFETIME."

UMM, I CAME HERE TO MEET HOT ISRAELI SOLDIERS.

BUT MY MIND IMMEDIATELY STARTS WANDERING AROUND THE GREEN-HOUSE WE SIT IN...IN ISRAEL!

ISRAELI ANTS. A FEW MONTHS AGO, I READ ABOUT AN ANT COLONY THAT WAS SO GIGANTIC IT STRETCHED FROM SPAIN TO ITALY.

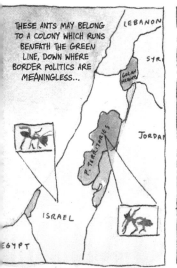

THESE ANTS MAY BELONG TO A COLONY WHICH RUNS BENEATH THE GREEN LINE, DOWN WHERE BORDER POLITICS ARE MEANINGLESS...

LEBANON

SYR

GOLAN HEIGHTS

JORDAN

P. TERRITORIES

ISRAEL

EGYPT

WITH BRAINS TOO SMALL TO CARE IN THE FIRST PLACE.

UH OH, I'M NEXT. WHAT DO I SAY?

HERE BECAUSE IT'S JUST A GREAT OPPORTUNITY TO SEE THIS PLACE WITH SUCH A FASCINATING HISTORY.

HI. I'M SARAH AND I'M HERE BECAUSE I'VE ALWAYS BEEN INTERESTED IN THE HISTORY AND POLITICS OF ISRAEL...

PALESTINE

...AND I WANTED TO, UH...

PASS JUDGMENT ON IT

...SEE IT FIRSTHAND.

WHAT YOU ALL HAVE IN COMMON IS THAT YOU'VE BEEN GIVEN A GIFT BY THE BIRTHRIGHT-ISRAEL FUND, OR AS IT'S CALLED IN ISRAEL, *TAGLIT*.

SINCE 1999, ABOUT 120,000 OTHER YOUNG JEWS FROM AROUND THE WORLD HAVE COME HERE ON A BIRTHRIGHT TOUR.

THE BIRTHRIGHT FUND RAISES MONEY FROM PRIVATE DONORS AND THE STATE OF ISRAEL WHICH IS THEN DISTRIBUTED TO PRIVATE TOUR COMPANIES LIKE OURS. WITH THEIR LICENSING COME SOME GUIDELINES SUCH AS REQUIRED VISITS TO PLACES LIKE MASADA AND YAD VASHEM.

AND BEN HERE IS ANOTHER REQUIREMENT. EVERY BIRTHRIGHT GROUP MUST BE ACCOMPANIED BY AN ARMED GUARD FOR YOUR SAFETY.

IT'S HARD FOR ME TO IMAGINE WHAT THIS GUY WOULD BE ABLE TO PROTECT US FROM, ESPECIALLY WITH A GUN THAT LOOKS LIKE THE RIFLES WE USED AT SUMMER CAMP.

DON'T WORRY, YOU ARE SAFE.

← TERRORISTS

IN A FEW DAYS YOU'LL BE JOINED BY SIX ISRAELI SOLDIERS, NOT TO PROTECT YOU, BUT TO TRAVEL WITH YOU AS PEERS.

BILL GOES ON TO APOLOGIZE FOR THE FACT THAT, DESPITE BEING ADULTS, WE ARE NOT TO LEAVE THE GROUP DUE TO SECURITY CONCERNS.

...EXCEPT FOR IN TEL AVIV AND JERUSALEM WHERE YOU WILL BE ALLOWED TO WANDER WITHIN A FEW DESIGNATED BLOCKS..

HE ALSO TELLS US THAT BECAUSE OF TERRORISM, ISRAELIS ARE VERY SENSITIVE ABOUT UNATTENDED BAGS.

IF WE LEAVE ANY POSSESSIONS OUT IN PUBLIC, SOMEONE WILL REPORT IT WITHIN MINUTES AND A ROBOT WILL BE SENT TO BLOW IT UP.

HALT!

KA-POW!

HEH HEH!

I'LL SEE YOU ALL IN A FEW DAYS. SHALOM AND WELCOME TO ISRAEL.

IT'S JUST LIKE THE POSTERS IN THE NEW YORK SUBWAY: "IF YOU SEE SOMETHING, SAY SOMETHING. THEN BLOW UP SOMETHING!"

NOT FUNNY.

WELL! THAT ORIENTATION WASN'T SO BAD AFTER ALL!

I WAS EXPECTING TO HEAR A WHOLE LOT MORE ABOUT HOW WE WERE SURELY GOING TO SOON "LOVE ISRAEL WITH ALL OUR HEARTS!"

SEE? MAYBE YOU'VE JUDGED BIRTHRIGHT PREMATURELY.

MAYBE. BUT SOONER OR LATER THEY'RE GOING TO HAVE TO ADDRESS "THE SITUATION" AND I'M CURIOUS TO SEE HOW THEY'LL HANDLE IT. I'M KEEPING AN OPEN MIND!

SUUUUURE YOU ARE.

AS WE DRIVE NORTH, GIL, A LIVING ENCYCLOPEDIA, IS ON THE MIC ANSWERING PEOPLE'S QUESTIONS ABOUT THE ISRAELI PARLIAMENT AND POPULATION STATISTICS.

I'M WAITING FOR THE SCENERY TO LOOK MORE LIKE HOW I'D IMAGINED ISRAEL AND LESS LIKE RURAL PENNSYLVANIA.

THAT MUST BE A LOCAL PRISON.

A REALLY LONG PRISON...

WAIT, THAT'S NOT A PRISON. IT'S THE **WALL**.

HOLY SHIT!

AND JUST LIKE THAT, ISRAEL HAS BECOME REAL. NOT PENNSYLVANIA, NOT A BUS FULL OF AMERICANS.

GIL! GIL!

AH YES. I WANT TO ADDRESS THIS WALL YOU SEE TO YOUR RIGHT.

THIS IS A VERY COMPLICATED ISSUE HERE. ON ONE HAND, AFTER IT WAS BUILT, THE TERRORIST ATTACKS IN TEL AVIV HAVE DROPPED FROM TWO A WEEK TO FOUR PER YEAR.

"ON THE OTHER HAND, A LOT OF IT HAS BEEN BUILT ON PALESTINIAN LAND AND IT'S CAUSED MANY PROBLEMS FOR INNOCENT PALESTINIAN PEOPLE."

"IT DOESN'T GO ALONG THE GREEN LINE BECAUSE IT'S A SECURITY FENCE, NOT A BORDER."

"SO SOME FARMERS HAVE HAD THEIR HOMES SEPARATED FROM THEIR FIELDS, AND THEY HAVE TO DRIVE FOR SEVERAL MILES TO A CHECKPOINT AND BACK AGAIN JUST TO GET TO THEIR OWN BACKYARDS."

ICH BIN EIN BERLINER

"AND WHEN THERE IS A SECURITY THREAT THE CHECKPOINT CLOSES AND IT HURTS THEIR LIVELIHOOD."

PEACE BE WITH YOU

SO THE FENCE DEFINITELY CAUSES PROBLEMS, BUT THE PALESTINIANS TAKE THESE DAY-TO-DAY ISSUES AND TURN THEM INTO VERY HARSH PROPAGANDA.

AND YOU NEED TO REALIZE THAT AND REMEMBER THE STATISTICS. BECAUSE OF THE WALL WE CAN TRAVEL SAFELY ON THIS ROAD.

MY PERSONAL OPINION IS THAT, WHILE I HATE HOW IT HURTS MANY PEOPLE, EVERY DAY THAT I WAKE UP AND THERE'S NO ATTACK ON THE NEWS, I THINK ABOUT THE WALL.

OH YES, THANK YOU, SHARON. I'D ALMOST FORGOTTEN TO GIVE YOU THESE MAPS.

THEY WILL HELP YOU LOOK AT THE SITUATION. PLEASE PASS THEM BACK.

YOU WILL SEE THE FENCE REPRESENTED BY THE BLACK DOTS AROUND THE JUDEAN AND SAMARIAN TERRITORIES.

AND BY THE WAY, ONLY TEN PERCENT OF IT IS CONCRETE LIKE YOU SEE HERE.

THE REST IS WIRE AND IT SENDS A SIGNAL TO THE I.D.F., THE ISRAELI DEFENSE FORCES, WHEN DISTURBED.

ISRAE ROAD MAP
with Compliments from ISRAEL EXPERTS

HAIFA

WHAT ARE ALL THESE PINK AND PURPLE BLOTCHES?

THE PINK AREAS ARE WHERE THE PALESTINIAN AUTHORITY HAS COMPLETE CONTROL AND THE PURPLE AREAS REPRESENT WHERE THE P.A. HAS AUTHORITY BUT ISRAEL CONTROLS SECURITY.

BUT IF THE P.A. HAS AUTHORITY, HOW CAN THE I.D.F. JUST GO IN AND IMPOSE A CURFEW?

OKAY, SO, AS PART OF THE OSLO ACCORDS THE ISRAELIS STILL CONTROL SOME AREAS AS PART OF WHAT WAS SUPPOSED TO BE A NEGOTIATION PROCESS TOWARDS A TWO-STATE SOLUTION.

Ramallah

BUT BECAUSE OF THE 2ND INTIFADA IN 2000, THE NEGOTIATIONS HAVE STOPPED AND IT'S VERY FRUSTRATING FOR BOTH SIDES.

Jerusalem

Bethlehem

WE WERE SO CLOSE. BUT WE HAVE A SAYING HERE: "THE PALESTINIANS NEVER MISS AN OPPORTUNITY TO MISS AN OPPORTUNITY."

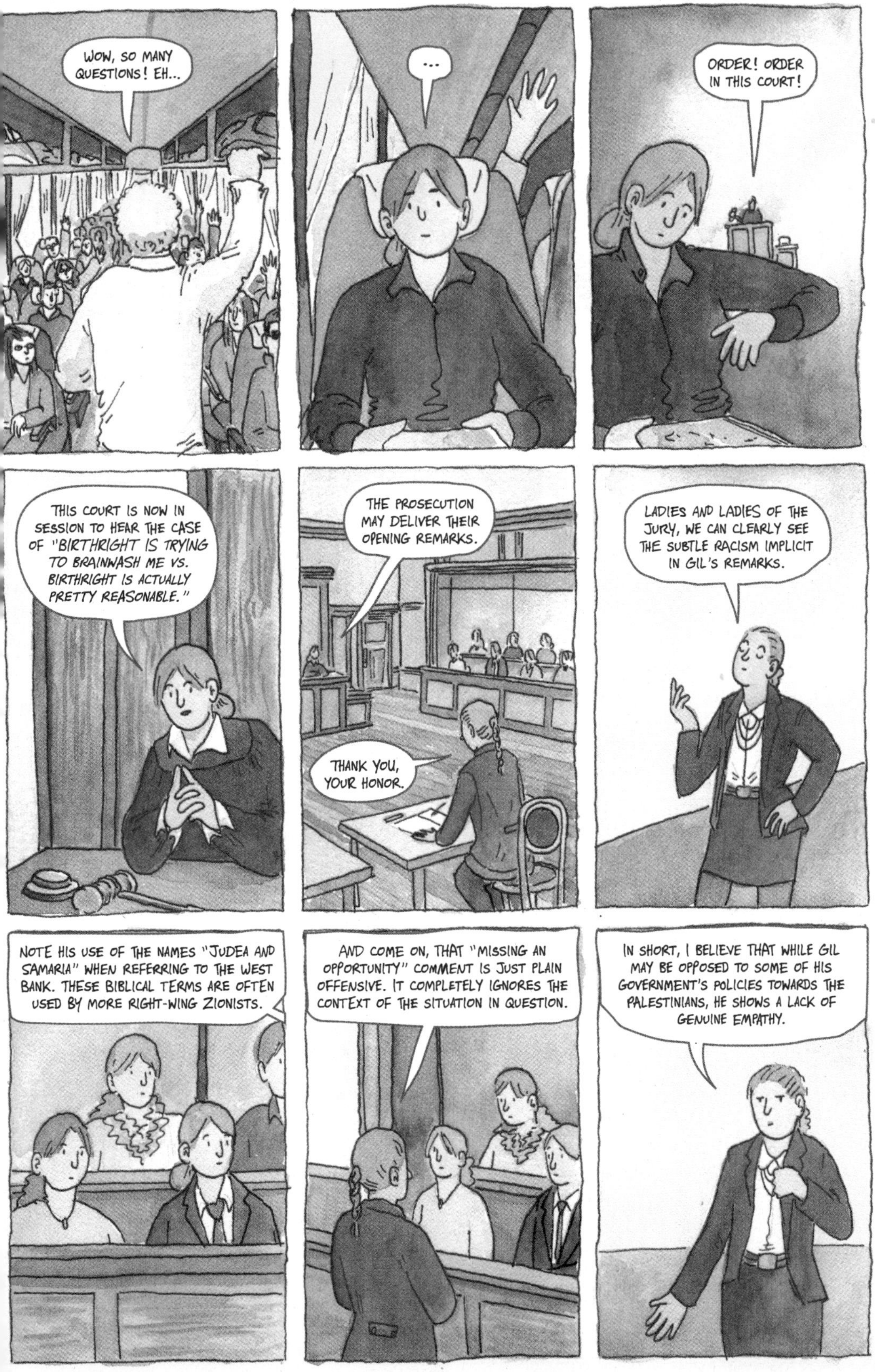
WOW, SO MANY QUESTIONS! EH...
...
ORDER! ORDER IN THIS COURT!
THIS COURT IS NOW IN SESSION TO HEAR THE CASE OF "BIRTHRIGHT IS TRYING TO BRAINWASH ME VS. BIRTHRIGHT IS ACTUALLY PRETTY REASONABLE."
THE PROSECUTION MAY DELIVER THEIR OPENING REMARKS.
THANK YOU, YOUR HONOR.
LADIES AND LADIES OF THE JURY, WE CAN CLEARLY SEE THE SUBTLE RACISM IMPLICIT IN GIL'S REMARKS.
NOTE HIS USE OF THE NAMES "JUDEA AND SAMARIA" WHEN REFERRING TO THE WEST BANK. THESE BIBLICAL TERMS ARE OFTEN USED BY MORE RIGHT-WING ZIONISTS.
AND COME ON, THAT "MISSING AN OPPORTUNITY" COMMENT IS JUST PLAIN OFFENSIVE. IT COMPLETELY IGNORES THE CONTEXT OF THE SITUATION IN QUESTION.
IN SHORT, I BELIEVE THAT WHILE GIL MAY BE OPPOSED TO SOME OF HIS GOVERNMENT'S POLICIES TOWARDS THE PALESTINIANS, HE SHOWS A LACK OF GENUINE EMPATHY.

THANK YOU. THE COURT NOW CALLS ON THE DEFENSE TO MAKE AN OPENING STATEMENT.

YOUR HONOR, JURISTS, I WOULD LIKE TO START BY MENTIONING HOW REFRESHING IT IS TO HEAR GIL SPEAK OF THE NEGATIVE ASPECTS OF THE WALL WITHOUT BEING PROMPTED.

THIS SHOWS HE IS BEING PROACTIVE IN FOSTERING A CRITICAL APPROACH TO DISCUSSIONS ON POLITICS DURING THIS TOUR.

IN ADDITION, HE SEEMS WILLING TO ANSWER TOUGH QUESTIONS HEAD-ON. IF THEY WANTED US TO GET A ONE-SIDED VIEW ON ISRAEL, THEY WOULDN'T HAVE CHOSEN THIS GUIDE. THANK YOU.

YOUR HONOR...

YES, BAILIFF?

THE DRIVER NEEDS TO REFUEL THE BUS, SO HE NEEDS TO STOP AT THIS GAS STATION...

THE COURT WILL NOW ADJOURN FOR A TEN-MINUTE BATHROOM BREAK AT THIS GAS STATION.

ALL RISE!

OOH! THEY HAVE A CAFÉ HERE. MAYBE THEY HAVE SOY MILK.

BEFORE I CAME HERE, I READ AS MANY FIRSTHAND ACCOUNTS OF THE BIRTHRIGHT EXPERIENCE AS I COULD ONLINE.

MANY OF THE ALUMNI WROTE THAT FROM THE MOMENT THEY SET FOOT IN THE LAND OF ISRAEL, THEY FELT A REAL CONNECTION.

A FEW EVEN SAID THAT THEY FELT LIKE THEY WERE "FINALLY HOME."

TO ME, IT'S MORE LIKE SPOTTING A CELEBRITY ON A CROWDED STREET.

SOMEONE WHOSE CRAZY LIFE HAS BEEN SPLASHED ALL OVER THE TABLOID PAGES FOR YEARS.

AND THERE THEY ARE...

...RIGHT IN FRONT OF YOU.

CHAPTER
TWO
THE GOLAN HEIGHTS

BUS ROUTE
HIGHWAY
UNITED NATIONS
DEMILITARIZED ZONE

LEBANON

MOUNT HERMON

AL QUNEITRA

HULA VALLEY

KATZRIN

ISRAEL

SYRIA

LAKE KINNERET OR SEA OF GALILEE

OHALO

JORDAN

OKAY, EVERYONE...

WE ARE ABOUT TO CROSS OVER THE JORDAN RIVER INTO THE GOLAN HEIGHTS. GET READY OR YOU MIGHT MISS IT!

התקדם לפס הצצירה

THERE IT IS..."THE MIGHTY JORDAN!"

THIS IS MORE OF A MUDDY STREAM THAN A "MIGHTY RIVER." IT MAY NOT BE AS IMPRESSIVE AS I HAD HOPED BUT IT DOESN'T MATTER, BECAUSE JUST LIKE THAT WE HAVE CROSSED THE BORDER..

TO THE GOLAN HEIGHTS!

FORMER SYRIA!

DISPUTED TERRITORY PROPER!

31

FOR A WHILE, ALL WE SEE IS BARREN HILLS SCATTERED WITH BASALT BOULDERS.

HEY, GIL? IF THIS IS SUCH CONTROVERSIAL LAND, HOW COME NO ONE'S BUILT ANYTHING ON IT?

WELL, BEFORE THE SIX-DAY WAR THESE WERE SYRIAN GRAZING LANDS, BUT NOW THEY ARE FULL OF MINES FROM BOTH ARMIES WHICH CAN'T BE REMOVED.

HMM. WHAT A WASTE.

FIGHTING OVER LAND THAT NO ONE CAN EVEN BUILD ANYTHING ON? IT'S RIDICULOUS!

SEE, MISSY, I KNEW YOU'D COME AROUND TO HOW MESSED UP THIS ALL IS.

ISRAEL SHOULD JUST GIVE IT BACK TO SYRIA, PLAIN AND SIMPLE.

WELL, I STILL DON'T KNOW A LOT ABOUT ALL OF THIS, SO I REALLY CAN'T SAY.

NOT ALL OF THE GOLAN HEIGHTS IS EMPTY, HOWEVER. SOON WE REACH KATZRIN, WHICH GIL TELLS US IS THE LARGEST TOWN IN THE REGION, AND STOP FOR LUNCH.

SARAH...

HURRY UP! I GOTTA GO!

JUST A MINUTE!

HMM...TWO LEVERS...

WHICH ONE DO I PUSH? THE SMALL ONE OR BOTH?

THE SMALL ONE, STUPID! WE AREN'T MADE OF WATER HERE!

WHY IS EVERYTHING IN THIS COUNTRY SO DAMNED CONFUSING?

FLOOOSH

GAH...GAH-LI-DAH?

HEBREW HAS ONLY BEEN A SPOKEN LANGUAGE FOR A LITTLE OVER 100 YEARS.

AFTER THE ROMANS EXPELLED THE JEWS IN THE 2ND CENTURY, IT FADED AWAY UNTIL IT WAS ONLY USED FOR RELIGIOUS TEXTS.

IT WAS ONLY IN THE LATE 1800'S THAT ELEIZER BEN-YEHUDA SET OUT TO REVIVE HEBREW AS A MODERN SPOKEN LANGUAGE FOR THE JEWS MOVING TO OTTOMAN PALESTINE.

WAVES OF IMMIGRANTS LEARNED THIS "NEW" HEBREW ONCE THEY MOVED HERE, USED TO ONLY SEEING IT IN PRAYER BOOKS AND THE TORAH.

THEY MUST HAVE FELT THEN LIKE I DO NOW: IT'S BIZARRE TO SEE ANCIENT CHARACTERS SCRAWLED ON CARDBOARD DESCRIBING VARIETIES OF ICE CREAM.

CAN I HAVE A FALAFEL, UM...BEVAKESHAH?

CHIPS?

CHIPS?

YES, CHIPS IN FALAFEL?

OH! FRENCH FRIES! OKAY, WHY NOT?

HUH! FRIES...

THERE'S GIL AND SHAI.

LET'S SIT WITH THEM AND THEN WE CAN ASK GIL ANY QUESTION WE WANT!

OKAY.

CAN WE SIT HERE?

OF COURSE!

SO, UM...

I WANTED TO ASK YOU ABOUT...

I WANT TO ASK GIL ALL SORTS OF QUESTIONS ABOUT THE CONFLICT, ABOUT WHAT HE DID IN THE ARMY, WHY HE DECIDED TO BECOME A GUIDE...BUT IT DAWNS ON ME THAT THIS IS HIS JOB AND I AM INTERRUPTING HIS LUNCH BREAK.

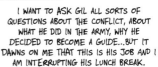

YES?

UM...WHAT'S OUR NEXT ACTIVITY?

WE ARE--EXCUSE ME--WE ARE GOING TO SEE A MOVIE ABOUT THE GOLAN HEIGHTS.

OH. COOL.

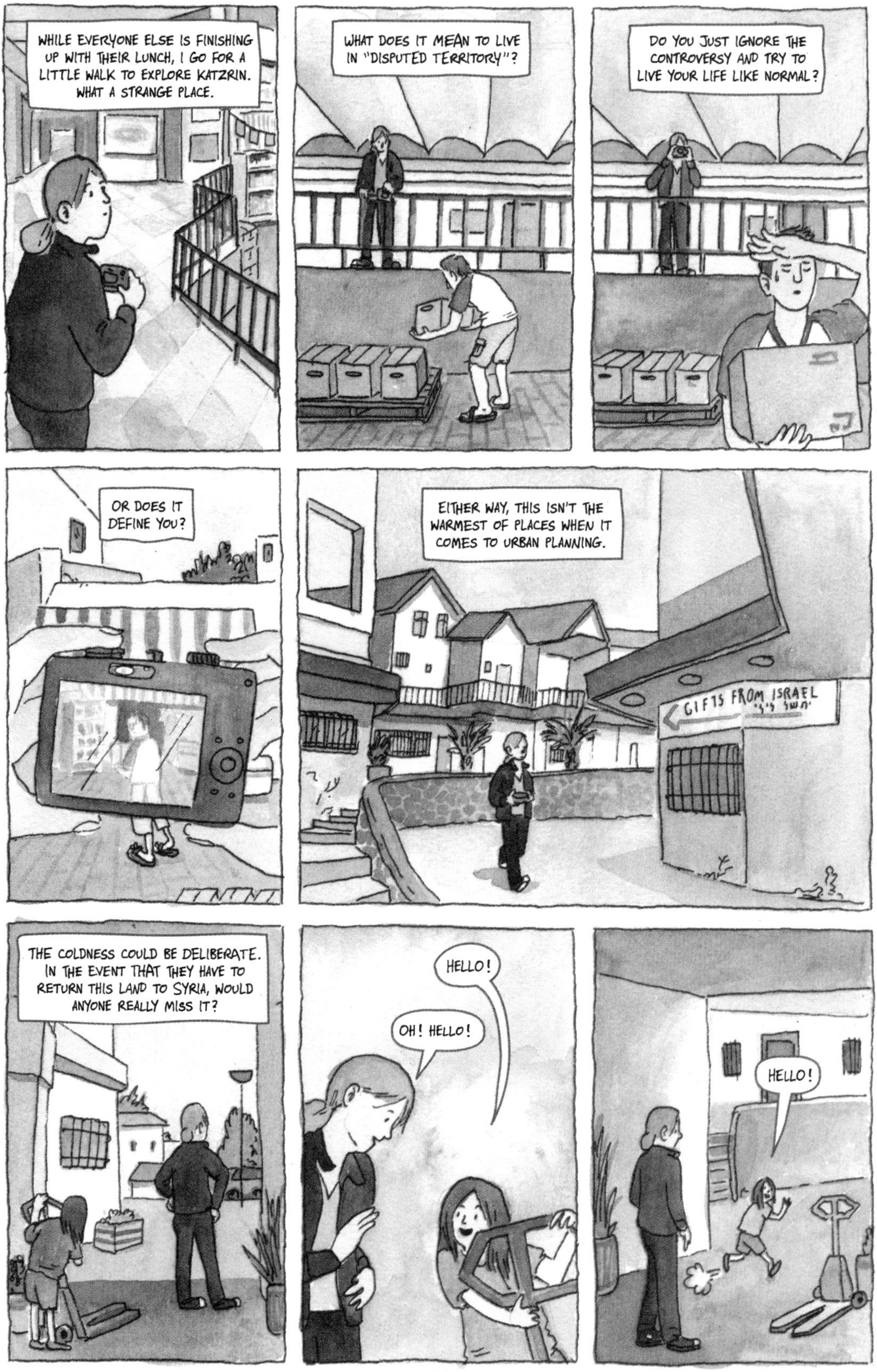
WHILE EVERYONE ELSE IS FINISHING UP WITH THEIR LUNCH, I GO FOR A LITTLE WALK TO EXPLORE KATZRIN. WHAT A STRANGE PLACE.
WHAT DOES IT MEAN TO LIVE IN "DISPUTED TERRITORY"?
DO YOU JUST IGNORE THE CONTROVERSY AND TRY TO LIVE YOUR LIFE LIKE NORMAL?
OR DOES IT DEFINE YOU?
EITHER WAY, THIS ISN'T THE WARMEST OF PLACES WHEN IT COMES TO URBAN PLANNING.
GIFTS FROM ISRAEL
THE COLDNESS COULD BE DELIBERATE. IN THE EVENT THAT THEY HAVE TO RETURN THIS LAND TO SYRIA, WOULD ANYONE REALLY MISS IT?
HELLO!
OH! HELLO!
HELLO!

WHEN GIL SAID WE WOULD BE WATCHING A MOVIE ABOUT THE GOLAN HEIGHTS I IMAGINED SOME KIND OF CHEESY FILMSTRIP.

I'M REEVALUATING MY PREDICTION NOW.

THIS PLACE IS SERIOUSLY INTENSE.

WHAT ARE WE IN FOR?

HEY, NADAN?

YES?

WHAT IS THIS PLACE?

GOLAN MAGIC!

HA HA. YES, I KNOW. IT'S VERY IMPRESSIVE. BUT WHAT IS IT?

NO, REALLY, THAT'S WHAT IT'S CALLED: "GOLAN MAGIC VISITOR CENTER!"

IT ALSO SAYS SO IN ENGLISH. SEE THERE?

GOLAN MAGIC VISITOR CENTER

כפר הגולן

OH.

WOW. NICE PLACE.

HEY, SARAH!

WHAT?

WOOSH

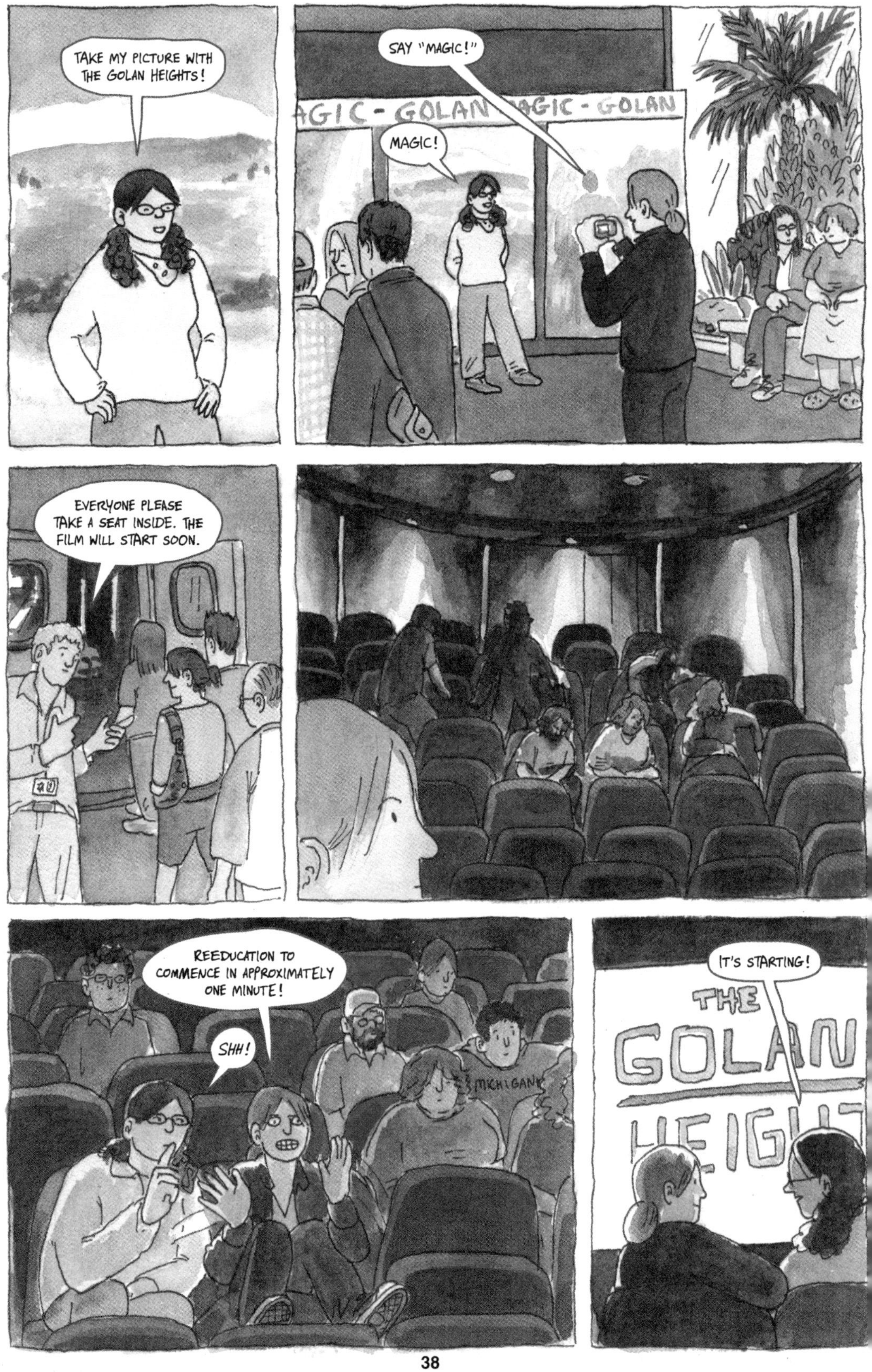
TAKE MY PICTURE WITH THE GOLAN HEIGHTS!
SAY "MAGIC!"
AGIC - GOLAN MAGIC - GOLAN
MAGIC!
EVERYONE PLEASE TAKE A SEAT INSIDE. THE FILM WILL START SOON.
REEDUCATION TO COMMENCE IN APPROXIMATELY ONE MINUTE!
SHH!
MICHIGAN
IT'S STARTING!
THE GOLAN HEIGHT

THE LIGHTS DIM AND THREE PROJECTORS LIGHT UP AN IMAX-STYLE SCREEN WITH A SWEEPING AERIAL SHOT OF THE GOLAN HEIGHTS IN FULL BLOOM.

THE GOLAN HEIGHTS...SINCE ISRAEL WON THIS LAND IN THE SIX-DAY WAR IT HAS BEEN AN IMPORTANT PART OF THIS NATION'S LIFEBLOOD.

IT SUPPLIES ALMOST A THIRD OF ISRAEL'S WATER SUPPLY AND IS A CENTER OF AGRICULTURE AND HERDING.

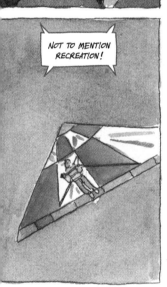

NOT TO MENTION RECREATION!

FROM THE SNOWY PEAK OF MOUNT HERMON...

...TO THE WORLD-FAMOUS VALLEY WINERIES...

CLINK!

THE GOLAN HEIGHTS' UNIQUE TERRAIN SUPPORTS ITS OWN POPULATION OF 30,000 AS WELL AS THE THOUSANDS OF VISITORS WHO COME TO SEE ITS MAJESTY.

MOST IMPORTANT, ITS GEOGRAPHIC POSITION MAKES IT INDISPENSABLE TO THE NATION'S SECURITY. BEFORE THE WAR, SYRIA SENT ROCKET ATTACKS INTO ISRAELI VILLAGES BELOW.

SYRIA

ROCKETS

ISRAEL

AND NOW...SYRIA WANTS IT BACK. ISRAEL HAS TRIED TO COMPROMISE WITH THE SYRIAN GOVERNMENT...

SYRIA

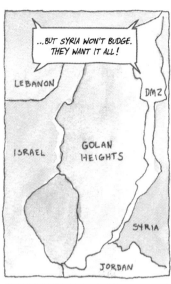

...BUT SYRIA WON'T BUDGE. THEY WANT IT ALL!

LEBANON

DMZ

ISRAEL

GOLAN HEIGHTS

SYRIA

JORDAN

EVERY BLADE OF GRASS, EVERY LAST PEBBLE, EVERY DROP OF WATER.

WOAH, SARAH...

YEAH. WOAH.

"MY FAMILY HAS LIVED HERE FOR FOUR GENERATIONS. THIS IS OUR HOME. TO GIVE IT UP WOULD BE TO GIVE UP MY HEART."

למסור את חגולן זה למסור אתלב'ני

HMPH. THAT'S A TOTAL LIE. FOR HER FAMILY TO HAVE BEEN THERE FOR FOUR GENERATIONS THEY WOULD HAVE HAD TO BE THERE FOR WAY MORE THAN THE FORTY YEARS ISRAEL HAD CONTROL OVER THE TERRITORY!

"WITHDRAWAL FROM THE GOLAN HEIGHTS IS UNTHINKABLE, EVEN IN TIMES OF PEACE. IT WOULD MEAN ABANDONING ISRAEL'S SECURITY."

זה מסכן את ביטחון ישראל

A GHOSTLY YITZHAK RABIN FLOATS OVER THE LANDSCAPE.

"LET ALL OF US FULFILL OUR OBLIGATIONS TO THE GOLAN HEIGHTS. AND TO YOU RESIDENTS THERE WHO MADE IT WHAT IT IS, YOU HAVE ALL MY RESPECT."

אני מכבד אותר

WHO CAN ARGUE WITH AN ASSASSINATED NOBEL PRIZE WINNER?

WHO CAN DISAGREE?

UM...

I KNEW IT! THIS WHOLE TRIP IS GOING TO BE A REGIONAL PROPAGANDA TOUR!

YOU GUYS THOUGHT IT WAS PROPAGANDA?

YOU DIDN'T?

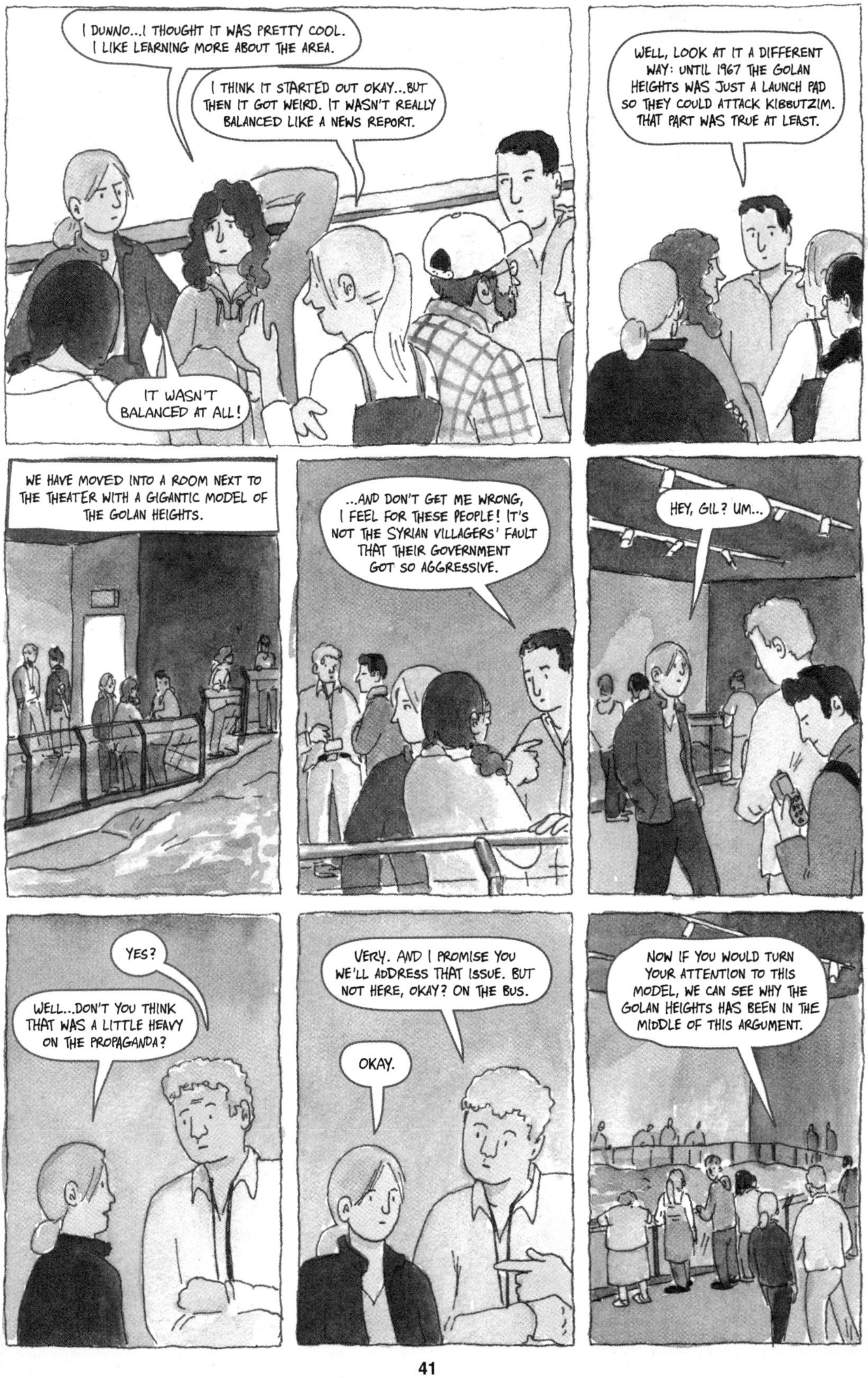
I DUNNO...I THOUGHT IT WAS PRETTY COOL. I LIKE LEARNING MORE ABOUT THE AREA.
I THINK IT STARTED OUT OKAY...BUT THEN IT GOT WEIRD. IT WASN'T REALLY BALANCED LIKE A NEWS REPORT.
IT WASN'T BALANCED AT ALL!
WELL, LOOK AT IT A DIFFERENT WAY: UNTIL 1967 THE GOLAN HEIGHTS WAS JUST A LAUNCH PAD SO THEY COULD ATTACK KIBBUTZIM. THAT PART WAS TRUE AT LEAST.
WE HAVE MOVED INTO A ROOM NEXT TO THE THEATER WITH A GIGANTIC MODEL OF THE GOLAN HEIGHTS.
...AND DON'T GET ME WRONG, I FEEL FOR THESE PEOPLE! IT'S NOT THE SYRIAN VILLAGERS' FAULT THAT THEIR GOVERNMENT GOT SO AGGRESSIVE.
HEY, GIL? UM...
YES?
WELL...DON'T YOU THINK THAT WAS A LITTLE HEAVY ON THE PROPAGANDA?
VERY. AND I PROMISE YOU WE'LL ADDRESS THAT ISSUE. BUT NOT HERE, OKAY? ON THE BUS.
OKAY.
NOW IF YOU WOULD TURN YOUR ATTENTION TO THIS MODEL, WE CAN SEE WHY THE GOLAN HEIGHTS HAS BEEN IN THE MIDDLE OF THIS ARGUMENT.

IN THE NINETEEN YEARS PRIOR TO THE SIX DAY-WAR, THERE WAS A LOT OF HARASSMENT FROM THE SYRIAN ARMY DOWN TO THE ISRAELI AREAS BELOW, AND THAT'S WHY ISRAEL DECIDED TO CAPTURE IT.

ACTUALLY, THE SIX DAY WAR WAS THREE DIFFERENT CAMPAIGNS. TWO DAYS AGAINST THE EGYPTIANS, TWO AGAINST THE JORDANIANS, AND THE LAST TWO AGAINST THE SYRIANS.

THIS RIDGE GOES ALL THE WAY FROM LEBANON TO ETHIOPIA, AND MOST OF THE BATTLES ON THE SYRIAN FRONT WERE FOUGHT ON THIS STEEP CLIFF WHERE IT RISES FROM THE KINNERET, WHAT YOU CALL THE SEA OF GALILEE.

BY THESE LAST TWO DAYS IN 1967, THE SYRIANS HAD HEARD THAT THE JORDANIAN AND EGYPTIAN ARMIES HAD BEEN DEFEATED.

THEY KNEW THEY COULD NOT HOLD BACK THE ISRAELI ARMY FOR LONG, SO THEY DECIDED TO PLAY A GAME WITH INTERNATIONAL POLITICS.

DAMASCUS

THE SYRIAN GOVERNMENT ANNOUNCED THAT THE ISRAELIS HAD ALREADY ADVANCED PAST THE CLIFFS AND WERE MARCHING TOWARDS DAMASCUS.

THEY HOPED THAT ONCE THE INTERNATIONAL COMMUNITY HEARD THIS FALSE REPORT THEY WOULD PRESSURE ISRAEL INTO A CEASE-FIRE.

UNITED NATIONS

AND IT WORKED. WITHIN 24 HOURS ISRAEL WAS COMPELLED TO STOP FIGHTING.

BUT WHAT HAPPENED *DURING* THAT 24 HOURS WAS VERY INTERESTING.

IMAGINE YOU ARE A SYRIAN CITIZEN LIVING IN A SMALL VILLAGE IN THE GOLAN HEIGHTS AND YOU HEAR ON THE OFFICIAL BROADCAST THAT YOU ARE SUDDENLY BEHIND ENEMY LINES.

WHAT WOULD YOU DO? YOU WOULD TAKE WHAT YOU CAN CARRY ON YOUR BACK AND EVACUATE!

AND BY THE WAY, ISRAELIS DID THE SAME THING LAST SUMMER WHEN HEZBOLLAH WAS FIRING ROCKETS OVER THE LEBANESE BORDER.

200,000 ISRAELIS MOVED TO CENTRAL ISRAEL UNTIL THE FIGHTING STOPPED AND THEN RETURNED TO THEIR HOMES.

THE SYRIAN PEOPLE DID THE SAME, AND WE'RE TALKING HALF A MILLION PEOPLE, ONLY THEY COULD NOT RETURN TO THEIR HOMES BECAUSE WE CAPTURED THE TERRITORY.

THIS JUNE IT WILL HAVE BEEN FORTY YEARS SINCE THEY HAVE NOT BEEN ABLE TO RETURN.

NOW THE SYRIAN *ARMY*, THAT WAS A DIFFERENT STORY.

WHEN THE OFFICERS HEARD THE TROUBLING NEWS THAT THEY WERE FIGHTING ON THE RIDGE BUT WERE NOW BEHIND ISRAELI UNITS, THEY PANICKED.

THEY RAN AWAY AND LEFT THEIR SOLDIERS BEHIND TO FIGHT THE ISRAELIS.

MY FATHER WAS A PARATROOPER DURING THIS WAR AND HE FOUGHT ON THE FRONT LINES HERE ON THIS RIDGE.

AS HE MADE HIS WAY UP THE CLIFFS, HE WAS VERY IMPRESSED BY THE BRAVERY OF THE SYRIAN TROOPS IN THEIR BUNKERS.

ALTHOUGH THEY WERE SUFFERING MANY CASUALTIES, NOT A SINGLE ONE CAME OUT TO SURRENDER.

WHEN MY FATHER FINALLY GOT INTO THE BUNKERS, ONLY THEN DID HE UNDERSTAND...

MOST OF THE SOLDIERS WERE EITHER DEAD OR INJURED, AND THEY HAD BEEN UNABLE TO LEAVE THEIR POSITIONS...

BEFORE THE OFFICERS LEFT THEY HAD CHAINED THEM TO THEIR BUNKERS BY THEIR FEET.

BY THE TIME THE FIRST LINE OF SYRIAN DEFENSE WAS CAPTURED, THERE WERE NO MORE SYRIAN FORCES IN THE REST OF THE GOLAN HEIGHTS.

THE ISRAELI ARMY THEN EASILY ADVANCED AS FAR AS THE TOWN OF AL QUNEITRA BEFORE THE UNITED NATIONS CEASE-FIRE WENT INTO EFFECT.

THE FIGHTING STOPPED, AND THAT WAS THE END OF THE SIX-DAY WAR.

BEFORE THE WAR, THERE WERE 500,000 PEOPLE LIVING HERE. NOW THERE ARE ABOUT 40,000. HALF OF THOSE ARE DRUZE, 18,000 ARE JEWS, AND 2,000 ARE MUSLIMS.

NOW, I HEARD SOME OF YOUR REMARKS ON THE FILM WE WATCHED. SOME OF YOU USED THE VERY HARSH WORD "PROPAGANDA." I AM GOING TO GET POLITICAL FOR A MOMENT AND TELL YOU THAT I AGREE. IT WAS PROPAGANDA.

YOU SEE, IN 1992 THERE WERE ONGOING NEGOTIATIONS ON THE RETURN OF THE GOLAN HEIGHTS TO THE SYRIANS.

TO TRY AND STOP THIS FROM HAPPENING, THE PEOPLE OF KATZRIN PRODUCED THIS FILM TO TRY AND SWAY THE OPINION OF THE REST OF ISRAEL.

...BY NOW, THINGS BEING WHAT THEY ARE WITH HEZBOLLAH, WHICH IS SUPPORTED BY SYRIA, NEGOTIATIONS ON THE GOLAN HEIGHTS ARE OUT OF THE QUESTION FOR THE TIME BEING.

THIS IS AS FAR NORTH AS WE'LL EVER GET ON THIS TRIP.

YOU CAN SEE SYRIA...

AND, IF YOU SQUINT, LEBANON...

...AND OVER THERE IS THE UNITED NATIONS BASE IN THE DEMILITARIZED ZONE.

IN THE LATE AFTERNOON LIGHT, MOUNT HERMON REMINDS ME OF "MOUNT DOOM" FROM THE LORD OF THE RINGS MOVIES, LOOKING IN THE DISTANCE.

MELISSA IS STILL DISCUSSING THE "SITUATION" WITH TAL, ONE OF THE FEW BIRTHRIGHT PARTICIPANTS AMONG US WHO HAVE BEEN TO ISRAEL BEFORE.

I DON'T THINK THERE CAN EVER BE PEACE. NOT IN A MILLION YEARS.

LOOK, THE PALESTINIANS DON'T HAVE A REAL HOMELAND AND THAT'S A HUGE PROBLEM! I THINK THEY SHOULD HAVE THE WEST BANK AND GAZA. EVERYONE THINKS THAT! BUT IT STILL WON'T BE ENOUGH FOR THEM.

AND THEY'VE BEEN SLAUGHTERED EVERYWHERE THEY GO, BUT NO ONE TALKS ABOUT IT UNLESS ISRAEL IS INVOLVED.

WELL, I DON'T KNOW...

THOSE ARAB NATIONS THAT REFUSE TO RECOGNIZE ISRAEL BECAUSE OF THE "PLIGHT OF THE PALESTINIANS?" THEY DON'T LIFT A FINGER TO HELP THEM. NOT ONE FINGER.

BELIEVE ME, I WANT PEACE AS MUCH AS ANYONE ELSE. I LOVE THIS COUNTRY! MY DAD'S SIDE OF THE FAMILY IS ISRAELI. THEY FOUGHT IN ALL THOSE WARS TO PROTECT IT.

...AND IT REALLY HURTS ME TO SEE HOW ISRAEL ACTS SOMETIMES. THEY GO TOO FAR. BUT BEHIND IT ALL THEY JUST WANT TO BE SAFE.

SO YOU'RE ISRAELI YOURSELF IN A WAY?

WELL, I CONSIDER MYSELF AMERICAN. I GUESS THIS IS MY COUNTRY TOO, BUT I'M AMERICAN.

WOULD YOU EVER LIVE HERE?

NO WAY. NEVER.

WHY NOT?

TO TELL YOU THE TRUTH? IT'S THE ISRAELIS. I CAN'T STAND THEM. THEY'RE SO RUDE!

GUYS! BACK ON THE BUS!

WHAT ABOUT GIL?

OF COURSE THEY'RE NOT ALL BAD! GIL SEEMS PRETTY COOL.

COME ON, WE'D BETTER GO.

COMING!

THE SUN IS FINALLY SETTING ON OUR FIRST DAY HERE AS WE DRIVE BACK THROUGH THE GOLAN HEIGHTS.

INSIDE THE BUS ARE FORTY TIRED PEOPLE WHO ARE MUCH TOO EXHAUSTED TO ASK ANY MORE QUESTIONS.

OUTSIDE THE BUS, THE LAND IS PRETTY EMPTY BESIDES THOSE BASALT ROCKS WHICH ARE EVERYWHERE.

SOMETIMES THEY'RE GROUPED IN WAYS THAT SUGGEST THEY USED TO BE WALLS OF BUILDINGS. THE FORMER HOMES OF FORMER SYRIANS?

AND THESE NEWER BUILDINGS, THEY MUST BE BUNKERS AND BARRACKS FROM THE WAR.

THAT STORY GIL TOLD ABOUT HIS FATHER CAN'T BE TRUE. IT'S PROBABLY A LEGEND MADE UP TO MAKE THE SYRIAN OFFICERS LOOK LIKE COWARDS.

BUT THEN AGAIN, HE DOESN'T REALLY SEEM LIKE THE LYING TYPE. I GUESS IT COULD BE A TRUE STORY.

I'M SURE THE ISRAELIS DID EQUALLY HORRIBLE THINGS, ALTHOUGH PROBABLY NOT TO THEIR OWN MEN. WARS DON'T BRING OUT THE BEST IN PEOPLE.

I DON'T EVEN KNOW ANYTHING ABOUT HOW THIS WAR WAS FOUGHT.

I HEAR ABOUT "FRONT LINES" THIS AND "ADVANCING" THAT, BUT WHEN I TRY TO IMAGINE THE LOGISTICS OF THE CONFLICT, IT GETS ALL HAZY.

AND I'M TOO DRAINED TO ASK RIGHT NOW.

THEY SHOULD MAKE A MOVIE ABOUT THE SIX-DAY WAR, LIKE ALL THOSE WORLD WAR TWO MOVIES. THEN MAYBE I WOULD UNDERSTAND.

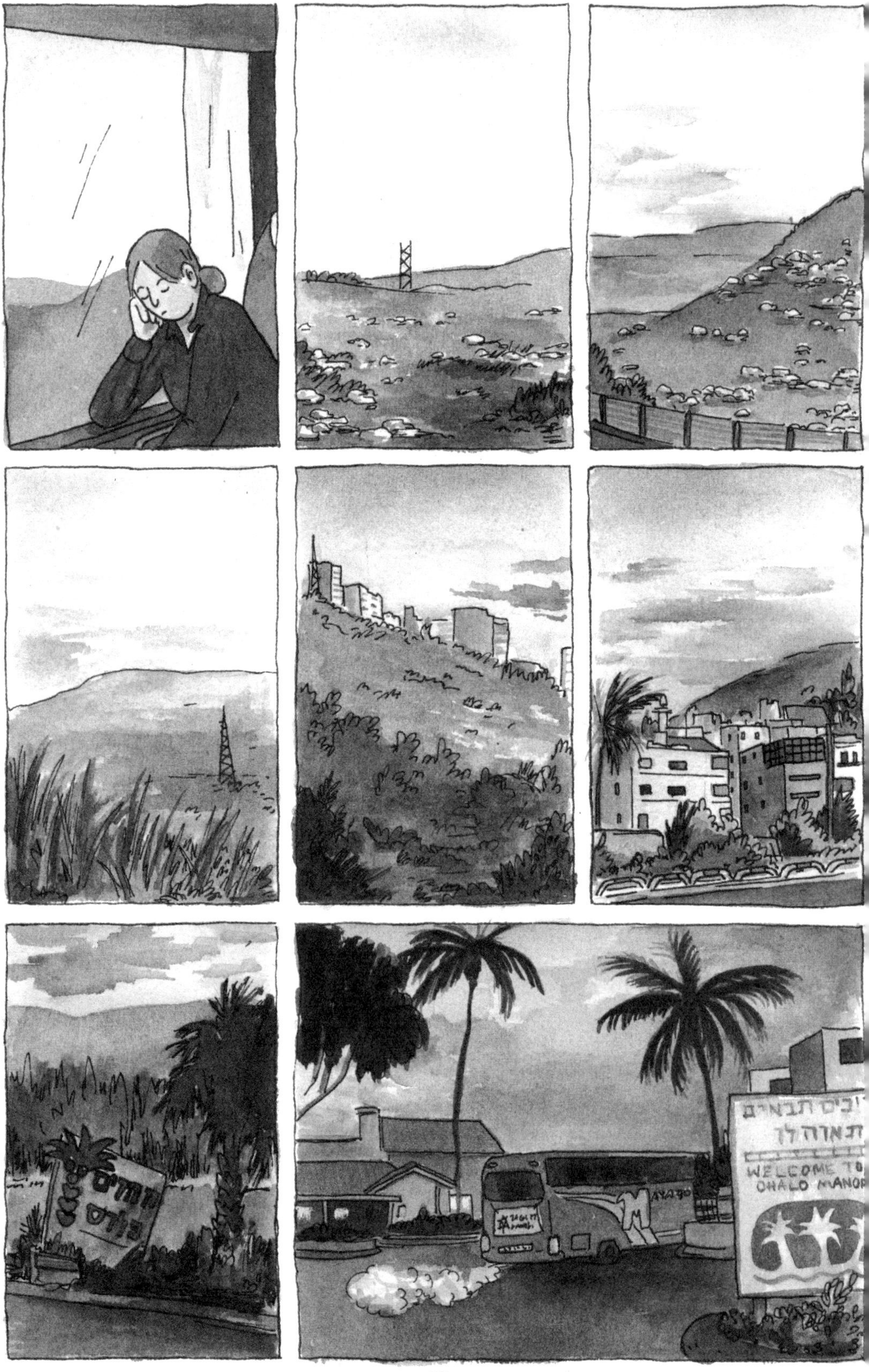
WELCOME TO
OHALO MANO

THIS COUNTRY HAS SAPPED ALL OF MY PHYSICAL AND MENTAL ENERGY IN JUST ONE DAY.

ON AUTOPILOT, I UNPACK IN OUR ROOM AT OHALO GUESTHOUSE.

DINNER IS SUBDUED AND WITHOUT VERY MUCH CONVERSATION.

CAN'T... THINK...ANY-MORE.

I KNOW. I DON'T THINK I'VE EVER BEEN SO TIRED.

CLICK

ISRAEL

THIS ROOM SMELLS LIKE AN OLD WOMAN ON A NIGHT OUT.

SNIFF

I'M TURNING OFF THE MAIN LIGHTS. GOODNIGHT, SARAH!

GOODNIGHT, MELISSA!

CLICK

I WAKE UP IN THE MIDDLE OF THE NIGHT AND CAN'T GO BACK TO SLEEP.

THIS PLACE HAS MY MIND OCCUPIED.

IT'S THE OLDEST PLACE I'VE EVER BEEN.

IN THIS LITTLE SQUARE OF SPACE OUR ROOM TAKES UP, ON THE GROUND BENEATH THE FOUNDATION...SO MANY PEOPLE MUST HAVE ALSO SLEPT HERE.

OR NOT BEEN ABLE TO SLEEP, LIKE ME, LYING AWAKE ON THE SHORES OF THE SEA OF GALILEE.

HUNDREDS OF PEOPLE OVER THOUSANDS OF YEARS IN THIS SQUARE OF LAND.

I WANT TO GO OUTSIDE AND LOOK AT THIS HISTORIC SCENERY, BUT IT'S STILL PITCH DARK.

SO I LIE HERE IN MY SQUARE, THE MOST RECENT LAYER OF SLEEPER, AND WAIT FOR THE SUN TO COME UP.

WITH THE PREHISTORIC NATUFIANS...

...AND THE EARLY JEWS...

...THE ROMAN FOOT SOLDIERS...

...THE OTTOMAN TAX COLLECTORS...

...THE ARAB FARMERS...

...THE TWENTIETH CENTURY JEWS...

AND AS SOON AS THE LIGHT CHANGES...

...I CAN GO.

FINALLY!

GOTTA SEE...
GOTTA SEE...

THE
SEA OF
GALILEEEEE

HUFF!

WAAAHHH!

LAKE
KINNERET

OR

SEA OF GALILEE

KINNERET CEMETERY

OHALO

NNERET
BBUTZ PUB

JORDAN RIVER

DEGANYA

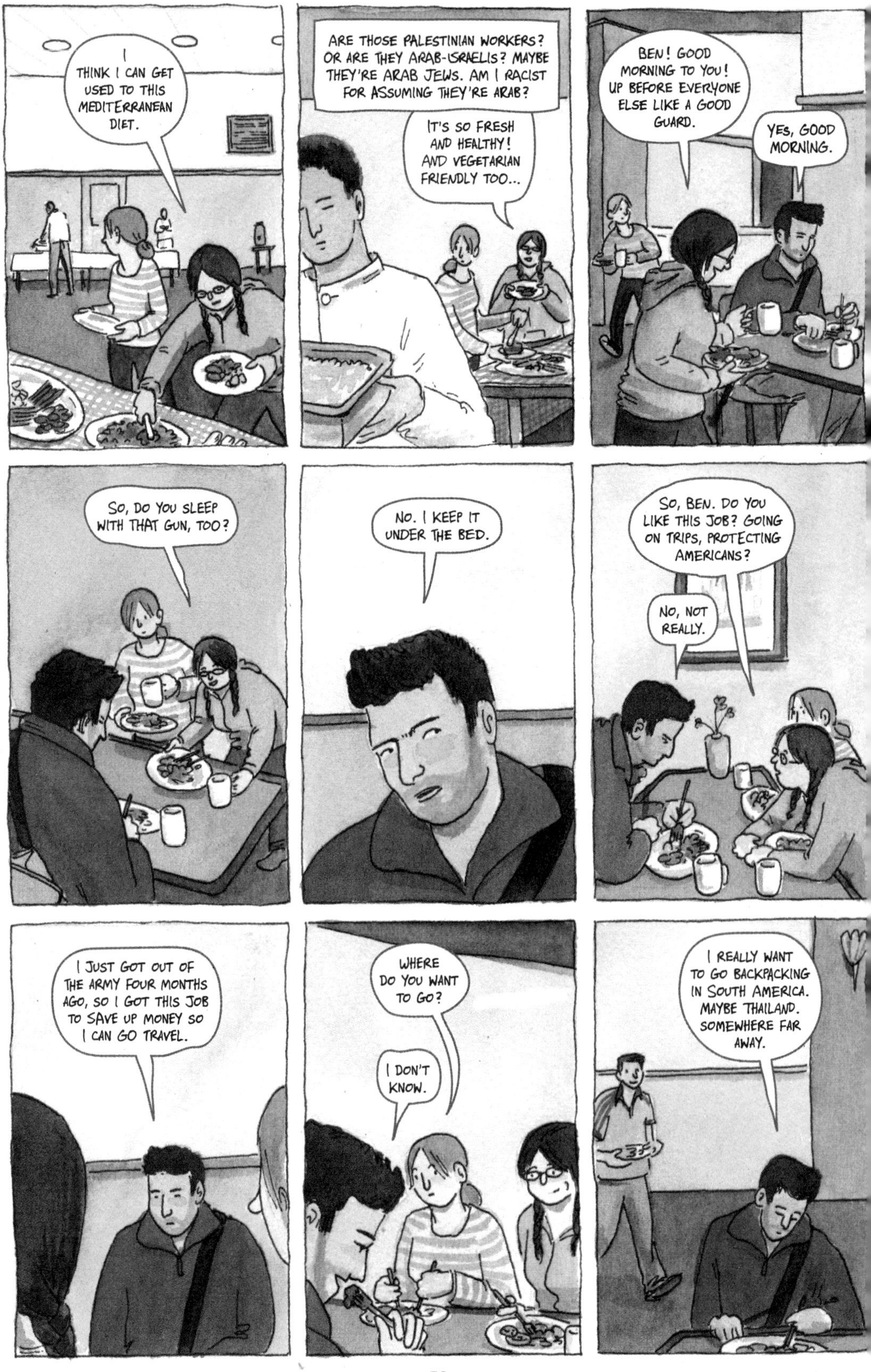
I THINK I CAN GET USED TO THIS MEDITERRANEAN DIET.
ARE THOSE PALESTINIAN WORKERS? OR ARE THEY ARAB-ISRAELIS? MAYBE THEY'RE ARAB JEWS. AM I RACIST FOR ASSUMING THEY'RE ARAB?
IT'S SO FRESH AND HEALTHY! AND VEGETARIAN FRIENDLY TOO...
BEN! GOOD MORNING TO YOU! UP BEFORE EVERYONE ELSE LIKE A GOOD GUARD.
YES, GOOD MORNING.
SO, DO YOU SLEEP WITH THAT GUN, TOO?
NO. I KEEP IT UNDER THE BED.
SO, BEN. DO YOU LIKE THIS JOB? GOING ON TRIPS, PROTECTING AMERICANS?
NO, NOT REALLY.
I JUST GOT OUT OF THE ARMY FOUR MONTHS AGO, SO I GOT THIS JOB TO SAVE UP MONEY SO I CAN GO TRAVEL.
WHERE DO YOU WANT TO GO?
I DON'T KNOW.
I REALLY WANT TO GO BACKPACKING IN SOUTH AMERICA. MAYBE THAILAND. SOMEWHERE FAR AWAY.

AHH, BREAKFAST! THE MOST IMPORTANT MEAL OF THE DAY! YOU GUYS LIKE ISRAELI FOOD YET? IT LOOKS PRETTY GOOD HERE.

NO BACON THOUGH. TOO BAD. I LIKE BACON.

YOU'RE NOT KOSHER?

NAH. DO I LOOK RELIGIOUS TO YOU?

I GUESS NOT...

SO HOW DO YOU LIKE WORKING FOR BIRTHRIGHT?

OH, THIS IS JUST A ONE-TIME THING FOR ME. BEING A MADRICH IS KIND OF LIKE A TREAT.

MADRICH?

IT'S LIKE A, WHADDAYACALLIT? "COUNSELOR."

I HELP SHANNON AND GIL ARRANGE THE HOTELS AND STUFF AND MAKE SURE NONE OF YOU GET LOST AND IN RETURN I GET TO GO ON A VACATION.

THIS WEEK, I'M A TOURIST TOO.

WELCOME TO THE KINNERET CEMETERY, EVERYONE! PLEASE HAVE A SEAT AND GET COMFORTABLE!

MY NAME IS JOEL. I'M ORIGINALLY FROM THE UNITED STATES LIKE YOU, BUT I COMMITTED ALIYAH IN 1986 AND HAVE BEEN DOING TIME EVER SINCE! HA HA!

YIKES, TOUGH CROWD. THIS GUY SHOULD KNOW BETTER THAN TO START HIS TALK WITH A BAD PUN.

FOR SOME TIME I'VE BEEN STUDYING THE LIVES OF THE PEOPLE BURIED IN THIS BEAUTIFUL SPOT.

MY OBSESSION BEGAN YEARS AGO, WHEN I WAS STUDYING HEBREW. MY TEACHER GAVE ME THE DIARY OF A YOUNG WOMAN NAMED FANYA.

THE NEXT DAY HE ASKED ME HOW I HAD SLEPT. THE DEVIL, HE KNEW I HADN'T SLEPT A WINK. I HAD BEEN UP ALL NIGHT READING ABOUT FANYA'S JOURNEY AND I WANTED TO KNOW MORE.

FANYA, AND THE OTHER AMAZING PEOPLE WHO SHARE HER STORY, WAS LAID TO REST HERE. YOU SEE, THEY WERE AMONG THE FIRST YOUNG JEWS TO SETTLE IN THE GALILEE IN THE EARLY 1900s.

THOSE KIDS CHANGED HISTORY. AND I WANT TO TELL YOU ABOUT THEIR COURAGEOUS STRUGGLE.

THEY WERE ZIONISTS FROM RUSSIA AND FROM EASTERN EUROPE AND THEY CAME HERE TO WORK THE LAND AND CREATE A NEW IDENTITY FOR THEMSELVES AS JEWS.

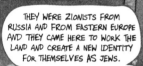

MOST OF THEM WERE EVEN YOUNGER THAN YOU FOLKS WHEN THEY ARRIVED.

BUT THE YISRAEL THEY FOUND WHEN THEY ARRIVED ISN'T WHAT YOU SEE NOW. INSTEAD OF THIS LUSH GREENERY AND FERTILE FARMLAND, THE GALILEE WAS A FETID SWAMP SURROUNDED BY DESERT.

MARK TWAIN, UPON VISITING ISRAEL A FEW DECADES EARLIER, HAD CALLED ISRAEL "A DESOLATE COUNTRY WHOSE SOIL IS RICH ENOUGH, BUT IS GIVEN OVER WHOLLY TO WEEDS...A DESOLATION IS HERE THAT NOT EVEN IMAGINATION CAN GRACE WITH THE POMP OF LIFE AND ACTION."

WELL LOOK AT IT NOW! WE HAVE CITRUS TREES! BANANAS! AVOCADOS! ALL BECAUSE THESE YOUNG PEOPLE SHARED A DREAM.

BUT I'M GETTING AHEAD OF MYSELF. WHY DID THEY COME HERE IN THE FIRST PLACE?

AT THE TURN OF THE CENTURY, JUST WHEN JEWS THOUGHT THEY HAD SUCCESSFULLY ASSIMILATED THEMSELVES INTO THE MODERN, MOSTLY SECULAR EUROPEAN SOCIETY, A SERIES OF EVENTS PROVED THIS WAS FAR FROM THE TRUTH.

DESPICABLE!

FIRST THE DREYFUS AFFAIR AND NOW THE KISHINEV POGROM. HAVE YOU READ BIALIK'S POEM OF THE RAPE OF OUR WOMEN BY THE COSSACKS?

"WITH BLOODY AXES IN THEIR PAWS COMPELLED THY DAUGHTERS YIELD: BEASTED AND SWIPED! NOTE ALSO DO NOT FAIL TO NOTE, IN THAT DARK CORNER, AND BEHIND THAT CASK CROUCHED HUSBANDS, BRIDEGROOMS, BROTHERS, PEERING FROM THE CRACKS..."

YOSEF...

"CRUSHED IN THEIR SHAME, THEY SAW IT ALL; THEY DID NOT STIR NOR MOVE...HOW DID THEIR MENFOLK BEAR IT, HOW DID THEY BEAR THIS YOKE? THEY CRAWLED FORTH FROM THEIR HOLES, THEY FLED TO THE HOUSE OF THE LORD, THEY OFFERED THANKS TO HIM!"

YOSEF, I HAVE READ THE POEM.

PAM!

WHAT HE WRITES IS TRUE. OUR OWN PEOPLE CANNOT STAND UP FOR THEMSELVES. WE ARE COWARDS, WAITING FOR THE MESSIAH TO RESCUE US FROM TYRANNY INSTEAD OF TAKING ACTION.

THE ZIONISTS ARE RIGHT! AS LONG AS THE JEWS DON'T HAVE A HOMELAND WE WILL ALWAYS BE AT THE MERCY OF HOSTS WHO DESPISE US.

WE MUST JOIN THE MOVEMENT IN PALESTINE. WITH THE OTHERS THERE WE CAN BUILD A NEW JEWISH IDENTITY OF STRENGTH AND FREEDOM!

WAIT, BUT WHAT ABOUT THE PEOPLE WHO LIVE THERE ALREADY?

THE ARABS? WHY, THEY WILL WELCOME US.

THEY CAME FROM RUSSIA, FROM MINSK, FROM LITHUANIA AND VIENNA, ALL SHARING A PASSION TO SHAPE THEIR DESTINIES. BUT FIRST THEY WOULD HAVE TO SHAPE THE LAND. AFTER MEETING IN A TRAINING FARM, TEN MEN AND TWO WOMEN CROSSED THE JORDAN RIVER AND BEGAN TO BUILD WHAT WOULD BECOME THE FIRST KIBBUTZ.

WE WILL ESTABLISH AN INDEPENDENT SETTLEMENT WITH NEITHER EXPLOITERS NOR EXPLOITED--A COMMUNE.

THREE THINGS ALMOST DID THEM IN. FIRST, THE HEAT AND HUMIDITY OF THE MEDITERRANEAN SUMMER TESTED THEIR WILLS.

THEN, ONE BY ONE, THEY ALL CONTRACTED MALARIA FROM THE TERRIBLE MOSQUITOES. WITH NO MEDICINE NEARBY, THEIR ONLY OPTION WAS TO WAIT OUT THE WEEKS OF FEVER, DELIRIUM AND DIARRHEA.

BUT MOST OF ALL THEY WERE HOMESICK. THEY MISSED THEIR PARENTS, MANY OF WHOM HAD SAT SHIVA AND NOW CONSIDERED THEIR CHILDREN DEAD TO THEM. THEY COULDN'T GO BACK.

BUT THEY DIDN'T GIVE UP. EACH MORNING AT DAWN THEY WOULD LEAP FROM THE HAYSTACK THEY ALL SHARED AS A BED AND THROW THEMSELVES INTO THE DAY'S WORK.

THEIR DREAM BECAME REALITY AND THEY NAMED IT DEGANYA AFTER THE PLENTIFUL GRAINS THEY GREW THERE. OTHERS LEARNED FROM THEM AND SOON THERE WERE KIBBUTZIM ALL OVER THE LAND OF ISRAEL.

NEVER AGAIN WILL WE BE OPPRESSED! WE HAVE CONTROLLED THE LAND AND NOW WE CONTROL OUR FUTURE. TO DEGANYA!

TO DEGANYA!

WAIT!

NONE OF YOU ARE THINKING OF THE CONSEQUENCES OF YOUR ACTIONS! WHAT YOU'RE A PART OF WILL ESCALATE INTO A WAR IN WHICH THOUSANDS WILL *LOSE THEIR HOMES!*

JEWS WILL LOSE THEIR HOMES?

NO, THE ARABS. YOUR NEIGHBORS!

WE NEED TO TAKE CARE OF OURSELVES NOW. IF WE DON'T, NO ONE WILL.

AND WE AREN'T HARMING THEM. QUITE THE OPPOSITE.

WE ONLY FIGHT THEM IN SELF-DEFENSE. THEY ARE THE ONES BEING HOSTILE TO US.

AH, THE FAMOUS POET RACHEL HAS WRITTEN ANOTHER POEM ABOUT DEGANYA! LET US LISTEN!

PERHAPS ALL THIS NEVER WAS.

PERHAPS I NEVER ROSE AT DAWN TO TILL THE GARDEN WITH THE SWEAT OF MY BROW... NEVER PURIFIED MYSELF IN THE QUIET BLUE AND INNOCENCE OF MY KINNERET.

♪ OH MY KINNERET DID YOU TRULY EXIST OR WERE YOU ONLY A DREAM?

NOW ALL I ASK OF YOU IS THAT YOU GO HOME AND SHARE THE STORY OF THESE PIONEERS WHO HELPED MAKE ISRAEL WHAT IT IS TODAY. AND THINK ABOUT THIS...

HAVE YOU FOUND THAT THING IN YOUR LIFE FOR WHICH YOU JUMP OFF THE HAYSTACK IN THE MORNING?

MAY YOU ALL TRANSFORM YOUR OWN REALITIES THE WAY THESE YOUNG PEOPLE DID.

WOW, THEY REALLY BOUGHT ALL OF THIS, HOOK, LINE AND SINKER!

I AM SO THANKFUL FOR THIS...I NOW HAVE SO MUCH TO BRING HOME WITH ME.

SO, WHAT DID YOU THINK OF JOEL'S LITTLE STORY?

THAT WAS REALLY INSPIRATIONAL. I'M JUST BLOWN AWAY!

WHAT? YOU DIDN'T THINK SO?

WELL, I MEAN... THERE WERE A FEW THINGS I...

JUST LITTLE THINGS. NOTHING REALLY. OVERALL, YEAH, VERY INSPIRING.

WASN'T IT THOUGH? IT MADE ME REALLY STOP AND THINK. WHAT DOES MAKE ME JUMP OFF THE HAYSTACK, YOU KNOW? I DON'T THINK I HAVE ANYTHING IN MY LIFE THAT I'M THAT PASSIONATE ABOUT.

EXACTLY!

GUYS, BECAUSE IT'S SHABBAT, SHAI IS OFF DUTY SO WE'LL WALK BACK TO OHALO. JUST FOLLOW NADAV.

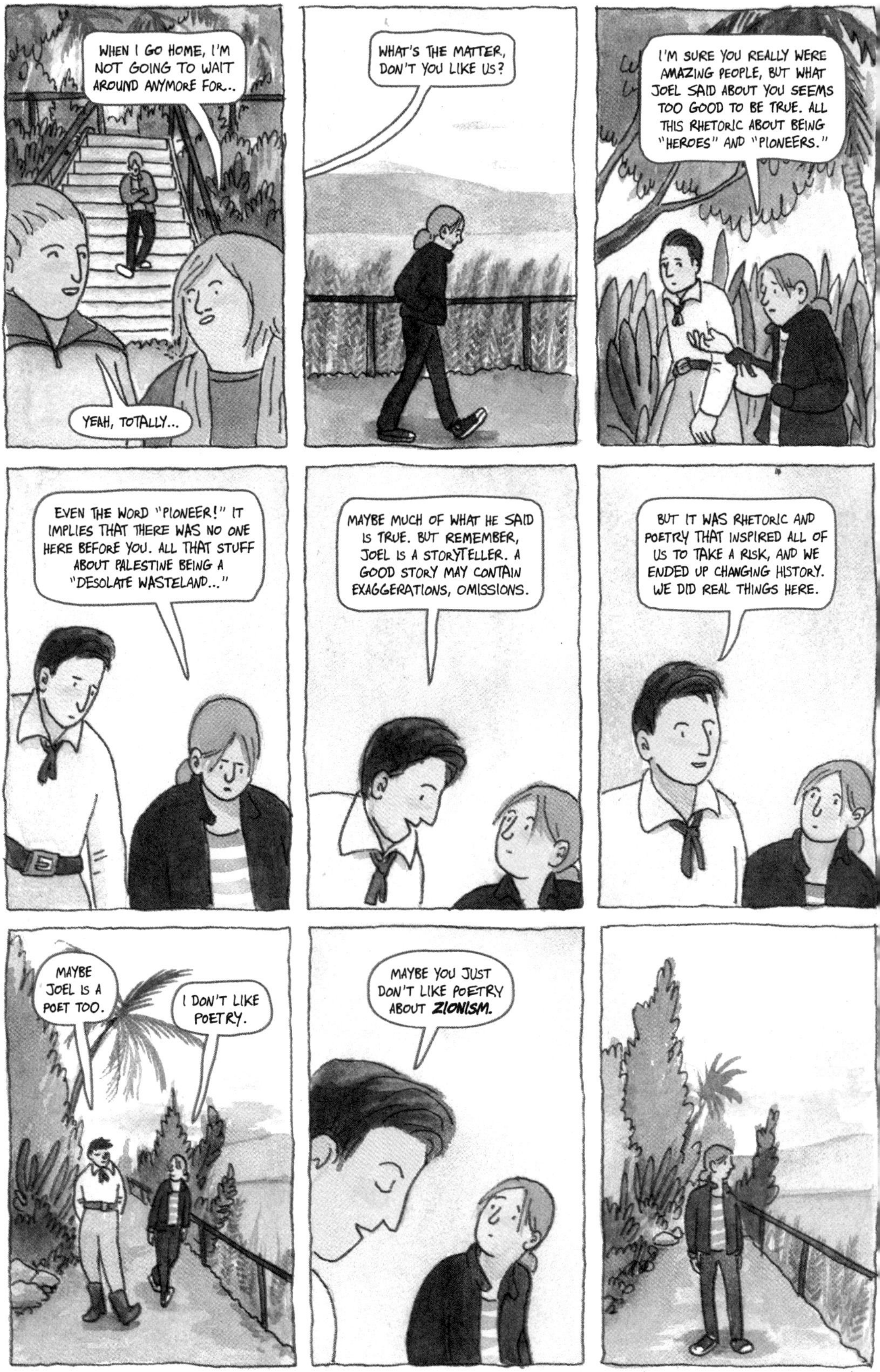
WHEN I GO HOME, I'M NOT GOING TO WAIT AROUND ANYMORE FOR..
YEAH, TOTALLY...
WHAT'S THE MATTER, DON'T YOU LIKE US?
I'M SURE YOU REALLY WERE AMAZING PEOPLE, BUT WHAT JOEL SAID ABOUT YOU SEEMS TOO GOOD TO BE TRUE. ALL THIS RHETORIC ABOUT BEING "HEROES" AND "PIONEERS."
EVEN THE WORD "PIONEER!" IT IMPLIES THAT THERE WAS NO ONE HERE BEFORE YOU. ALL THAT STUFF ABOUT PALESTINE BEING A "DESOLATE WASTELAND..."
MAYBE MUCH OF WHAT HE SAID IS TRUE. BUT REMEMBER, JOEL IS A STORYTELLER. A GOOD STORY MAY CONTAIN EXAGGERATIONS, OMISSIONS.
BUT IT WAS RHETORIC AND POETRY THAT INSPIRED ALL OF US TO TAKE A RISK, AND WE ENDED UP CHANGING HISTORY. WE DID REAL THINGS HERE.
MAYBE JOEL IS A POET TOO.
I DON'T LIKE POETRY.
MAYBE YOU JUST DON'T LIKE POETRY ABOUT **ZIONISM.**

SHALOM ALEICHEM MALACHEI HA-SHAREIS...

AT SUNDOWN, A GUEST RABBI ARRIVES TO LEAD US THROUGH A SHORT SHABBAT SERVICE.

WITH THESE CANDLES, WE WELCOME THE SHABBAT, AS DO JEWS ALL OVER THE WORLD.

WE THINK OF THE SHABBAT AS A BEAUTIFUL BRIDE. EVERY WEEK WE WAIT FOR HER TO GRACE US WITH HER BLESSINGS...

THAT WAS SO LOVELY, DON'T YOU THINK?

I GUESS. I THOUGHT THIS WAS SUPPOSED TO BE A NON-RELIGIOUS BIRTHRIGHT TOUR, THOUGH.

AND SHABBAT FOOD IS ALWAYS SUCH A DOWNER. BLECH. REHEATED LEFTOVERS.

GLOP

I WOULDN'T KNOW. THIS WAS MY FIRST SHABBAT EVER. I THOUGHT IT WAS NICE.

WOAH, *REALLY?*

HEY NADAN, DID YOU KNOW THAT NOT ONLY IS THIS MELISSA'S FIRST TRIP OUTSIDE THE U.S., IT'S HER FIRST SHABBAT AS WELL!

SHABBAT SHALOM, MELISSA!

UH, THANKS.

WE ARE TOLD TO GO TO "MEETING ROOM ALEPH" FOR AN EVENING DISCUSSION SESSION.

BILL IS TAKING OVER FOR THE NIGHT AND HAS ASKED US TO SPLIT INTO GROUPS OF PEOPLE WE DON'T KNOW YET.

I'M SURE I'M NOT ALONE IN DREADING THE "BONDING ACTIVITY" THEY MUST HAVE IN STORE FOR US.

TONIGHT I'M GOING TO ASK YOU SOME QUESTIONS ABOUT WHAT IT MEANS TO BE JEWISH AND I WANT YOU TO ALL DISCUSS THEM TOGETHER. THERE ARE NO WRONG ANSWERS.

OKAY, FOR YOUR FIRST DISCUSSION, FILL IN THE BLANK: "I AM A JEW BECAUSE..."

GROAAAAAAN.

UM...I'M A JEW BECAUSE MY PARENTS ARE JEWISH, I GUESS.

I'M A JEW BECAUSE HALF MY BLOOD IS JEWISH AND HALF IS PROTESTANT, BUT MY MOM'S SIDE IS JEWISH SO I, LIKE, AM OFFICIALLY A JEW.

SUDDENLY THE DISCUSSION STARTS TO GET INTERESTING.

I'M A JEW BECAUSE...WELL, FIRST OF ALL, I WAS RAISED CHRISTIAN IN UKRAINE. WE IMMIGRATED TO THE U.S. WHEN I WAS FOURTEEN. ONE DAY I WENT TO A SYNAGOGUE WITH A FRIEND AND FELT LIKE I REALLY BELONGED THERE. A FEW YEARS LATER, I CONVERTED.

MY MOM CONVERTED TO JUDAISM TOO! I GREW UP HAVING TO DEFEND BEING A JEW BECAUSE WHERE I LIVED IN ARKANSAS WE WERE THE ONLY JEWS AROUND. NOW I FEEL LIKE IT'S SOMETHING WORTH PRESERVING, YOU KNOW?

WELL, MY FAMILY ISN'T EXACTLY RELIGIOUS, BUT I DEFINITELY INHERITED AN INTEREST IN SOME OF THE CULTURAL ASPECTS OF JUDAISM FROM THEM. THEY TAUGHT ME HOW TO LOVE LEARNING, EATING AND ARGUING.

RELIGION IS ONE OF THOSE FORBIDDEN TOPICS WHICH YOU'RE NOT SUPPOSED TO DISCUSS AT DINNER PARTIES. BUT ASK A BUNCH OF PEOPLE WHO HAVE ALMOST NOTHING IN COMMON TO TALK ABOUT IT AND YOU START TO GET TO KNOW THEM PRETTY QUICKLY.

EVERYONE IN MY TOWN WAS JEWISH. IN COLLEGE I JOINED A JEWISH FRATERNITY. IT WASN'T UNTIL AFTER GRADUATION THAT I STARTED GETTING TO KNOW NON-JEWS.

OKAY. NEXT DISCUSSION POINT, FILL IN THE BLANK: "THE ONE THING I DON'T GET ABOUT JUDAISM IS..."

EVERYTHING!

HA HA

WE SHOULD HAVE HAD THIS CONVERSATION ON THE FIRST DAY OF THE TRIP.

WHAT I DON'T GET ABOUT JUDAISM? WHY ARE JEWS ALWAYS QUESTIONING THEMSELVES?

HEY, GIRLS, WE'RE HAVING A PARTY IN OUR ROOM. ROOM 28. DAVID GOT SOME ISRAELI BOOZE. YOU SHOULD COME.

WHAT DO YOU THINK? DROP BY FOR ONE DRINK?

I GUESS I COULD HAVE JUST ONE...

ROOM PARTY, DUDE!

I FEEL LIKE I DON'T HAVE ANYTHING IN COMMON WITH THESE PEOPLE.

PFFT! JOIN THE CLUB! NEITHER DO I!

YOU DO THOUGH. YOU WENT TO SUNDAY SCHOOL, YOU KNOW THE SHABBAT SONG. I WAS THE ONLY ONE IN MY DISCUSSION GROUP THAT NEVER HAD A BAT MITZVAH.

YOU DIDN'T MISS MUCH. TRUST ME.

WELL...IT WOULD HAVE BEEN NICE TO HAVE A CHANCE TO CHOOSE. IT JUST NEVER *HAPPENED* IN MY FAMILY.

YOU MEAN THEY WEREN'T RELIGIOUS?

MORE THAN THAT. IT'S HARD TO EXPLAIN...IT'S LIKE THEY WERE AFRAID OF SOMETHING IN IT. LIKE THERE WAS SOMETHING IN BEING JEWISH THAT WAS NOBODY'S BUSINESS, THAT PEOPLE SHOULDN'T KNOW ABOUT.

SO WE JUST KIND OF AVOIDED IT ALTOGETHER.

OHH, SAY IT AIN'T SO!

NO COFFEE ON SHABBAT?

HE TRULY IS A VENGEFUL GOD.

IS EVERY- ONE ELSE STILL ASLEEP?

I'M NOT SURPRISED. THAT WAS SOME NASTY STUFF DAVID WAS PASSING AROUND LAST NIGHT. I WOULD NEVER DRINK SOMETHING CALLED "TACO TACO TEQUILA."

HEY, LOOK, IT'S THAT GUY, FRANK.

FRANK WHO DOESN'T BELIEVE IN GAY PEOPLE?

YEAH, I'VE BEEN KIND OF AVOIDING HIM THIS WHOLE TIME.

WELL, IT WOULD BE RUDE NOT TO SIT WITH HIM. THERE'S NO ONE ELSE HERE.

MORNING! YOU'RE FRANK, RIGHT?

YEAH...SARAH... AND MELISSA?

SO I HEAR YOU DON'T BELIEVE IN GAY PEOPLE. WHAT DOES THAT EVEN MEAN?

WHO DID YOU HEAR THAT FROM?

WE, UM...OVERHEARD A CERTAIN CONVERSATION IN THE AIRPORT.

AH, I REMEMBER NOW. BECCA WAS GIVING ME A PRETTY HARD TIME ABOUT THAT. REALLY IT WAS JUST A BIG MISUNDERSTANDING.

"SHE HEARD ME TELLING SOMEONE THAT I'M A REPUBLICAN SO SHE ASKED ME IF I THOUGHT GAY PEOPLE SHOULD BE ABLE TO GET MARRIED. I STARTED TO TELL HER THAT I DON'T BELIEVE IN MARRIAGE BUT SHE NEVER LET ME FINISH MY SENTENCE."

"WAIT, YOU DON'T BELIEVE IN MARRIAGE? FOR ANY-ONE?"

"NO, I DON'T. IT DOESN'T MATTER IF YOU'RE GAY OR STRAIGHT, IT JUST DOESN'T WORK. IT'S A BROKEN SYSTEM."

RRRRRR!

SURE, GAY PEOPLE SHOULD BE ABLE TO GET MARRIED, SAME AS EVERYONE ELSE. I JUST DON'T KNOW WHY THEY WOULD WANT TO.

OH! WELL, THAT MAKES SENSE THEN, I GUESS.

BUT YOU'RE A REPUBLICAN?

GUILTY AS CHARGED!

AND CHRISTIAN TOO?

HUH? OH, MY TATTOO?

I GREW UP IN FOSTER CARE, AND MY FOSTER PARENTS WERE CATHOLIC. I THOUGHT THAT WAS WHO I WAS, BUT THEN I STARTED ASKING MYSELF QUESTIONS. HOW COULD I REALLY KNOW THAT CATHOLICISM WAS RIGHT FOR ME UNLESS I HAD TRIED ALL THE OTHER RELIGIONS?

SO I LOOKED AT OTHER FORMS OF CHRISTIANITY. I LOOKED AT ISLAM. BUT THEN I SAW THAT ALL OF THESE HAD ROOTS IN JUDAISM, SO I TRIED THAT AND IT JUST FELT RIGHT. THEN I CONVERTED.

I WAIT FOR THE REST OF THE GROUP TO FINISH BREAKFAST AND WONDER HOW MANY OTHER PEOPLE ON THIS TRIP I'VE COMPLETELY MISJUDGED.

I THINK WE'RE LEAVING.

WHERE ARE WE GOING? WE CAN'T DRIVE ANYWHERE.

WE'RE GOING TO A KIBBUTZ! AND GET THIS...IT'S DEGANYA!

BRUSH BRUSH

GIL LEADS THE WAY TO A PATH THROUGH THE PALMS AND UNDERBRUSH AT THE EDGE OF OHALO'S GROUNDS.

WOW, DEGANYA...THE WAY JOEL DESCRIBED IT YESTERDAY I CAN'T EVEN IMAGINE IT AS A REAL PLACE.

I'M GLAD WE CAN'T USE THE BUS TODAY. THIS IS JUST WHAT I NEEDED: A NATURE WALK THOUSANDS OF MILES AWAY FROM NEW YORK CITY.

OUR WALK TAKES US ALONG THE JORDAN RIVER. WE SEE SOME NATIVE WILDLIFE.

AND WHERE THE RIVER SWELLS, SOME VISITING WILDLIFE.

BY THE POWER OF JESUS, YOU ARE SAVED!

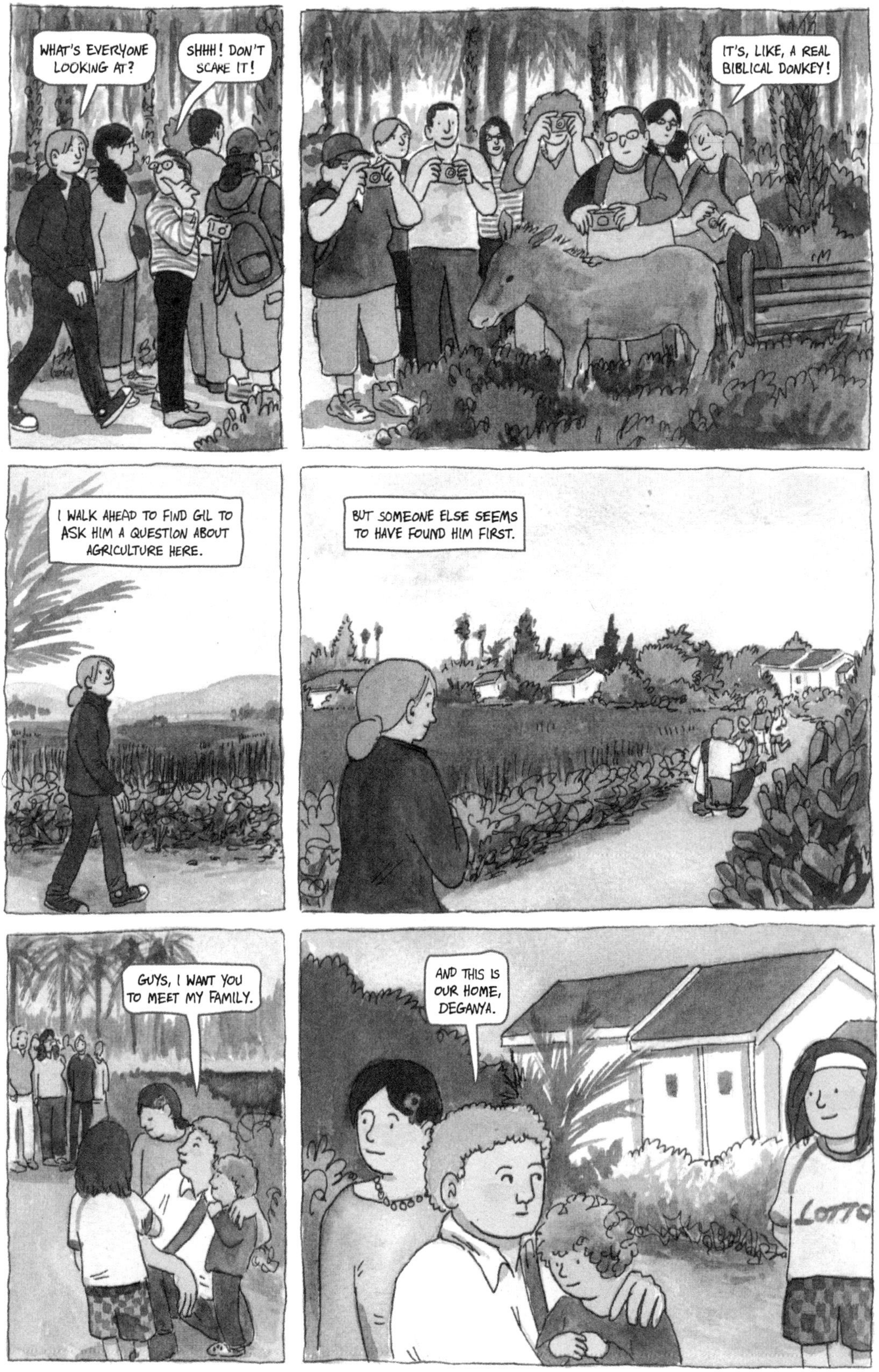
WHAT'S EVERYONE LOOKING AT?
SHHH! DON'T SCARE IT!
IT'S, LIKE, A REAL BIBLICAL DONKEY!
I WALK AHEAD TO FIND GIL TO ASK HIM A QUESTION ABOUT AGRICULTURE HERE.
BUT SOMEONE ELSE SEEMS TO HAVE FOUND HIM FIRST.
GUYS, I WANT YOU TO MEET MY FAMILY.
AND THIS IS OUR HOME, DEGANYA.
LOTTO

DEGANYA IS A BIT DIFFERENT NOW THAN THE TIME THAT JOEL DESCRIBED TO YOU YESTERDAY. OVER THERE IS A FACTORY WHERE THEY MAKE DIAMOND-TIPPED TOOLS.

BUT WE HAVE ALWAYS MADE SURE THAT WE REMEMBER OUR PAST. THESE ARE THE ORIGINAL BUILDINGS FROM WHEN DEGANYA WAS FIRST BUILT.

THIS ONE WE MADE INTO A MUSEUM SO OUR CHILDREN CAN ALWAYS KNOW THE HISTORY OF THEIR HOME.

PLEASE TAKE YOUR TIME AND LOOK AROUND.

IS WHAT JOEL TOLD US TRUE? WAS IT REALLY A SWAMP?

WELL, IT STILL DOESN'T MEAN THAT THERE WAS NO ONE ALREADY LIVING HERE.

THESE MUST BE THE ORIGINAL "PIONEERS" THAT JOEL WAS TALKING ABOUT.

THEY WERE SO YOUNG!

IT'S HARD NOT TO ROMANTICIZE THIS PLACE.

A COMMUNE IS SUPPOSED TO BE ABOUT AS LEFT WING AS YOU CAN GET.

HOWEVER, MOSHE DAYAN WAS DEGANYA'S SECOND CHILD.

HE ENDED UP BEING ONE OF ISRAEL'S MOST IMPORTANT AND CONTROVERSIAL MILITARY FIGURES. NOT EXACTLY A DOVE.

THEY SAY THAT KIBBUTZ LIFE ENDED IN 1912 HERE.

A MEMBER OF THE COMMUNITY, AN AUSTRIAN WOMAN, WANTED TO HAVE HER OWN TEAPOT. DELIBERATION OVER THAT TEAPOT ALMOST BROKE UP THE COMMUNITY!

AT DEGANYA PEOPLE HAD ALWAYS SHARED EVERYTHING, JUST LIKE AT EVERY KIBBUTZ THAT CAME AFTER THEM.

BUT NOW WE ARE IN THE NEWS BECAUSE JUST A FEW WEEKS AGO WE VOTED TO PRIVATIZE DEGANYA.

YOU'RE GOING CAPITALIST? HOW COULD DEGANYA JUST GIVE UP ON ITSELF LIKE THAT?

YOU'RE NOT THE FIRST ONE TO SAY THAT. A LOT OF PEOPLE WHO DON'T LIVE HERE ARE OUTRAGED.

TIMES ARE CHANGING. MORE OF US WORK OUTSIDE OF THE FIELDS AND FACTORIES OF THE KIBBUTZ. SOME ARE LAWYERS. OR TOUR GUIDES.

UNTIL NOW EVERYONE CONTRIBUTED THEIR WHOLE SALARY TO THE KIBBUTZ AND THEN GOT SERVICES LIKE ELECTRICITY, FOOD AND EDUCATION BACK.

BUT THE REALITY IS THAT NOT EVERYONE CONTRIBUTES ACCORDING TO HIS ABILITIES AND TAKES ACCORDING TO HIS NEEDS.

WITH THE CHANGES WE JUST VOTED ON, THERE WILL BE A NEW TAX TO PROVIDE FOR THE ELDERLY MEMBERS, OR THOSE WHO DO NOT MAKE ENOUGH MONEY TO LIVE OTHERWISE. WE WILL STILL HAVE SOME MEALS TOGETHER.

MUCH OF ISRAEL IS DISAPPOINTED IN US FOR FOLLOWING IN THE FOOTSTEPS OF OTHER KIBBUTZIM THAT HAVE GIVEN UP THE OLD WAY OF LIFE. BUT THEY ARE JUST NOSTALGIC FOR ANOTHER ISRAEL THAT EXISTS IN THE PAST AND WHICH THEY WERE NEVER A PART OF.

FOR US, THIS IS REAL LIFE.

AFTER LEAVING GIL WITH HIS FAMILY AT DEGANYA AND HAVING DINNER, OUR GROUP IS BUSSED OVER TO ANOTHER LOCAL KIBBUTZ WHICH HAS ITS OWN BAR. IT'S PURIM, WHICH IS KIND OF LIKE JEWISH HALLOWEEN, SO EVERYONE IS DRESSED UP.

THE LOCALS SEEM TO TOLERATE OUR GROUP.

BUT MELISSA IS A HIT WITH THE U.N. PEACEKEEPERS WHO ARE STATIONED IN THE DEMILITARIZED ZONE BETWEEN SYRIA AND THE GOLAN HEIGHTS AND HAVE COME ALL THIS WAY FOR SOME R&R.

THERE'S A LUNAR ECLIPSE TONIGHT SO NADAN AND I GO OUTSIDE TO CHECK IT OUT. NADAN ASKS ME WHAT I THINK OF ISRAEL.

SO WHAT DO YOU THINK OF ISRAEL?

WELL, I LIKE IT MORE THAN I THOUGHT I WOULD...BUT I'M SORRY...

...THE WHOLE **PALESTINIAN** SITUATION REALLY MAKES IT HARD TO FOCUS ON THE GOOD.

UGH. THE SITUATION, THE SITUATION. ALWAYS IT'S THE SITUATION. CAN'T YOU THINK ABOUT ANYTHING ELSE?

WELL, IT'S KIND OF A BIG DEAL, DON'T YOU THINK?

LIKE, WHY DO YOU HAVE TO BULLDOZE PEOPLE'S HOUSES? AND KEEP BUILDING SETTLEMENTS? IT MAKES THINGS WORSE AND WORSE!

LOOK, I'M WHAT YOU WOULD CALL A LEFT-WING ISRAELI, BUT IT'S MORE COMPLICATED THAN YOU THINK. NOBODY'S BULLDOZING FOR FUN.

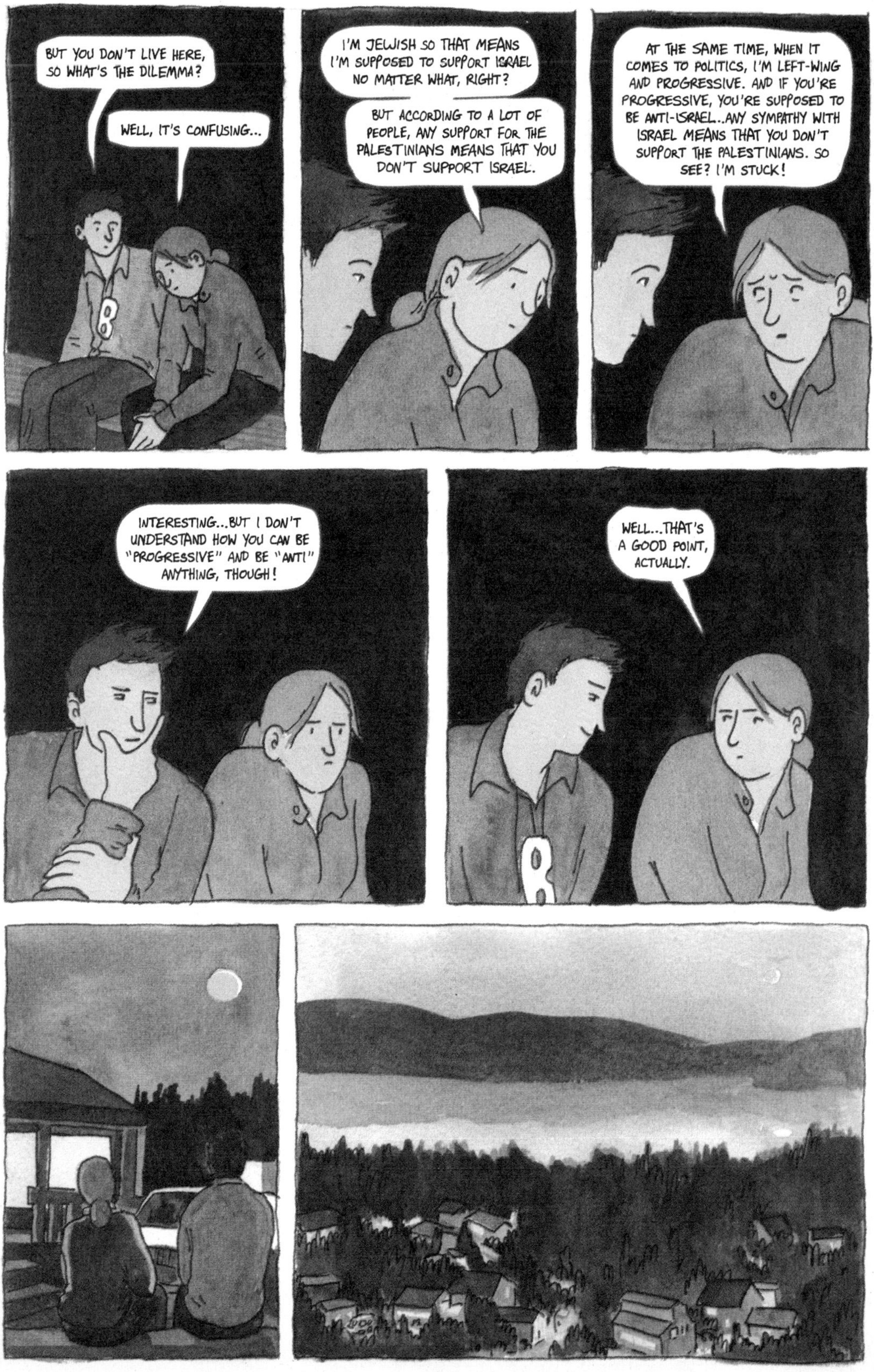
BUT YOU DON'T LIVE HERE, SO WHAT'S THE DILEMMA?
WELL, IT'S CONFUSING...
I'M JEWISH SO THAT MEANS I'M SUPPOSED TO SUPPORT ISRAEL NO MATTER WHAT, RIGHT?
BUT ACCORDING TO A LOT OF PEOPLE, ANY SUPPORT FOR THE PALESTINIANS MEANS THAT YOU DON'T SUPPORT ISRAEL.
AT THE SAME TIME, WHEN IT COMES TO POLITICS, I'M LEFT-WING AND PROGRESSIVE. AND IF YOU'RE PROGRESSIVE, YOU'RE SUPPOSED TO BE ANTI-ISRAEL...ANY SYMPATHY WITH ISRAEL MEANS THAT YOU DON'T SUPPORT THE PALESTINIANS. SO SEE? I'M STUCK!
INTERESTING...BUT I DON'T UNDERSTAND HOW YOU CAN BE "PROGRESSIVE" AND BE "ANTI" ANYTHING, THOUGH!
WELL...THAT'S A GOOD POINT, ACTUALLY.

CHAPTER
FOUR
TEL AVIV AND ENVIRONS

RABIN SQUARE

HOTEL

MEDITERRANEAN SEA

MIKE'S PLACE

MIRI ALONI SQUARE

INDEPENDENCE HALL

JAFFA

HOLON

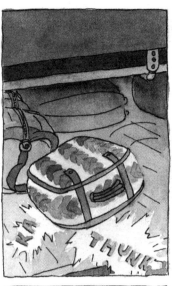

URLLGGH...YA GOTTA THROW IT SO LOUDLY, SHAI? I HAVE A HEADACHE.

YOU AMERICANS REALLY DRINK A LOT, DON'T YOU?

WHAT, LIKE ISRAELIS DON'T?

NAH, NOT SO MUCH.

HUH. OH, IS IT BECAUSE YOU'RE NOT ALLOWED TO DRINK WHILE YOU'RE IN THE ARMY? AND PEOPLE USUALLY FORM DRINKING HABITS BETWEEN THE AGES OF EIGHTEEN AND TWENTY-TWO?

INTERESTING THEORY. BUT I DON'T THINK THAT HAS ANYTHING TO DO WITH IT. JEWS JUST DON'T DRINK VERY MUCH. PERIOD.

OH.

HEY, COOL SWEATSHIRT, BEN. WHERE'D YOU GET THAT?

THIS? OH, IT'S THE SWEATSHIRT OF MY UNIT IN THE ARMY.

OOOH! I LIKE IT! CAN I HAVE IT?

WHAT? NO. IT'S LIKE A SOUVENIR. A KEEPSAKE. EVERY UNIT MAKES THEIR OWN WITH A DRAWING. MY UNIT FOUGHT IN THE WAR WITH LEBANON.

WOW, YOU WERE *THERE?* WAS IT SCARY?

NO. NOT SCARY. BUT THERE WAS ONE TIME...

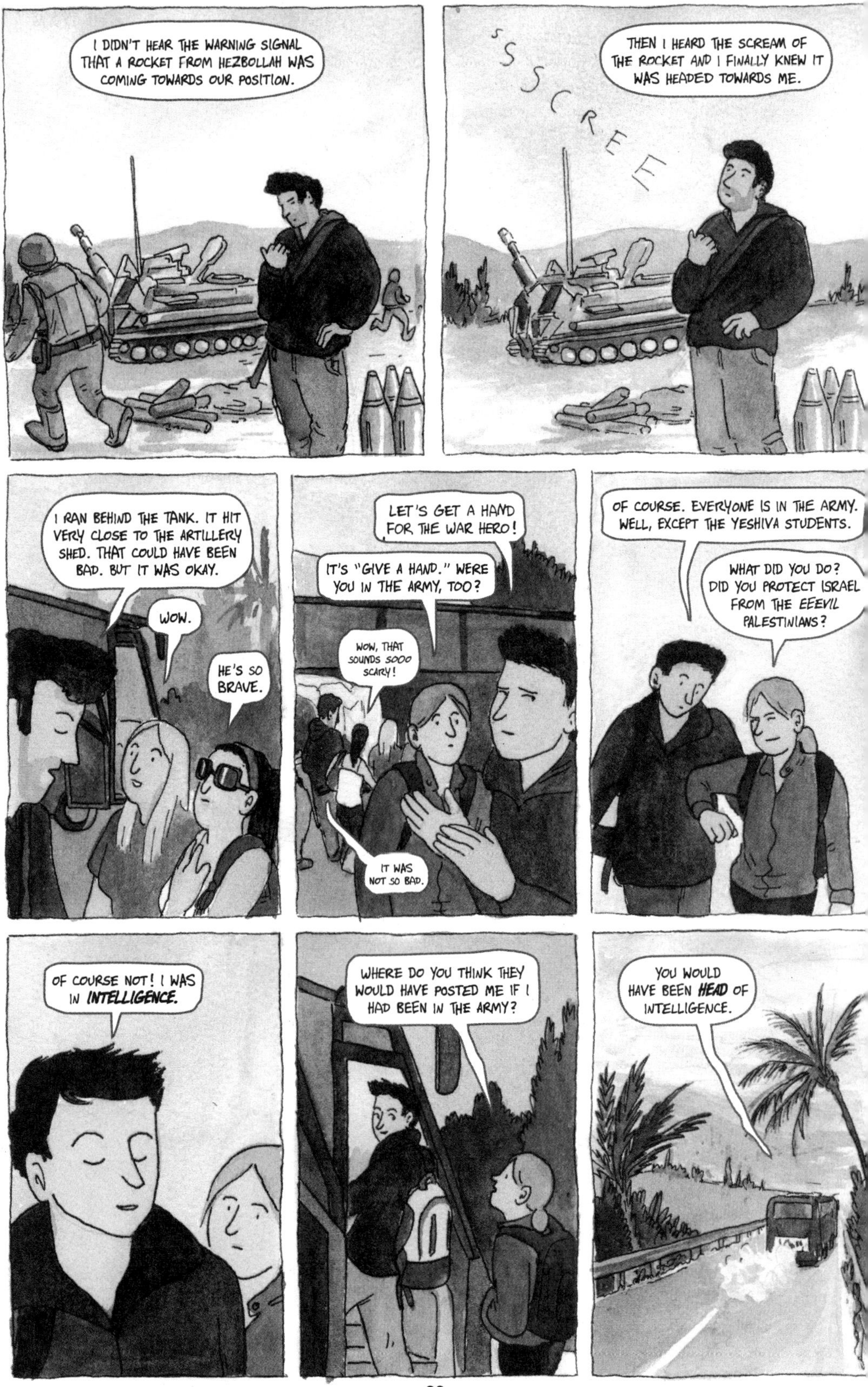
I DIDN'T HEAR THE WARNING SIGNAL THAT A ROCKET FROM HEZBOLLAH WAS COMING TOWARDS OUR POSITION.
SSCREE
THEN I HEARD THE SCREAM OF THE ROCKET AND I FINALLY KNEW IT WAS HEADED TOWARDS ME.
I RAN BEHIND THE TANK. IT HIT VERY CLOSE TO THE ARTILLERY SHED. THAT COULD HAVE BEEN BAD. BUT IT WAS OKAY.
WOW.
HE'S SO BRAVE.
LET'S GET A HAND FOR THE WAR HERO!
IT'S "GIVE A HAND." WERE YOU IN THE ARMY, TOO?
WOW, THAT SOUNDS SOOO SCARY!
IT WAS NOT SO BAD.
OF COURSE. EVERYONE IS IN THE ARMY. WELL, EXCEPT THE YESHIVA STUDENTS.
WHAT DID YOU DO? DID YOU PROTECT ISRAEL FROM THE EEEVIL PALESTINIANS?
OF COURSE NOT! I WAS IN INTELLIGENCE.
WHERE DO YOU THINK THEY WOULD HAVE POSTED ME IF I HAD BEEN IN THE ARMY?
YOU WOULD HAVE BEEN HEAD OF INTELLIGENCE.

WE ARE HEADED TO TEL AVIV, BUT FIRST MAKE A DETOUR TO HOLON, A CITY JUST TO THE SOUTH WHICH IS HAVING ITS FAMOUS PURIM PARADE TODAY.

UGGH. I HATE PARADES. I DON'T SEE WHY I CAN'T JUST STAY ON THE BUS.

AW, DON'T SAY THAT. PARADES ARE FUN! IT'S PURIM!

WHATEVER.

OKAY, EVERYONE, SO THIS IS THE BIGGEST PURIM PARADE IN ISRAEL. I DON'T THINK IT'S POSSIBLE THAT WE WILL ALL STAY TOGETHER..

...SO LET'S TRY TO MEET BACK HERE IN TWO HOURS, OKAY?

IT'LL BE NICE TO ACTUALLY SEE SOME PEOPLE. I FEEL LIKE WE'VE BEEN OUT IN THE WOODS THIS WHOLE TIME.

YIKES!

COME ON, IT'LL BE JUST LIKE WALKING THROUGH TIMES SQUARE!

AW, BUT I *HATE* TIMES SQUARE!

OOF!

HEY!

ISRAELI STEREOTYPE #142: "ISRAELIS ARE PUSHY." STATUS: CONFIRMED.

WOOPS! SORRY!

WELL, WHEN IN ROME, DO AS THE ROMANS DO!

UPS! EXCUSE ME! HAHA!

HEY, I'M GETTING THE HANG OF THIS! IT'S LIKE A MOSH PIT!

I THINK SOMEONE JUST GOOSED ME, BUT I'M NOT SURE.

WE MADE IT ACROSS THE STREET! VICTORY IS OURS!

I'M GOING TO DUCK INTO THAT BODEGA FOR A SEC AND GET A BOTTLE OF WATER.

'KAY. I'LL BE HERE.

THIS IS OUR FIRST TIME EXPERIENCING AN URBAN ISRAELI ENVIRONMENT AND THE CROWDS THAT GO WITH IT. I'M FEELING SOMETHING STRANGE MISSING...

THE FEELING OF FOREIGNNESS, THE STICKING-OUT-LIKE-A-SORE-THUMBNESS THAT I NORMALLY HAVE WHILE TRAVELING...SOMEHOW I DON'T FEEL IT HERE.

ONE THING I LOVE ABOUT TRAVELING IS FEELING DISORIENTED AND REMOVED FROM MY COMFORT ZONE.

BUT IT'S NEVER COOL TO STAND OUT AS A TOURIST. TRY AS I MIGHT, THERE'S ALWAYS SOMETHING TO GIVE ME AWAY. SOMETIMES IT'S MY COMPLETE LACK OF SOPHISTICATION.

PARIS, FRANCE

IN SOME PLACES PHYSICAL DIFFERENCES MAKE ASSIMILATION IMPOSSIBLE, BUT DISCOMFORT CAN BE SLIGHTLY OFFSET BY ASSUMING THE TRADITIONAL COSTUME OF MY HOST NATION.

HEH. NI HAU MAH?

GUANGZHOU, CHINA

AND THEN THERE ARE THE PLACES WHERE I COULD NEVER BE SEEN AS ANYTHING BUT AN OUTSIDER.

ÖVÖRKHANGAI, MONGOLIA

BUT I COULD EASILY BE ONE OF THESE PEOPLE.

IN FACT, THE ONLY REASON I'M **NOT** ONE OF THEM RIGHT NOW IS BECAUSE WHEN MY GREAT-GRANDPARENTS FLED EASTERN EUROPE AND CONSIDERED THEIR TWO OPTIONS, THEY CHOSE THE UNITED STATES.

סליחה, מתי מתחילה התהלוכה?

I'M SORRY, I DON'T SPEAK HEBREW.

CRAP. MY COVER'S BEEN BLOWN.

83

SARAH, LOOK! I FOUND US SOME PURIM COSTUMES!

THEEEERE YA GO.

I BETTER NOT LOOK LIKE A FREAK.

YOU ARE MY GREATEST CREATION!

SO IT LOOKS LIKE PURIM REALLY DOES HAVE A LOT IN COMMON WITH HALLOWEEN BACK IN THE STATES...

IT'S JUST AN EXCUSE FOR GIRLS TO DRESS LIKE SLUTS.

AWW, BUT LOOK AT THE LITTLE FALAFEL!

BANG

CRACK

I GOTTA GET A PICTURE OF TH--

POM

WHAT WAS *THAT?*

OH, HA HA, IT'S JUST FIRECRACKERS.

I KNEW IT WAS FIRECRACKERS.

OOF, 'SCUSE ME... BEVAKESHAH.

THE THEME OF THIS PARADE SEEMS TO BE...THE WORLD? UNITED?

OR AT LEAST, THE WORLD OF COUNTRIES WITH DIPLOMATIC TIES TO ISRAEL.

THEY ARE NOT SHY ABOUT STEREOTYPES, IT SEEMS.

A GROTESQUE CHINA FLOAT ARRIVES...

ALONG WITH SOME ADDITIONAL VOICES.

MY KNEE-JERK REACTION IS TO SAY...

KIND OF LIKE THE POT CALLING THE KETTLE BLA--

BUT I CATCH MYSELF. WHAT AM I THINKING? NO MATTER WHAT A COUNTRY'S OWN PROBLEMS ARE, DON'T THEY HAVE THE RIGHT AND DUTY TO CALL OUT THE HUMAN RIGHTS VIOLATIONS OF OTHERS?

CERTAINLY MY OWN COUNTRY IS FAR FROM INNOCENT. THERE AREN'T ANY ANTI-WAR BALLOONS FOR US TODAY, THOUGH.

WE SHOULD PROBABLY GET BACK TO THE BUS...

OKAY.

UM...WHERE ARE WE ANYWAY?

STADIUM? BASKETBALL STADIUM? BUSES? BUS?

HABLAS ESPAÑOL? FRANÇAIS?

THERE YOU ARE! STOP FLIRTING WITH THE POLICE AND GET BACK TO THE BUS.

HEY, DON'T BE RUDE, YOU JUST INTERRUPTED A VERY INTERESTING CONVERSATION!

WE PARK ON A BLUFF OVERLOOKING THE MEDITERRANEAN SEA.

UNDERNEATH THIS PARK ARE THE REMAINS OF THOUSANDS OF YEARS OF CIVILIZATION.

HERE, ONE OF THE OLDEST LAYERS IS BEING EXCAVATED. THESE WERE THE WALLS OF AN EGYPTIAN FORTRESS.

AS GIL EXPLAINS BY PILING HATS ON BRENDAN, WE ARE STANDING ON A TEL, AN ARTIFICIAL HILL MADE UP OF THE ARCHEOLOGICAL STRATA OF ONE OF THE OLDEST PORT CITIES IN THE WORLD, JAFFA.

...SO AS YOU CAN SEE, WHEN YOU PILE LAYER UPON LAYER OF DEBRIS, IT ADDS UP OVER LONG PERIODS OF TIME.

FROM HERE THERE'S A GREAT VIEW OF TEL AVIV RIGHT ACROSS THE BAY.

THE PRESENCE OF A TEL IS A SUREFIRE SIGN THAT A PIECE OF LAND HAS CHANGED HANDS MANY, MANY TIMES, AND JAFFA HAS, AT ONE POINT OR ANOTHER, BELONGED TO JUST ABOUT EVERYONE.

JAFFA WASN'T EVER THE SEAT OF A GREAT CIVILIZATION LIKE EGYPT, BABYLON OR SUMER, BUT ITS LOCATION BETWEEN ALL THESE ON THE MEDITERRANEAN MADE IT PRIME REAL ESTATE FOR CULTURES WITH A GROWING INTEREST IN TRADE.

PEOPLE OVERSIMPLIFY THE CURRENT CONFLICT IN ISRAEL AND SAY "IT'S BEEN A HOLY WAR FOR THOUSANDS OF YEARS." ACTUALLY, IT SEEMS THAT IT'S NEVER REALLY BEEN ABOUT RELIGION BUT ABOUT LAND.

JAFFA IS A GOOD EXAMPLE OF A PLACE THAT'S BEEN FOUGHT OVER LONG BEFORE THE DEVELOPMENT OF MONOTHEISM. IT STARTED AS A CAANANITE PORT CITY.

BUT THEN THE EGYPTIANS TOOK OVER. PHARAOH THUTMOSE III TRICKED THE CITY GOVERNOR BY HIDING HIS WARRIORS IN GIANT GIFT BASKETS. FROM THEN ON IT WAS TAKEN AND RETAKEN AS EMPIRES EXPANDED AND BORDERS SHIFTED.

MAMLUKS, CRUSADERS, OTTOMANS...EACH CAME THROUGH AND ADDED TO THE TEL WITH THE RUBBLE OF A FRESHLY RAZED JAFFA AND ITS INHABITANTS.

NAPOLEON SPENT THREE DAYS RANSACKING THE CITY IN 1799. MOST OF THE CIVILIANS HE AND HIS ARMY DIDN'T MASSACRE THEMSELVES DIED FROM THE DISEASES HIS TROOPS CARRIED.

THINGS HAD FINALLY SETTLED DOWN FOR A WHILE IN JAFFA WHEN THE NEW JEWISH NEIGHBORS FROM EUROPE STARTED MOVING IN AT THE TURN OF THE CENTURY. MANY OF THEM, FEELING THAT JAFFA WAS TOO CROWDED, BEGAN WORK ON A SUBURB NEARBY WHICH THEY NAMED TEL AVIV.

THERE WAS TENSION BETWEEN THE JEWS AND THE ARABS, AND THIS ONLY INCREASED WHEN THE BRITISH TOOK CONTROL OF PALESTINE AFTER WORLD WAR ONE.

THE CONFLICT BETWEEN THE THREE GROUPS BECAME SO INTENSE THAT THE BRITISH DECIDED TO END THEIR MANDATE IN 1947, LEADING TO A FULL-SCALE WAR.

DURING THE INDEPENDENCE WAR IN 1948, 60,000 PEOPLE, OR 95% OF JAFFA'S ARAB POPULATION, FLED THE CITY WHEN ISRAEL BECAME A NATION.

I'VE READ A LOT ABOUT THE EVENTS THAT LED UP TO THIS. JAFFA'S TAKEOVERS HAVE NEVER BEEN PEACEFUL, AND THIS ONE WAS NO EXCEPTION.

ARABS MURDERED JEWS, JEWS SHOT ARABS. THE JEWISH TERRORIST STERN GANG AND THE IRGUN, AN EXTREME BRANCH OF ISRAEL'S FLEDGLING PARAMILITARY GROUP, CARRIED OUT BOMBINGS AND RAIDS.

IT DOESN'T SEEM LIKE GIL IS GOING TO GO INTO ANY OF THESE UNPLEASANT DETAILS. THERE ARE MORE ENTERTAINING STORIES SET IN JAFFA, WHOSE OLD CITY HAS IN THE PAST FEW DECADES BECOME A POPULAR TOURIST ATTRACTION.

IN THE BIBLE STORY, JONAH HEARD GOD'S COMMAND AND DECIDED INSTEAD TO FLEE. SO HE SET SAIL FROM THE PORT OF JAFFA...

PALESTINIANS LIVED HERE

← WE WILL BE BACK

exiled in 1948
we won't forget

UM...WHAT'S THAT?

I'M NOT SURE, BUT...

IT LOOKS LIKE AN INDIAN CHIEF.

BUT WHY?

MELISSA AND I HAVE BEEN GETTING TO KNOW EMILY AND JULIA, TWO STYLISH GIRLS IN OUR GROUP WHO ARE ALSO FROM NEW YORK CITY.

SO THIS IS TEL AVIV...DOES THIS MEAN WE'LL FINALLY GET TO SEE SOME ISRAELI HIPSTERS?

HONEY, I THINK "ISRAELI HIPSTER" MAY BE AN OXYMORON. THIS WHOLE COUNTRY IS A FASHION "DON'T" SO FAR.

EMILY! WHAT IF THEY HAVE THE STREETS BUGGED? YOU'RE GOING TO GET US THROWN INTO JAIL FOR INSULTING ISRAEL'S SENSE OF STYLE!

SOMETIMES IT'S NICE TO TALK ABOUT SOMETHING BESIDES MIDDLE EASTERN POLITICS FOR A BIT. OUR NEW FRIENDS ARE A NICE DISTRACTION.

HAHAHAHA

THIS NEIGHBORHOOD IS SO EUROPEAN-LOOKING. IT REMINDS ME A LITTLE OF BARCELONA.

KNOW HOPE NO HOPE

THAT'S SO FUNNY! I WAS JUST ABOUT TO SAY IT LOOKS LIKE MEXICO CITY!

OMIGOD, IT REMINDS *ME* OF CHILE!

OKAY, GIRLS, WE HAVE AN HOUR OF FREE TIME. SHOPPING?

YEAH, I HAVE, LIKE, TEN PEOPLE I NEED TO BUY PRESENTS FOR.

NAH, WE'RE SAVING OUR GIFT SHOPPING FOR JERUSALEM. LET US KNOW IF YOU FIND YOUR HIPSTERS THOUGH.

WHAT DO YOU THINK THAT GUY'S SO UPSET ABOUT?

I DON'T KNOW, BUT I'M GUESSING IT'S EITHER ABOUT POLITICS OR RELIGION. HEY, THERE'S NADAV, MAYBE HE KNOWS.

HEY, GUYS, YOU SEE THAT WOMAN THERE PLAYING GUITAR?

YEAH.

THAT'S MIRI ALONI.

WHO'S THAT?

YOU DON'T KNOW MIRI ALONI? SHE WAS LIKE THE JONI MITCHELL OF ISRAEL IN THE EARLY '90s!

AT THE PEACE RALLY WHERE YITZHAK RABIN WAS KILLED? SHE'S THE ONE WHO SANG "A SONG FOR PEACE." DO YOU KNOW IT? IT'S KIND OF LIKE AN ANTHEM NOW.

ANYWAY, HER HUSBAND WAS CRAZY AND HE RUINED HER. NOW SHE HAS NO MONEY SO SHE HAS TO PLAY HERE.

WOW, THAT'S... REALLY DEPRESSING.

YES, IT'S REALLY DEPRESSING.

AND WHAT'S THAT GUY YELLING ABOUT?

HIM? HE SAYS HE WILL TAKE YOUR PHOTOGRAPH WITH THAT BOARD YOU CAN PUT YOUR HEAD IN.

OH.

91

MY COUSIN MATT AND I DECIDED TO GET A DRINK WHILE I'M IN TEL AVIV. SINCE WE AREN'T ALLOWED TO TAKE TAXIS OR BUSES ON OUR OWN, WE HAVE TO MEET UP AT A TOURISTY BAR, WHICH IS WITHIN WALKING DISTANCE OF THE HOTEL.

אין בעיה שני׳ גולדסטואר בבקשה.

WOW, YOUR HEBREW SOUNDS PRETTY GOOD!

THANKS. IT'S PRETTY **BAD** ACTUALLY...BUT I'M LEARNING.

SO, WHAT DO YOU THINK OF ISRAEL SO FAR?

OY. I DON'T EVEN KNOW. IT'S NOT WHAT I EXPECTED, I KNOW THAT MUCH.

THERE'S SO MUCH THAT I'M ANGRY ABOUT, AND I DON'T THINK THAT WILL EVER CHANGE. BUT I AM KIND OF SEEING THIS OTHER SIDE TO ISRAEL. LIKE, THE PEOPLE? THE ONES WE'VE MET SO FAR ARE PRETTY COOL.

MOSTLY THOUGH, I THINK THIS PLACE IS JUST FASCINATING. I MEAN, IT'S SO BIZARRE! THERE'S JUST SO MUCH HISTORY RUNNING THROUGH IT, AND THEN ADD IN THE SOLDIERS ALL OVER THE PLACE, THE FERAL CATS, BEING SURROUNDED BY OTHER JEWS...

I WOULD NEVER MAKE ALIYAH OR ANYTHING...BUT I KIND OF LIKE IT HERE. MAYBE I'D COME BACK HERE TO STUDY ANCIENT MIDDLE EASTERN HISTORY OR SOMETHING.

YOU CAN GET A MASTER'S IN THAT, RIGHT?

AHH, YOU'RE EXPERIENCING THE "BIRTHRIGHT GLOW."

"BIRTHRIGHT GLOW"?

YEAH. DON'T WORRY, IT HAPPENS TO EVERYONE. IT'LL WEAR OFF.

YOU COME HERE WITH A BUNCH OF OTHER PEOPLE YOUR AGE, THEY LEAD YOU AROUND, YOU DON'T HAVE TO PLAN ANYTHING AT ALL. IT'S FREE. IT'S AN IDEAL TRAVEL EXPERIENCE SO YOU'RE GUARANTEED TO HAVE A GOOD TIME.

THEN YOU GO BACK TO THE STATES AND WHEN YOU THINK ABOUT ISRAEL, YOU THINK ABOUT THAT GREAT TIME YOU HAD ON YOUR BIRTHRIGHT TRIP.

IT'S ACTUALLY PRETTY BRILLIANT.

BUT...I'M NOT...

...BIRTHRIGHT GLOW...

WELL, YOU'VE BEEN HERE ALMOST A YEAR...WHAT DO YOU THINK ABOUT IT?

LOOK, THERE ARE A LOT OF GREAT THINGS ABOUT ISRAEL. I LIKE MY UNIVERSITY. I LIKE A LOT OF THE PEOPLE...

BUT THERE ARE A LOT OF PROBLEMS BEYOND THE OCCUPATION THAT YOU WON'T SEE ON A BIRTHRIGHT TRIP, THAT'S ALL I'M SAYING.

THEY TREAT ARAB ISRAELIS LIKE SECOND-CLASS CITIZENS. NO, THIRD- OR FOURTH-CLASS CITIZENS!

EVEN OTHER JEWS, IF THEY'RE OF MIDDLE EASTERN OR ETHIOPIAN BACKGROUND, GET TREATED MUCH WORSE THAN EUROPEAN ASHKENAZI JEWS.

THE SETTLERS ARE OUT OF CONTROL, AND THE GOVERNMENT WON'T STAND UP TO THEM.

THE GOVERNMENT IS CORRUPT ANYWAY. THEY WON'T LET PALESTINIANS GET BASIC LIFE-SAVING MEDICAL TREATMENT SOMETIMES.

AND THE YOUNG ISRAELIS, PEOPLE OUR AGE, THEY DON'T REALLY WANT TO DO ANYTHING ABOUT IT. THEY JUST WANT TO HAVE A NORMAL LIFE.

AND I CAN'T BLAME THEM FOR THAT. LIVING UNDER THE THREAT OF TERRORISM IS NO SMALL THING. WHEN I WAS ON MY BIRTHRIGHT TRIP A FEW YEARS AGO THERE WAS A NIGHTCLUB BOMBING JUST A QUARTER MILE DOWN THE STRIP FROM HERE. AND EVEN THIS BAR WAS HIT BY A BOMBING A FEW YEARS AGO.

WOAH.

I DON'T MEAN TO BE SO NEGATIVE, MED SCHOOL IS JUST KIND OF STRESSFUL. USUALLY I TRY NOT TO THINK ABOUT THIS STUFF BECAUSE IT'S TOO DISTRACTING.

WHAT DO YOUR ISRAELI FRIENDS THINK ABOUT ALL THIS?

WE TRY NOT TO TALK ABOUT POLITICS TOO MUCH.

I'M UP AT SIX AGAIN. WAY TOO EARLY.

AT LEAST I HAVE SOMETHING PRETTY TO LOOK AT WHILE I RUMINATE.

I GUESS WE SHOULD HEAD TO THE LOBBY SOON...

HEY, IS SOMETHING WRONG? YOU'VE EATEN LIKE TWO PIECES OF CUCUMBER.

NAH, I'M JUST NOT THAT HUNGRY.

OOOH, THE DESERT. I AM REALLY LOOKING FORWARD TO THAT.

YEAH. ME TOO.

TAGLIT BUS 16

9 AM INDEPENDENCE HALL
11 MEET SOLDIERS
12 RABIN SQUARE
1 DRIVE TO DESERT

WELCOME, GUYS. SHALOM.

THIS IS INDEPENDENCE HALL. IT WAS HERE THAT THE STATE OF ISRAEL WAS DECLARED ON MAY 14TH, 1948. BUT ALLOW ME TO START AT THE BEGINNING...

YOU VISITED JAFFA YESTERDAY, DIDN'T YOU? WELL LET ME TELL YOU, A HUNDRED YEARS AGO THOSE STREETS WERE NOT SO QUIET. JAFFA WAS A CROWDED CITY AND BECAME EVEN MORE SO AS IT WAS THE PORT WHERE ALL JEWISH IMMIGRANTS LANDED BY BOAT.

ANOTHER SPEECH ABOUT THE POOR VICTIMIZED JEWS WHO BRAVELY BUILT SOMETHING OUT OF NOTHING.

WE HAD NOWHERE ELSE TO GO! WE WOULD HAVE BEEN KILLED IF WE STAYED IN EUROPE!

IN 1909, SIXTY-SIX FAMILIES, LED BY A MAN NAMED MEIR DIZENGOFF, BOUGHT LAND HERE, JUST OUTSIDE OF JAFFA, AND STARTED BUILDING A SUBURB TO HOUSE ALL THE JEWISH REFUGEES.

THEIR VISION WAS FOR A COMMUNITY BASED ON JEWISH VALUES, AT PEACE WITH THEIR ARAB NEIGHBORS IN JAFFA.

YEAH. SO PEACEFUL THEY WOULDN'T EMPLOY ANY ARAB WORKE-- *OOF!*

SHH!

AFTER WORLD WAR ONE, THE BRITISH TOOK CONTROL OF PALESTINE FROM THE OTTOMANS, AND TENSIONS BETWEEN THE JEWS AND THE ARABS IN JAFFA BEGAN TO INCREASE AS MORE JEWS SOUGHT REFUGE HERE.

INTELLECTUALS, POETS, ARTISTS OF ALL SORTS CAME TO TEL AVIV, FLEEING THE RISE OF THE NAZIS.

YOU WOULD HAVE COME HERE TOO.

I WOULD HAVE GONE TO THE U.S.

MAYBE NOT. THE UNITED STATES HAD QUOTAS FOR JEWS AFTER 1925, REMEMBER?

OH YEAH...

PLEASE, HAVE A SEAT.

WE ARE BEING WATCHED BY A GIANT PORTRAIT OF THEODOR HERZL, THE FOUNDER OF THE ZIONIST MOVEMENT IN THE 1800'S.

96

SO, IT SOON BECAME CLEAR THAT THEY COULD NOT LIVE IN PEACE TOGETHER. IN NOVEMBER OF 1947, THE UNITED NATIONS DRAFTED A PLAN TO PARTITION THE LAND INTO TWO STATES: ONE FOR THE JEWS AND ONE FOR THE ARABS.

THIS WAS THE DECISION OF THE WORLD, AND THIS IS WHAT WE WERE SUPPOSED TO LOOK LIKE. IT WASN'T MUCH, BUT THE JEWS WERE OVERJOYED. WHY? BECAUSE ONLY TWO YEARS AFTER THE WORST DISASTER IN JEWISH HISTORY, THEY FINALLY HAD A JEWISH STATE.

IF THIS PLAN HAD HAPPENED, GUYS, THEN OUR WHOLE HISTORY WOULD BE DIFFERENT. BUT IF ONE SIDE DOESN'T WANT IT, IT DOESN'T WORK. AND THE ARABS DID NOT WANT THIS PLAN. THEY DID NOT WANT TO GIVE UP ANY OF THEIR LAND. THEY ARE OUR NEIGHBORS AND WE HAVE TO HAVE BOTH SIDES AGREE.

FOR SIX MONTHS THE JEWS AND THE ARABS FOUGHT EACH OTHER AND AGAINST THE BRITISH WHO WERE IN THE MIDDLE. THEN THE BRITISH DECIDED TO GIVE UP THEIR MANDATE AND LEAVE.

WHEN IT WAS ANNOUNCED THAT NO ONE WOULD BE RULING, THE JEWS DECIDED IT WAS THEIR CHANCE TO DECLARE THEMSELVES A STATE. THE UNITED STATES ENCOURAGED THEM TO DO THIS.

BECAUSE JERUSALEM WAS UNDER SIEGE, THE PROVISIONAL GOVERNMENT, HEADED BY DAVID BEN-GURION, CHOSE THIS MUSEUM TO COME TOGETHER AND DECLARE THEIR INDEPENDENCE TO THE WORLD.

I AM OFTEN ASKED "WHAT RIGHT DID THE JEWISH PEOPLE HAVE TO DECLARE A JEWISH STATE?" ALL THE ANSWERS ARE HERE IN THIS DOCUMENT THEY SIGNED THAT DAY, THE DECLARATION OF INDEPENDENCE.

THE WAR CONTINUED UNTIL WE SUCCEEDED IN GAINING THAT INDEPENDENCE. ISRAEL WAS ON ITS WAY TO BECOMING WHAT IT IS TODAY.

ALL THAT IS MISSING HERE IS PEACE. AND WE WANT PEACE. WE WANT "SHALOM."

THIS WOMAN IS A VERY GOOD SPEAKER. SHE'S MAKING IT SEEM LIKE SHE HASN'T GIVEN THIS SAME SPEECH TEN TIMES A DAY FOR YEARS AND YEARS. IT FEELS LIKE IT'S SOME PRIVATE STORY ONLY FOR US.

EVERYONE THINKS THAT ISRAELIS ARE SO TOUGH. BUT YOU DON'T GET USED TO TERRORISM, GUYS. WE GET INTO OUR CARS IN THE MORNING AND WE TURN ON THE RADIO TO HEAR WHAT KIND OF SONG IS PLAYING. YOU KNOW, THEY DON'T PLAY A HAPPY SONG IF THERE HAS BEEN AN ATTACK.

WHEN OUR CHILDREN ARE EIGHTEEN YEARS OLD WE SEND THEM TO THE ARMY. IT IS NOT NORMAL, AND IT IS NOT EASY. DO YOU THINK THAT I LIKE IT? THERE ISN'T ANY MOTHER IN THE WORLD THAT WANTS TO SEND HER CHILD TO THE ARMY.

BUT WE ARE PROUD OF THEM. IN ISRAEL, EVERY PERSON IS A SOLDIER, IT'S TRUE. BUT EVERY SOLDIER IS A PERSON.

AND MAYBE WE MAKE MISTAKES. AND MAYBE WE DO THINGS YOU DON'T LIKE, BUT WE LOVE THIS COUNTRY. IT HAS PROBLEMS, YES, BUT WE WANT TO SOLVE THEM.

THE LAST THING I WANT TO TELL YOU IS WHY YOU CAME HERE. YOU ARE HERE BECAUSE THE STATE OF ISRAEL BELONGS TO THE WHOLE JEWISH WORLD. THIS IS YOUR COUNTRY TOO.

YOU ARE THE AMBASSADORS OF THE ISRAELI STATE. YOU CAME HERE TO FEEL THE STATE OF ISRAEL. YOU CAME HERE BECAUSE YOU HAVE COME HOME.

I AM NOT GOING TO LET THIS GET TO ME...THIS WHOLE SPEECH IS DESIGNED TO MAKE ME EMOTIONAL.

THANK YOU.

CLAP CLAP CLAP CLAP CLAP CLAP CLAP CLAP

I AM NOT GOING TO LET THIS GET TO ME...I'M NOT...

THE DECLARATION OF INDEPENDENCE

I'M GOING TO GET SOME AIR.

OKAY, SEE YOU OUTSIDE.

I'M NOT GETTING EMOTIONAL, I JUST NEED SOME AIR, I NEED SOME--

ARE *THESE* OUR SOLDIERS?

MY GOD, THEY'RE SO *YOUNG.*

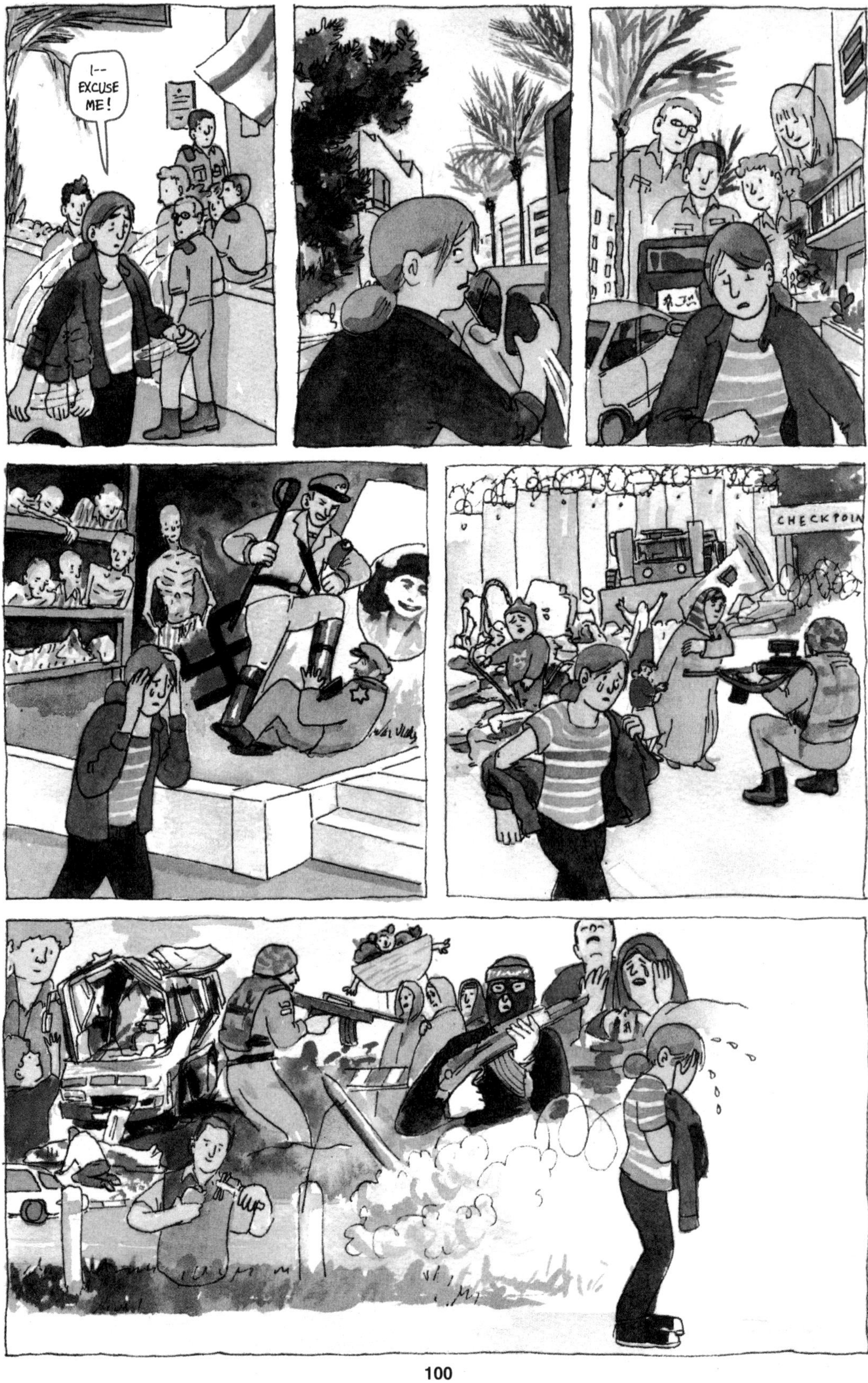
I--
EXCUSE
ME!
CHECKPOIN

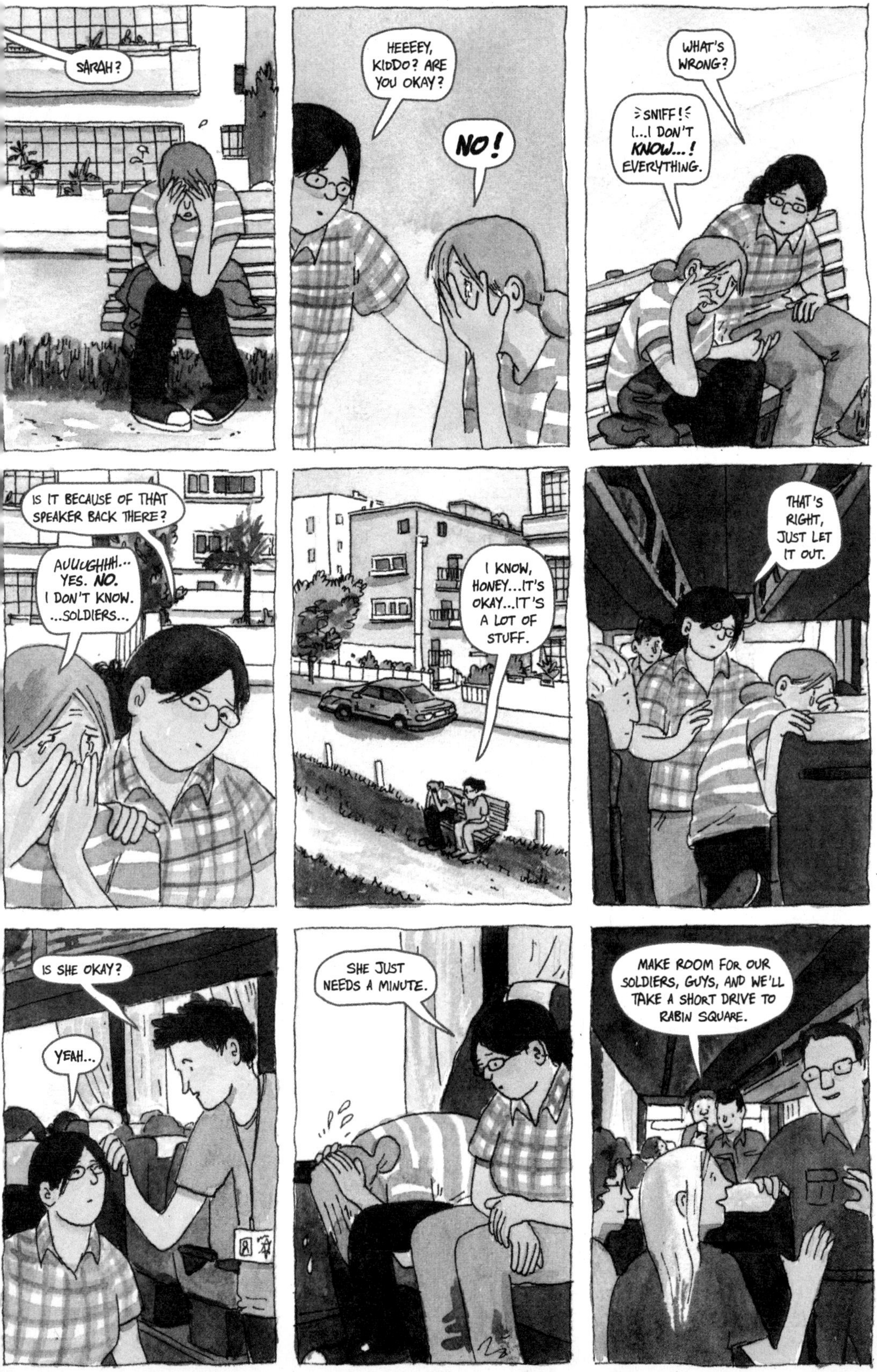
SARAH?
HEEEEY, KIDDO? ARE YOU OKAY?
NO!
WHAT'S WRONG?
SNIFF! I...I DON'T KNOW...! EVERYTHING.
IS IT BECAUSE OF THAT SPEAKER BACK THERE?
AUUUGHHH... YES. NO. I DON'T KNOW. ...SOLDIERS...
I KNOW, HONEY...IT'S OKAY...IT'S A LOT OF STUFF.
THAT'S RIGHT, JUST LET IT OUT.
IS SHE OKAY?
YEAH...
SHE JUST NEEDS A MINUTE.
MAKE ROOM FOR OUR SOLDIERS, GUYS, AND WE'LL TAKE A SHORT DRIVE TO RABIN SQUARE.

OKAY, EVERYONE! LET'S GET IN A CIRCLE! WE'RE GOING TO PLAY A LITTLE GAME SO OUR SOLDIERS CAN GET TO KNOW US A LITTLE BETTER.

EACH PERSON WILL COME TO THE CENTER OF THE CIRCLE AND TELL THE GROUP THEIR NAME AND SOMETHING ABOUT THEMSELVES.

I'LL GO FIRST. HI, MY NAME IS SHARON AND I'M...

HEY... ARE YOU ALL RIGHT?

YEAH, I'M FINE, NADAN. I JUST...I CAN'T HANDLE AN ICEBREAKER GAME RIGHT NOW.

PEOPLE THOUGHT MAYBE YOU GOT A PHONE CALL FROM HOME WITH BAD NEWS OR SOMETHING. THEY'RE WORRIED.

NO, IT'S NOTHING LIKE THAT.

I DON'T KNOW. YOU'RE GONNA THINK I'M CRAZY. I JUST THOUGHT I KNEW WHAT I FELT ABOUT THIS PLACE AND NOW I'M ALL MESSED UP.

I KNOW THE PALESTINIANS ARE WRONG SOMETIMES. BUT... I ALWAYS THOUGHT THAT ISRAEL WAS *MORE* WRONG BECAUSE IT HAS ALL THE POWER.

AND NOW ALL THESE PEOPLE HERE ARE TELLING ME THAT THIS IS *MY* HOME? WELL, MAYBE I DON'T WANT IT!

I CAME HERE...I THINK I WANTED TO KNOW FOR SURE THAT ISRAEL WAS THE BAD GUY. I WANTED TO KNOW THAT I COULD CUT IT OUT OF MY LIFE FOR GOOD.

BUT NOW I DON'T KNOW. I DON'T KNOW ANYTHING. I CAN SEE WHY ISRAEL DID SOME OF WHAT THEY DID. YOU GUYS ARE GOOD PEOPLE. AT LEAST, SOME OF YOU ARE.

OR MAYBE I'M JUST BEING BRAINWASHED JUST LIKE EVERYONE SAID I WOULD BE!

JAMIL'S DAD WILL TURN OUT TO BE RIGHT AFTER ALL.

WHO'S JAMIL?

MY BOYFRIEND. HIS DA-

HE'S AN ARAB?

HUH? NO, HIS DAD IS FROM PAKISTAN. BUT WOULD IT MATTER IF HE WAS?

DON'T ANSWER THAT.

ANYWAY, WHEN HE TOLD HIS DAD I WAS JEWISH, AND HIS DAD, HE'S PRETTY CONSERVATIVE, YOU KNOW? HE SAID, "OH, SO SHE MUST SUPPORT ISRAEL."

SO JAMIL SAID, "ACTUALLY, SHE'S PRETTY CRITICAL OF ISRAEL." BUT HIS DAD SAID, "WELL, SHE'LL END UP BEING AN ISRAEL SUPPORTER, EVENTUALLY. ALL AMERICAN JEWS ARE."

WHEN JAMIL TOLD ME THAT HE SAID THAT, I WAS FURIOUS. AND NOW...

SNIFF! THANKS.

SO YOU GUYS WIN! I FEEL A CONNECTION, OKAY? I HOPE YOU'RE HAPPY.

HOW CAN I FEEL A CONNECTION TO A PLACE THAT CAUSES SO MUCH SUFFERING?

OR MAYBE I DON'T REALLY FEEL THIS CONNECTION. MAYBE IT'S JUST IMPOSSIBLE NOT TO, AFTER SOMEONE TALKS TO YOU ABOUT HOLOCAUST REFUGEES AND TEENAGED SOLDIERS!

UH...WOW.

I'M SORRY. ₹SNIFF!₹ I KNOW I SOUND LIKE A CRAZY PERSON.

LOOK, NO ONE IS BRAINWASHING YOU OR TRYING TO MAKE YOU THINK SOMETHING YOU DON'T WANT TO THINK. THE SPEAKER AT INDEPENDENCE HALL, GIL, THEY'RE JUST TELLING YOU FACTS.

YEAH, THEY'RE ONLY TELLING YOU ONE SIDE OF THE STORY, THE ISRAELI SIDE OF THE STORY. THE PALESTINIANS HAVE THEIR OWN STORY.

LIFE ISN'T SUCH A TRAGEDY, EH? COME ON NOW.

BUT IT IS A TRAGEDY!

OKAY, IF YOU SAY SO. BUT IT'S NOT ALL OUR FAULT.

I KNOW...

I DON'T EVEN KNOW WHY I CARE ABOUT THIS SO MUCH.

AND WHY DO YOU HAVE A ROLL OF TOILET PAPER IN YOUR POCKET?

OH, YOU KNOW...ONE SHOULD ALWAYS BE PREPARED.

...RABIN'S ASSASSINATION WAS ONE OF THE GREATEST TRAGEDIES IN ISRAEL'S HISTORY. HE WAS SHOT HERE, AS HE CAME DOWN THE STEPS AFTER ADDRESSING A GIGANTIC CROWD ASSEMBLED IN THE SQUARE. THE RALLY HAD BEEN IN SUPPORT OF THE OSLO PEACE ACCORDS.

ALTHOUGH HIS AIDES HAD URGED HIM TO WEAR A BULLETPROOF VEST, HE HAD REFUSED THAT DAY, SAYING THAT "IF THERE COMES A TIME WHEN I WOULD NEED A BULLETPROOF VEST, I NO LONGER WANT TO BE PRIME MINISTER OF THIS COUNTRY."

THE ASSASSIN WAS YIGAL AMIR, AN ORTHODOX JEW FROM THE EXTREME RIGHT WHO OPPOSED THE PEACE TALKS.

MURDERER

HE WAITED FOR RABIN AND HIS BODYGUARDS TO COME DOWN THESE STAIRS AND THEN HE FIRED SEVERAL SHOTS. RABIN'S LAST WORDS BEFORE HE SUCCUMBED TO HIS WOUNDS WERE "I CAN'T BELIEVE IT'S A JEW."

HEY, IS THERE A BATHROOM NEAR HERE?

YEAH, IN THE MALL OVER THERE.

CAN A TRAGEDY BE NOBODY'S FAULT?

OR IS THIS A STORY IN WHICH THERE ARE JUST NO "GOOD GUYS"?

ORDER! ORDER!

THE CASE OF "BIRTHRIGHT IS BRAINWASHING ME VS. BIRTHRIGHT IS NOT BRAIN-WASHING ME" IS RESUMING!

THE COURT NOW CALLS--

WHERE IS EVERYONE?

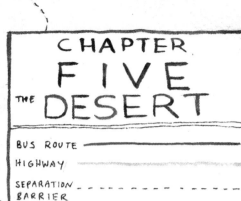

CHAPTER
FIVE
THE DESERT

BUS ROUTE	————————
HIGHWAY	
SEPARATION BARRIER	– – – – – – –

WEST BANK

DEAD SEA

MASADA

BEDOUIN CAMP

SWIM SP.

KIBBUTZ MASHAVEI SADE

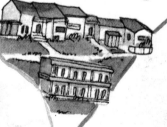

DIMONA

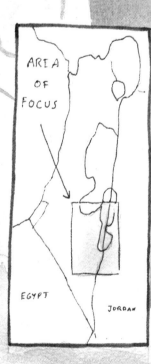

AREA OF FOCUS

EGYPT

JORDAN

KIBBUTZ SDE BOKER
AND BEN GURION BURIAL SITE

WE'RE LEAVING THE INTENSITY OF TEL AVIV TO EXPLORE THE DESERT FOR A FEW DAYS.

HOW YA FEELIN', BABE?

OH, I'M FINE. REALLY. READY FOR THE NEXT THING.

MY EYES STILL STING FROM MY EMOTIONAL OUTBURST.

I KNOW MINE ISN'T A UNIQUE EXPERIENCE. CATHARTIC MOMENTS, EPIPHANIES AND NERVOUS BREAKDOWNS ARE PROBABLY BUILT INTO A BIRTHRIGHT ITINERARY LIKE LUNCH STOPS ON A CLASS FIELD TRIP.

OF ALL THE FORTY DAYS OF CRAMMING AND READING I DID BEFORE THIS TRIP, THERE'S ONE ANALOGY BY MELANIE KAYE THAT'S STICKING OUT IN MY MIND RIGHT NOW.

"SOME OF US EXPERIENCE ISRAEL AS A CRAZY UNCLE... SOMEONE OVER WHOM WE HAVE NO CONTROL, BUT WHOSE BEHAVIOR WE'RE SOMEHOW RESPONSIBLE FOR.

"TO PUBLICLY REJECT HIM WOULD EXPOSE OUR FAMILY'S SHAME."

I--I'D LIKE TO MAKE...A TOAST!

ACCORDING TO OUR ITINERARY, WE ARE ON OUR WAY TO EXPERIENCE BEDOUIN CULTURE WITH A CAMEL RIDE AND AN OVERNIGHT IN A BEDOUIN TENT.

THERE IS GENERAL EXCITEMENT VIS-À-VIS CAMEL RIDING.

MY FRIEND ANNIE? SHE SAID THE CAMEL RIDE WAS HER FAVORITE PART.

OMAGAWD I CANNOT WAIT!

IT WOULD BE NICE IF WE ACTUALLY DID GO TO A REAL BEDOUIN VILLAGE, BUT I'VE HEARD THINGS ABOUT THIS CAMP WE'RE HEADED TOWARDS.

NOT THE MOST AUTHENTIC?

SOUNDS MORE LIKE A THEME PARK.

THEME PARK IS RIGHT...IT'S AS IF A PIECE OF EPCOT CENTER BROKE APART FROM THE MAINLAND AND SOMEHOW CAME TO REST IN THE MIDDLE OF THE NEGEV.

A GOAT HAIR TENT! WELL, THE *SMELL* IS AUTHENTIC AT LEAST.

WHERE SHOULD WE SET UP OUR SLEEPING BAGS?

THERE'S A GOOD SPOT BY THAT POLE ACROSS FROM THE AIR CONDITIONER.

NOW, WHEN YOU GET ON THE CAMEL, DON'T BE AFRAID! BUT HANG ON TIGHT BECAUSE WHEN THEY STAND UP IT CAN BE SURPRISING!

BECAUSE WE DON'T HAVE ENOUGH CAMELS FOR EVERYONE, WE WILL PUT SOME OF YOU ON THE MULES AND THEN WE WILL SWITCH ON THE WAY BACK.

THE OUTRAGE EXPRESS IS PULLING OUT OF THE STATION AND I'VE GOT A GREAT VIEW...

...360 DEGREES OF BITTER, DEPRESSING IRONY FROM THE BACK OF AN ASS.

OH MY GOD!

THE WAY THEY'RE HITTING THE CAMELS IS SO MEAN!

I KNOW. IT'S CRUEL!

HEP! LET'S GO!

THE STORY OF THE NEGEV BEDOUINS IS AN ESPECIALLY SAD ONE. WHILE THE PALESTINIAN STRUGGLE IS ONGOING AND FULL OF COLORFUL LUNATICS WHO MAKE FOR COLORFUL HEADLINES, THE EVAPORATION OF THE BEDOUIN WAY OF LIFE IS KIND OF SEEN AS A FAIT ACCOMPLI AND THEREFORE DOESN'T GET MUCH ATTENTION IN INTERNATIONAL PRESS. IN FACT, I ALMOST MISSED IT ALTOGETHER DURING MY CLUMSY, HURRIED "RESEARCH."

IN LEADING OUR PATHETIC CARAVAN, THESE GUYS ARE TAKING US ON A TOUR OF THEIR PEOPLE'S OWN DEFEAT.

AND THEY'RE LUCKY TO HAVE A JOB AT ALL! UNEMPLOYMENT IN THE BEDOUIN COMMUNITY IS AS HIGH AS 60% IN SOME PLACES.

BUT TO HAVE TO DISPLAY A BASTARDIZED VERSION OF THEIR NEARLY DEAD CULTURE TO THE COUSINS OF THE VERY PEOPLE RESPONSIBLE FOR ITS DEATH IS JUST CRUEL.

NOT TO MENTION THE FACT THAT THESE ANIMALS DON'T LOOK TOO HAPPY EITHER.

IT'LL BE OVER SOON...

WHAT? YOU DON'T LIKE THE DONKEY RIDE?

NO. THESE PEOPLE HATE US. THE CAMELS HATE US.

AND LOOK AT *HIM*! HE **DEFINITELY** HATES ME.

AW, COME ON, JUST TRY TO ENJOY IT!

OKAY! TIME TO SWITCH! CAREFUL AS YOU DISMOUNT.

OKAY, I GO...? OKAY.

BRAAAA!

WO-*OAH*!

OKAY, I'LL TRY TO ENJOY THIS. THESE THINGS ARE TALLER THAN I THOUGHT.

I TRY TO FOCUS ON HOW BEAUTIFUL THE DESERT IS... IF I BLOCK OUT THE SOUNDS OF MY TRAVEL-MATES' SQUEALING AND THE CAMELS' LOWING I COULD BE IN ANY TIME IN HISTORY.

I AM T.E. LAWRENCE!

BRAAAAHHHHHH

CAN WE MAKE THE JOURNEY ACROSS THE DESERT BY DAYBREAK?

PERHAPS. BUT I DOUBT WE SHALL BE SUCCESSFUL WITHOUT BACKUP.

WE CAN RECRUIT SUPPORT! OUR CAUSE IS TRUE!

NEVER. RESISTANCE IS STRONG... *TOO* STRONG.

BUT IT *IS* POSSIBLE! DON'T YOU TRUST ME?

AND WHY SHOULD WE TRUST YOU, ENGLISH?

≥SIGH≤

HEY, SARAH!

HUH?

SAY "CAMEL!"

CAMEL!

OH, THAT'S A GOOD ONE!

OURS KEPT WAVING ITS HEAD AROUND! I THINK IT WAS CRAZY OR RETARDED.

IS IT JUST ME? OR DID THOSE GUYS LOOK REALLY DEPRESSED?

HEY, CHECK IT OUT! RUSSIAN BIRTHRIGHT.

HI!

IT WAS NICE MEETING YOU!

SO MUCH FOR JEWISH UNITY.

WELCOME, WELCOME! PLEASE HAVE A SEAT! WELCOME!

I AM SALEEM, YOUR HOST FOR THIS EVENING! AND I WANT TO WELCOME YOU AND SHOW YOU SOME OF THE HOSPITALITY WE BEDOUIN ARE FAMOUS FOR.

THE TENT WE ARE IN IS CALLED A BAYT CHAR, OR "HOUSE OF HAIR." ANY VISITOR IS WELCOMED INTO IT. WHY? BECAUSE IN THE DESERT, WE DON'T OFTEN SEE MANY PEOPLE. HAVING A GUEST IS CAUSE FOR CELEBRATION!

OUR COFFEE IS CENTRAL TO WELCOMING A GUEST. IT IS BLACK LIKE THE NIGHT, STRONG LIKE A MAN, AND BITTER LIKE A MOTHER-IN-LAW!

THANK YOU.

SALEEM IS A PRACTICED STORYTELLER, BUT I WISH HE WOULD TALK ABOUT WHAT THE LIFE OF THE BEDOUIN HAS *BECOME* INSTEAD OF WHAT IT *USED* TO BE...

UNTIL VERY RECENTLY, WE RULED AS KINGS OF THE DESERT, MASTERED NATURE'S HARSHEST CONDITIONS.

PLEASE STAND BY

FOR CENTURIES WE WERE NOMADS, SURVIVING THROUGH HERDING AND FISHING, GUIDING PILGRIMS, AND YES, EVEN RAIDING IF YOU GO BACK FAR ENOUGH. WE LIVED IN A WORLD WITHOUT TIME.

EVERYTHING CHANGED IN 1948. MANY OF US FLED OR WERE EXPELLED. THOSE WHO REMAINED HAVE HAD EVERYTHING TAKEN FROM THEM.

WE WERE STRIPPED OF OUR LAND. ISRAEL FORCIBLY RELOCATED US TO THIS SMALL TRIANGLE CALLED SIYAG OR "ENCLOSURE." IT IS ONLY 2% OF THE NEGEV AND EVEN HERE WE HAVE NO PROPERTY RIGHTS.

N

JERUSALEM

JORDAN

NEGEV

EGYPT

THE ISRAELIS WANTED US TO MOVE TO NEW TOWNS BUILT BY THE STATE, TO BECOME URBAN, ASSIMILATE. HALF OF US WENT TO THESE POOR TOWNS WITH NO VIABLE ECONOMY AND GAVE UP OUR TRADITIONS.

BUT MANY OF US WANTED TO STAY IN OUR TRADITIONAL VILLAGES. ISRAEL CALLS THESE "UNRECOGNIZED." THEY REFUSE TO PROVIDE THESE VILLAGES WITH THE MOST BASIC HUMAN SERVICES SUCH AS ELECTRICITY OR SANITATION.

AND BECAUSE THEY ARE "ILLEGAL" THE GOVERNMENT CAN, AND DOES, DEMOLISH OUR HOMES, SPRAY PESTICIDES ON OUR CROPS, AND CONFISCATE OUR LIVESTOCK AT ANY TIME.

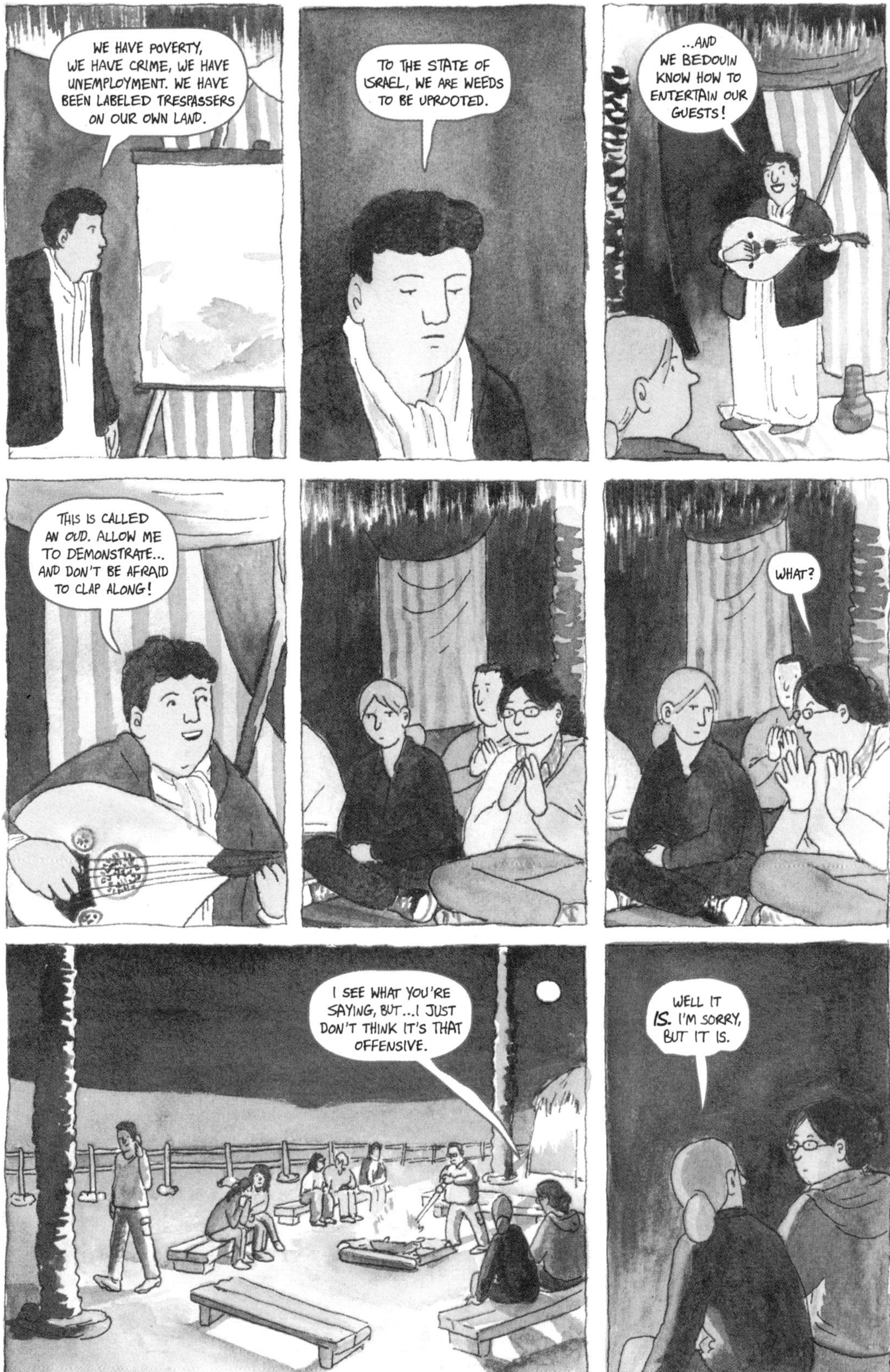
WE HAVE POVERTY, WE HAVE CRIME, WE HAVE UNEMPLOYMENT. WE HAVE BEEN LABELED TRESPASSERS ON OUR OWN LAND.
TO THE STATE OF ISRAEL, WE ARE WEEDS TO BE UPROOTED.
...AND WE BEDOUIN KNOW HOW TO ENTERTAIN OUR GUESTS!
THIS IS CALLED AN OUD. ALLOW ME TO DEMONSTRATE... AND DON'T BE AFRAID TO CLAP ALONG!
WHAT?
I SEE WHAT YOU'RE SAYING, BUT...I JUST DON'T THINK IT'S THAT OFFENSIVE.
WELL IT IS. I'M SORRY, BUT IT IS.

YOU KNOW THIS PLACE IS A STOP ON ALMOST EVERY BIRTHRIGHT TOUR. IT'S SO WE CAN GO BACK AND SAY WE MET A HAPPY ARAB WHO DOESN'T HATE ISRAEL LIKE THOSE NASTY PALESTINIANS.

THE ISRAELI WHO OWNS THIS PLACE PROBABLY SCRIPTED THAT SPEECH FOR HIM. LIKE THE PART WHERE HE HOLDS UP HIS CELL PHONE AND SAYS "WELL, THESE DAYS MANY OF US ARE LEAVING BEHIND THE OLD WAYS FOR THE COMFORTS OF MODERN LIFE!"

AND JUST WHEN I WAS STARTING TO SYMPATHIZE WITH SOME THINGS THEY DO...

WELL...YOU DON'T HAVE TO AGREE WITH EVERYTHING.

COME ON, LET'S CALL IT A NIGHT. WE HAVE THAT THREE A.M. WAKE-UP CALL FOR THE MASADA SUNRISE HIKE.

OKAY.

OKAY, GUYS! I'M GONNA TURN OFF THE LIGHTS NOW. GOODNIGHT.

GOODNIGHT!

GOODNIGHT!

GOODNIGHT!

GOODNIGHT!

HEY, HOW ARE YOU FEELING NOW? BETTER THAN THIS MORNING?

WOW, WAS THAT ONLY THIS MORNING? HUH! IT SEEMS LIKE DAYS AGO.

BUT BETTER..YEAH, I FEEL A LITTLE BETTER. I'M KIND OF CYCLING THROUGH THE WHOLE CATALOGUE OF EMOTIONS TODAY.

ARE YOU ON A...WHAT DO YOU CALL IT..."EMOTIONAL ROLLER COASTER"?

YES, EMOTIONAL ROLLER COASTER IS A FINE PHRASE FOR IT.

I HEARD YOU TALKING TO MELISSA...ABOUT THIS PLACE BEING RIDICULOUS?

YEAH? WHAT DO *YOU* THINK ABOUT IT?

OH, WELL, I AGREE WITH YOU. I DON'T THINK IT'S POSSIBLE TO BELIEVE THIS PLACE IS AUTHENTIC. IT WOULD BE LIKE YOU TAKING ME TO A CASINO TO SHOW ME WHAT AMERICAN INDIAN CULTURE IS LIKE.

GOOD, SO I'M NOT GETTING ALL AGITATED OVER NOTHING.

NO, NO. WHAT'S BECOME OF THE BEDOUINS IS REALLY SAD...BUT IT'S NOT AS SIMPLE AS YOU THINK..

I *KNOW!* IT'S HORRIBLE!

SHHH!

SORRY!

IT'S HORRIBLE. THEY'RE TRYING TO KEEP THEM CONTAINED, RIGHT? AND TO PREVENT THEM FROM BEING A PART OF THE "DEMOGRAPHIC TIME BOMB," RIGHT?

DEMOGRAPHIC TIME BOMB?

YEAH, YOU KNOW...THE KOENIG MEMORANDUM AND ALL THAT?

HOW ISRAELI JEWS ARE AFRAID THAT THE ARABS HAVE A HIGHER BIRTHRATE AND WILL EVENTUALLY BECOME THE MAJORITY IN ISRAEL PROPER AND THEREFORE NEED TO BE "CONTAINED."

AH, YES.

AND THAT'S WHY THEY DON'T WANT TO ALLOW THE PALESTINIAN REFUGEES THE RIGHT TO RETURN...

RIGHT. BECAUSE THEN JEWS WOULDN'T BE THE MAJORITY IN ISRAEL.

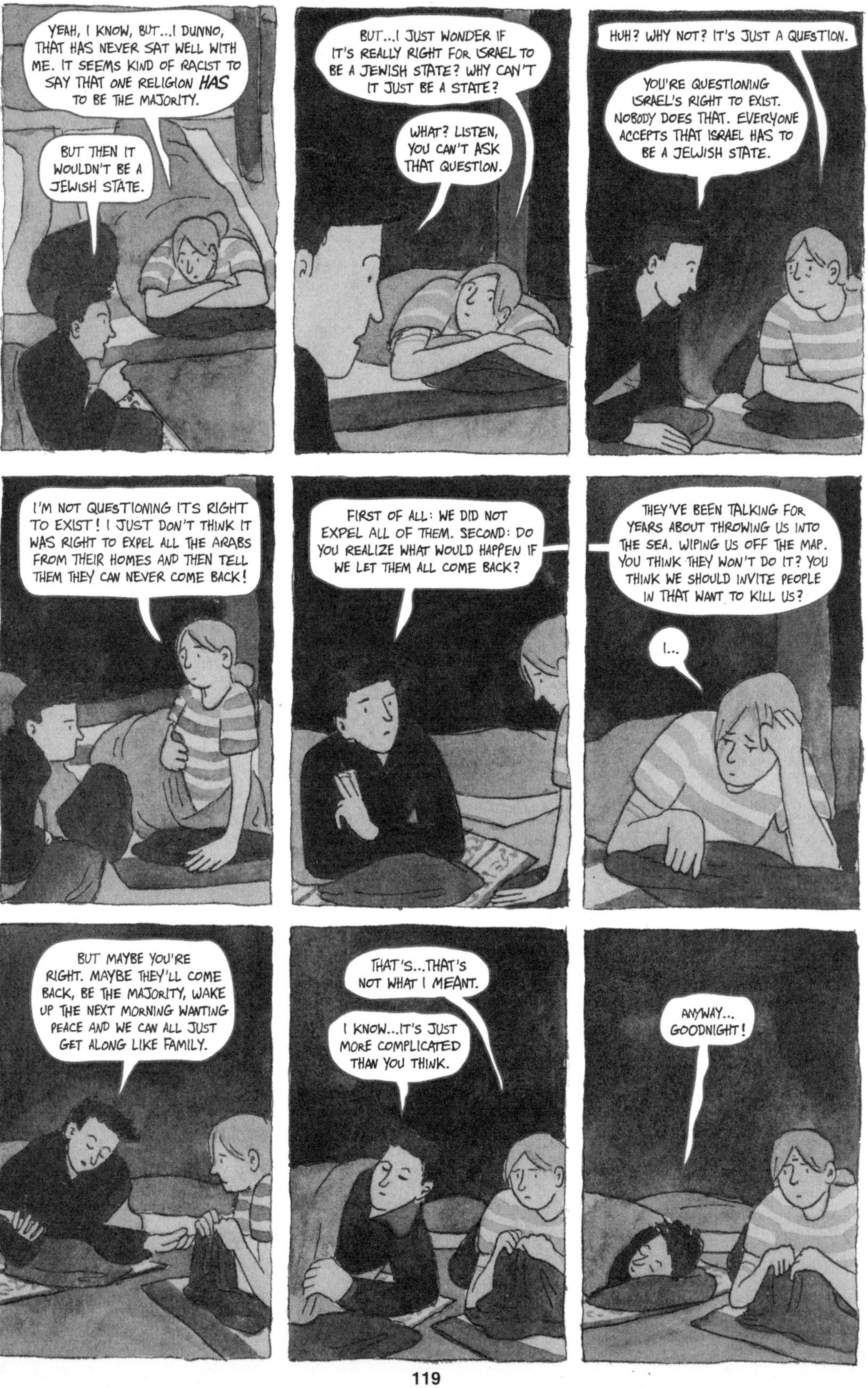
YEAH, I KNOW, BUT...I DUNNO, THAT HAS NEVER SAT WELL WITH ME. IT SEEMS KIND OF RACIST TO SAY THAT ONE RELIGION HAS TO BE THE MAJORITY.
BUT THEN IT WOULDN'T BE A JEWISH STATE.
BUT...I JUST WONDER IF IT'S REALLY RIGHT FOR ISRAEL TO BE A JEWISH STATE? WHY CAN'T IT JUST BE A STATE?
WHAT? LISTEN, YOU CAN'T ASK THAT QUESTION.
HUH? WHY NOT? IT'S JUST A QUESTION.
YOU'RE QUESTIONING ISRAEL'S RIGHT TO EXIST. NOBODY DOES THAT. EVERYONE ACCEPTS THAT ISRAEL HAS TO BE A JEWISH STATE.
I'M NOT QUESTIONING ITS RIGHT TO EXIST! I JUST DON'T THINK IT WAS RIGHT TO EXPEL ALL THE ARABS FROM THEIR HOMES AND THEN TELL THEM THEY CAN NEVER COME BACK!
FIRST OF ALL: WE DID NOT EXPEL ALL OF THEM. SECOND: DO YOU REALIZE WHAT WOULD HAPPEN IF WE LET THEM ALL COME BACK?
THEY'VE BEEN TALKING FOR YEARS ABOUT THROWING US INTO THE SEA. WIPING US OFF THE MAP. YOU THINK THEY WON'T DO IT? YOU THINK WE SHOULD INVITE PEOPLE IN THAT WANT TO KILL US?
I...
BUT MAYBE YOU'RE RIGHT. MAYBE THEY'LL COME BACK, BE THE MAJORITY, WAKE UP THE NEXT MORNING WANTING PEACE AND WE CAN ALL JUST GET ALONG LIKE FAMILY.
THAT'S...THAT'S NOT WHAT I MEANT.
I KNOW...IT'S JUST MORE COMPLICATED THAN YOU THINK.
ANYWAY... GOODNIGHT!

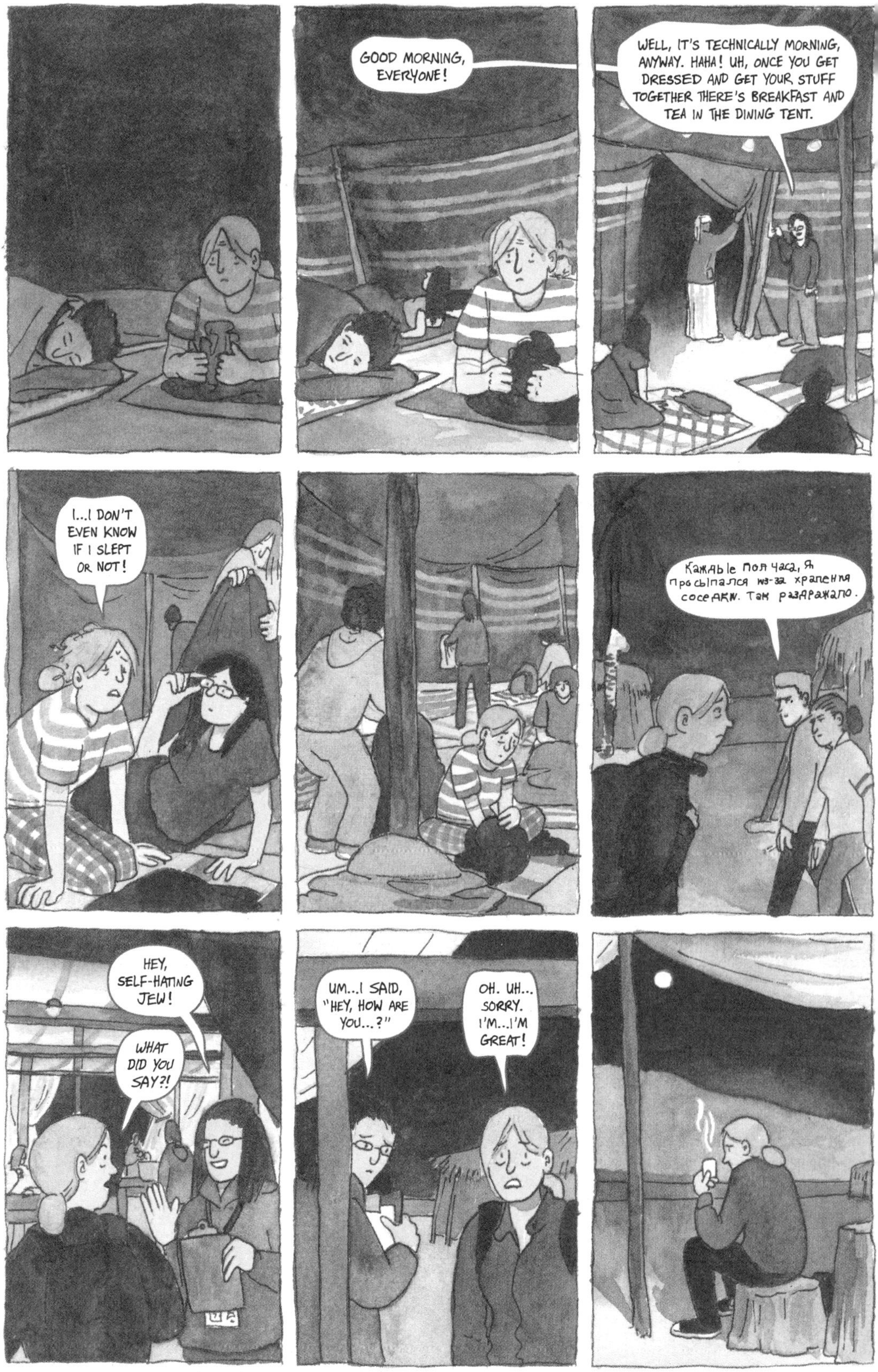
GOOD MORNING, EVERYONE!
WELL, IT'S TECHNICALLY MORNING, ANYWAY. HAHA! UH, ONCE YOU GET DRESSED AND GET YOUR STUFF TOGETHER THERE'S BREAKFAST AND TEA IN THE DINING TENT.
I...I DON'T EVEN KNOW IF I SLEPT OR NOT!
Каждые пол часа, я просыпался из-за храпения соседки. Так раздражало.
HEY, SELF-HATING JEW!
WHAT DID YOU SAY?!
UM...I SAID, "HEY, HOW ARE YOU...?"
OH. UH... SORRY. I'M...I'M GREAT!

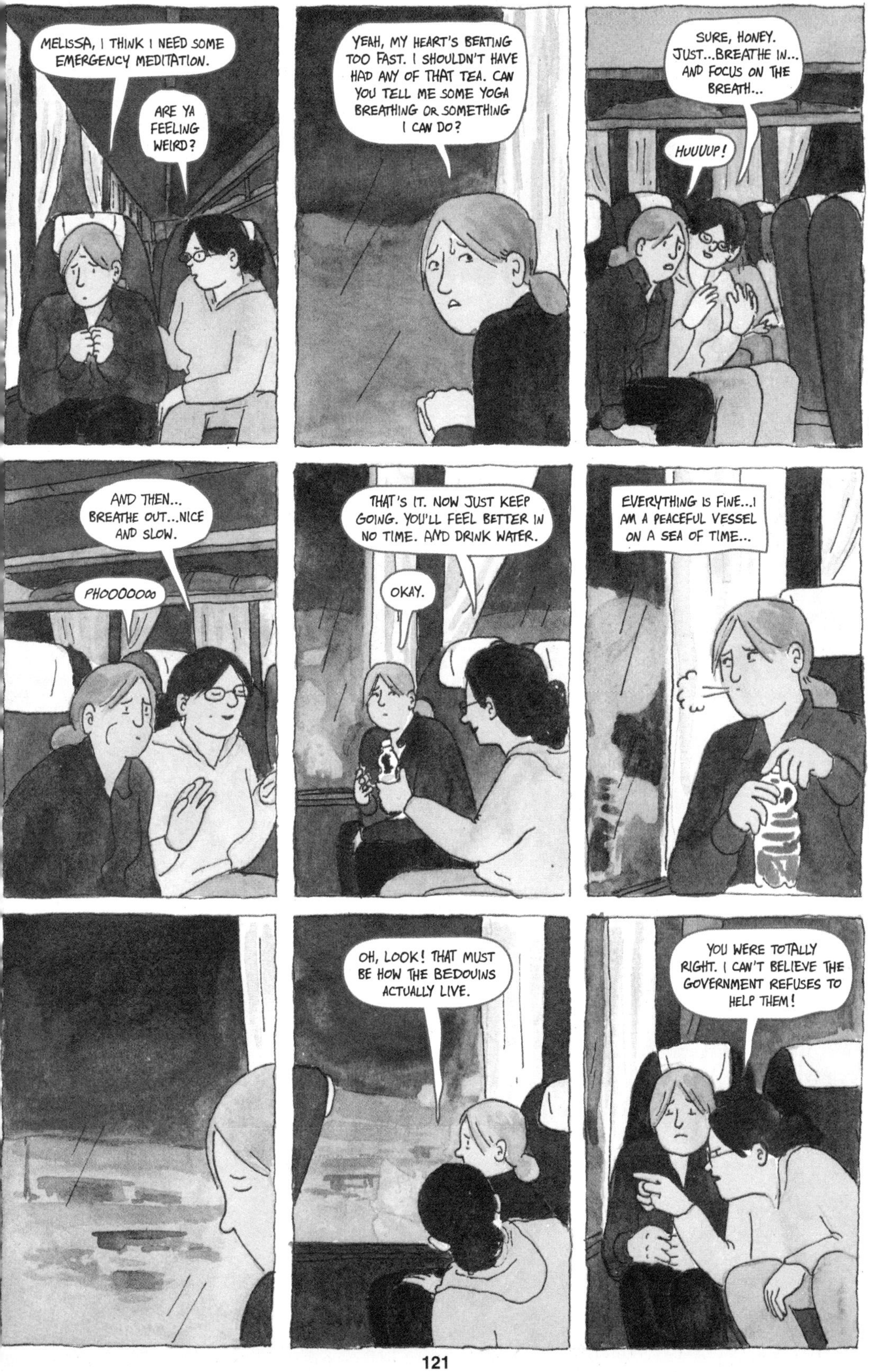
MELISSA, I THINK I NEED SOME EMERGENCY MEDITATION.
ARE YA FEELING WEIRD?
YEAH, MY HEART'S BEATING TOO FAST. I SHOULDN'T HAVE HAD ANY OF THAT TEA. CAN YOU TELL ME SOME YOGA BREATHING OR SOMETHING I CAN DO?
SURE, HONEY. JUST...BREATHE IN... AND FOCUS ON THE BREATH...
HUUUUP!
AND THEN... BREATHE OUT...NICE AND SLOW.
PHOOOOOOO
THAT'S IT. NOW JUST KEEP GOING. YOU'LL FEEL BETTER IN NO TIME. AND DRINK WATER.
OKAY.
EVERYTHING IS FINE...I AM A PEACEFUL VESSEL ON A SEA OF TIME...
OH, LOOK! THAT MUST BE HOW THE BEDOUINS ACTUALLY LIVE.
YOU WERE TOTALLY RIGHT. I CAN'T BELIEVE THE GOVERNMENT REFUSES TO HELP THEM!

AFTER SOME MORE BREATHING EXERCISES I'M FINALLY ABLE TO GET IN A POWERNAP.

I WAKE UP WITH THE VAGUE FRAGMENTS OF SOME NIGHTMARE DISAPPEARING QUICKLY INTO GIL TELLING US ABOUT MASADA ON THE BUS MIC.

WE SHOULD BE ABLE TO MAKE IT TO THE TOP BY SUNRISE. IT'S WORTH YOUR LACK OF SLEEP, BELIEVE ME!

I QUICKLY FORGET ABOUT MY APPARENT ANTI-SEMITIC TENDENCIES AS I REMEMBER WHERE WE'RE HEADED AT SUCH AN UNGODLY HOUR.

MASADA!

EVERYONE PLEASE MAKE SURE YOU BRING A HAT WITH YOU...ONCE THE SUN COMES OUT YOU WILL REALLY NEED IT.

OH MAN, I'VE BEEN LOOKING FORWARD TO THIS SO MUCH. DID I TELL YOU ALREADY ABOUT THE MASADA STORY?

YEAH...I REMEMBER. YOU WERE TALKING ALL ABOUT IT AT THE BAR A FEW WEEKS AGO. SOME ANCIENT JONESTOWN STUFF, RIGHT?

WELL, NOT REALLY. BUT FASCINATING ANYWAY. IT WAS DURING THE FIRST JEWISH REVOLT AGAINST THE ROMANS IN THE FIRST CENTURY C.E. THE ONLY RECORD WE HAVE OF ANY OF THAT WHOLE WAR IS FROM THIS GUY JOSEPHUS.

WELL, HE USED TO BE CALLED YOSEF BEN MATITYAHU, HE WAS PART OF THE REVOLT BUT WHEN HE GOT CAPTURED HE BECAME A ROMAN. HE WAS THE BIGGEST JEWISH TURNCOAT EVER!

ANYWAY, HIS ACCOUNT OF MASADA IS THE ONLY RECORD OF IT ANYWHERE, AND EVEN THAT IS A SECONDARY SOURCE. DO YOU WANT TO READ IT? I PHOTOCOPIED THE PARTS ABOUT MASADA.

I, UM...CAN I READ IT WHEN WE GET TO THE TOP?

YEAH, NO PROBLEM! I WANTED TO GO BACK OVER IT ANYWAY BEFORE WE GO UP THERE.

ALL I KNEW ABOUT MASADA BEFORE I BEGAN PREPARING FOR THIS TRIP WAS THAT IT WAS SOME KIND OF LIFE-CHANGING TOURIST DESTINATION IN THE DESERT.

BACK BEFORE BIRTHRIGHT-ISRAEL WAS FOUNDED, MY LITTLE BROTHER WENT ON A TOUR OF ISRAEL WITH THE SYNAGOGUE YOUTH GROUP.

LISTEN TO WHAT DAN WROTE: "AS WE WATCHED THE SUN RISE FROM THE TOP OF MASADA, WE HEARD THE INCREDIBLE STORY OF THE HEROIC FREEDOM FIGHTERS WHO TOOK THEIR OWN LIVES RATHER THAN SUBMIT TO ROMAN RULE. LOOKING OUT UPON THE DESERT, I FELT CONNECTED TO THESE BRAVE JEWS." I THINK HE'S REALLY GROWING UP DURING THIS JOURNEY.

SOUNDS LIKE ZIONIST PROPAGANDA TO ME, MAH! I TOLD YOU HE'S TOO YOUNG TO GO ON ONE OF THOSE TRIPS.

DAN'S EXPERIENCE WAS EXACTLY WHY I HAD AVOIDED BIRTHRIGHT-ISRAEL FROM ITS INCEPTION.

IT'S A FREE TRIP! WHY WOULDN'T YOU WANT TO GO?

YEAH, RIGHT, MOM, SO I CAN HAVE SOME PSEUDO-RELIGIOUS NATIONALIST CONVERSION ON TOP OF AN OLD ROCK LIKE DAN DID? I DON'T THINK SO.

SO YEARS LATER WHEN MASADA SHOWED UP ON ISRAEL EXPERTS' SAMPLE ITINERARY, IT WAS KIND OF A RED FLAG.

UH OH. I'D BETTER LOOK INTO THIS... "MASADA."

THE GRUESOME STORY I READ ON WIKIPEDIA HAD ME HOOKED. I PICKED UP A TRANSLATION OF JOSEPHUS' ORIGINAL TEXT TO GET MORE DETAILS ON THE VIOLENT TAIL-END OF THE JEWISH REVOLT.

BY THE TIME I WAS DONE WITH JOSEPHUS, I WONDERED HOW THIS STORY COULD BE INSPIRATIONAL TO ANYONE.

IN A NUTSHELL, A VIOLENT FANATICAL SPLINTER GROUP WHO EVEN MURDERED OTHER JEWS COMMITTED MASS SUICIDE WHEN THE ROMANS FOUND THEIR HIDING PLACE AT THE END OF THE FIRST REVOLT.

BUT IT TURNS OUT THAT JOSEPHUS' VERSION OF THE STORY GOT A MAKEOVER PRETTY RECENTLY. FOR MORE THAN 1800 YEARS IT HAD BEEN BURIED BY DIASPORA JUDAISM.

THEN, IN 1933, A YOUNG, EXCITABLE GUY NAMED SHMARIA GUTTMAN WENT ON A HIKE TO MASADA WITH A FEW FRIENDS. HE ALSO BROUGHT HIS COPY OF JOSEPHUS.

THEY HAD A DIFFICULT CLIMB TO THE TOP, BUT THERE, SHMARIA REALIZED THAT MASADA HAD MAJOR STAR POWER. HE WAS PART OF A ZIONIST YOUTH GROUP WITH TIES TO THE BURGEONING ISRAELI STATEHOOD MOVEMENT, AND HE WAS CONVINCED THAT THE MASADA WOULD HELP RALLY MORE JEWS TO THE CAUSE.

THE HEAD OF THE JEWISH NATIONAL COMMITTEE WAS NOT IMPRESSED WHEN SHMARIA PROPOSED ORGANIZED TRIPS TO THE SUMMIT.

WHY ARE YOU SO EXCITED? NINE HUNDRED JEWISH ROBBERS RAN FROM JERUSALEM TO MASADA AND COMMITTED SUICIDE. SO WHAT?

BUT SHMARIA WAS PERSISTENT AND BECAUSE OF HIM, A HIKE UP MASADA PAIRED WITH A TELLING OF THE STORY OF ITS BRAVE DEFENDERS BECAME COMMON AMONG YOUTH GROUPS AND, TODAY, BIRTHRIGHT TRIPS.

FROM ERWIN ROMMEL'S AFRIKAKORPS DURING WORLD WAR TWO TO HAMAS, HEZBOLLAH AND IRAN TODAY, SHMARIA'S VERSION OF THE STORY INSPIRES WHOEVER HEARS IT TO BE PREPARED TO DEFEND AGAINST THE ENEMY AT ALL COSTS.

BEFORE OUR EYES, THE WORLD IS ON FIRE. WE SEE NATIONS DISINTEGRATE WHEN THEY CONFRONT THE DIABOLIC NAZI POWER...WE MUST STRENGTHEN OURSELVES AND STAND ON GUARD FOR OUR FREEDOM WITH ALL OUR MIGHT AS THE BRAVE SICARII STOOD AGAINST THE ROMANS.

BY NOW, THE MASADA NARRATIVE HAD BEEN SO PERFECTLY TAILORED TO FIT THE NEEDS OF ITS NEW IDENTITY THAT FEW PEOPLE ARE EVEN FAMILIAR WITH THE ORIGINAL TEXT ANYMORE.

BUT THAT'S WHY I BROUGHT OLE JOSEPHUS WITH ME. I'M INTERESTED TO SEE HOW GIL'S VERSION OF THE STORY WILL COMPARE.

HE STARTS WITH MASADA'S BEGINNINGS. A CENTURY BEFORE THE REVOLT, HEROD BUILT A PALACE FORTRESS WHICH SPRAWLED ACROSS THE NATURALLY FLAT TOP OF A MOUNTAIN IN THE DESERT.

THAT BODY OF WATER TO THE EAST YOU SEE IS THE DEAD SEA. JERUSALEM LIES THIRTY MILES TO THE NORTHWEST.

THERE WAS A PALACE, AN ARMORY AND A RAINWATER COLLECTION SYSTEM WHOSE DESIGN IS A MARVEL OF ENGINEERING.

IT COULD COLLECT ENOUGH IN AN HOUR OF RAIN TO PROVIDE 1,000 PEOPLE WITH WATER FOR THREE YEARS. INCREDIBLE!

BASICALLY, MASADA IS WHAT HAPPENS WHEN A PARANOID SCHIZOPHRENIC RULES A TROUBLED KINGDOM. HE WAS CERTAIN HIS SUBJECTS WOULD TURN ON HIM AND NEEDED A REFUGE IN CASE OF REVOLT.

HE SO FEARED FOR HIS LIFE THAT HE HAD HIS OWN CHILDREN TRIED FOR TREASON AND EXECUTED.

HEROD ENDED UP DYING OF KIDNEY DISEASE. HE NEVER SET FOOT ON MASADA.

OKAY, HERE WE GO...

NOW, THE JEWISH REVOLT BEGAN IN 66 C.E. WHEN THE ZEALOTS BEGAN ENCOURAGING OTHER JEWS TO REBEL AGAINST THE ROMAN RULERS...

WHEN THE REVOLT AGAINST THE ROMANS STARTED, THE SICARII WERE ALIGNED WITH THE ZEALOTS, BUT THEY WERE MORE EXTREME. THEY GOT THEIR NAME FROM THE SPECIAL DAGGERS CALLED "SICARS" THAT THEY HID IN THEIR ROBES. WITH THESE THEY WOULD MURDER THEIR POLITICAL ENEMIES.

JOSEPHUS AGREES. HE SAYS THAT THE SICARII MURDERED THE HIGH PRIEST OF JERUSALEM "IN BROAD DAYLIGHT AND IN THE MIDDLE OF THE CITY."

THEY CAME HERE TO MASADA AFTER A JOURNEY FROM JERUSALEM.

ACCORDING TO JOSEPHUS, THE SICARII DIDN'T JUST "JOURNEY" FROM JERUSALEM, THEY WERE CHASED OUT BY THE ZEALOTS. THE GROUP HAD BECOME "UNBEARABLY TYRANNICAL," AND THE ZEALOTS AGREED THAT IT WAS "ABSURD TO REVOLT FROM ROME AND THEN HAND OVER THAT LIBERTY TO AN EXECUTIONER."

IT WAS A LITTLE NEGLECTED, BUT THE STORES WERE FULL OF FOOD AND THE CISTERNS FULL OF WATER. THEIR LEADER, ELIAZER, MADE A HOME FOR THEM HERE. THEY BUILT MIKVAH BATHS SO THEY COULD PRACTICE THEIR RELIGION.

JOSEPHUS' TEXT DOESN'T SAY ANYTHING ABOUT AN ABANDONED MASADA. HE WRITES THAT THE SICARII "CAPTURED IT BY STEALTH AND EXTERMINATED THE ROMAN GARRISON, PUTTING THEIR OWN IN ITS PLACE."

FOR TWO YEARS THEY LIVED HERE, SURVIVING ON THE GRAIN IN THE STORAGE SHEDS AND THEN BY PLANTING FIELDS TO GROW CROPS WHICH THEY IRRIGATED WITH THE CISTERNS.

SOMETHING GIL DOESN'T MENTION IS THAT THE SICARII PROCURED ADDITIONAL FOOD THROUGH RAIDS. DURING PASSOVER, "THEY MADE A NIGHT RAID ON A LITTLE TOWN CALLED EIN GEDI. THOSE WHO COULD NOT FLEE, WOMEN AND CHILDREN MORE THAN 700 IN NUMBER, WERE BUTCHERED. THEN THEY STRIPPED THEIR HOUSES BARE AND SEIZED THE RIPEST OF THE CROPS."

ONE NIGHT THEY LOOKED WEST AND SAW THE SKIES GLOW RED. IT WAS JERUSALEM BURNING. THEY KNEW THEN THAT THE REBELLION WAS OVER.

THE ROMANS SENT OUT FORCES TO "MOP UP" ANY REMAINING REBEL GROUPS. AFTER CONQUERING THE SMALLER TOWNS, THEY MARCHED ON MASADA.

"FOR THE ROMAN COMMANDER SILVA, MASADA WAS THE VERY LAST TASK IN THE WAR AGAINST THE JEWS."

AFTER STEALING FOOD AND WATER FROM EIN GEDI, THE ROMANS BUILT A WALL AND LAID SIEGE ON MASADA. THEY WAITED FOR THREE MONTHS FOR THE SICARII TO SURRENDER. THEN THE ROMANS BEGAN BUILDING A MASSIVE RAMP. THAT'S THE RAMP WE WALKED UP TO GET HERE.

ONE DAY THE ROMANS CALLED TO THEM TO SURRENDER, SAYING THEY MUST BE SOON RUNNING OUT OF WATER. IN RESPONSE, THE SICARII POURED GIGANTIC JUGS OF WATER DOWN THE CLIFF TO SHOW THAT THEY WOULD NEVER RUN OUT OF WATER AND NEVER SURRENDER.

AS THE ROMANS BUILT THE RAMP, THE DEFENDERS THREW ROCKS AND WEAPONS DOWN ON THE ROMANS BUT WHEN THEY SAW THAT THEY WERE USING JEWISH SLAVES TO BUILD THE RAMP, THE SICARII HAD TO STOP FIGHTING BACK, LEST THEY KILL THEIR OWN PEOPLE. THE RAMP TOOK A YEAR TO BUILD.

THERE'S NO MENTION OF SLAVES IN THE JOSEPHUS TEXT-- ALTHOUGH I SUPPOSE IT COULD JUST BE ASSUMED--ONLY THAT THEY BUILT THE RAMP WITH "WILL AND AMPLE MANPOWER." THEN THEY BROUGHT IN A TOWER WITH A BATTERING RAM UP THE RAMP TO BREAK THE FORTRESS DOOR DOWN.

AFTER TWO AND A HALF YEARS THE BATTLE FINALLY STARTED. THE SICARII BUILT AN EXTRA WALL TO FORTIFY MASADA, BUT THE ROMANS SET FIRE TO IT AND IT BECAME APPARENT THAT THEY WOULD NOT BE ABLE TO DEFEND THEMSELVES ONCE IT WAS GONE.

"AS ELIAZER SAW HIS WALL GOING UP IN FLAMES, HE COULD THINK OF NO MEANS OF ESCAPE OR HEROIC ENDEAVOR...DEATH SEEMED TO HIM LIKE THE RIGHT CHOICE FOR THEM ALL."

HERE IN THE SYNAGOGUE, ELIAZER HAD TO GIVE TWO SPEECHES TO CONVINCE HIS MEN, BUT EVENTUALLY THEY UNDERSTOOD THAT TAKING THEIR OWN LIVES WAS PREFERABLE TO THE TORTURE THAT AWAITED THEM AND THE RAPE AND SLAVERY WAITING FOR THEIR WIVES AND CHILDREN.

ELIAZER'S SPEECHES WERE EFFECTIVE. "AS IF POSSESSED THEY RUSHED OFF, SO IRRESISTIBLE A DESIRE HAD SEIZED THEM TO SLAUGHTER THEIR WIVES, THEIR CHILDREN, AND THEMSELVES. IN THE END NOT A MAN FAILED TO CARRY OUT HIS TERRIBLE RESOLVE. THE LAST MAN SET FIRE TO THE FORTRESS AND DROVE HIS SWORD THROUGH HIS BODY."

MEANWHILE, THE ROMANS WAITED FOR THE FIRE TO DO ITS WORK ON THE WALL. THEN, "EXPECTING FURTHER RESISTANCE, THE ROMANS ARMED THEMSELVES AT DAWN AND MADE THEIR ASSAULT."

"SEEING NO ENEMY, BUT DREADFUL SOLITUDE ON EVERY SIDE, FIRE WITHIN, AND SILENCE, THEY WERE AT A LOSS TO GUESS WHAT HAPPENED."

TWO WOMEN AND SOME CHILDREN HAD HIDDEN IN THE CISTERNS AND TOLD THE ROMANS WHAT HAPPENED.

WOAH.

I *TOLD* YOU IT WAS A CRAZY STORY.

BUT THE SIEGE DIDN'T LAST THREE YEARS, IT PROBABLY LASTED THREE MONTHS. SEE? THEY CHANGED THE STORY TO MAKE IT SOUND MORE IMPRESSIVE. HE LEFT OUT THE EIN GEDI MASSACRE TOO. AND THAT WATER-POURING STORY IS MADE UP.

WE'VE JUST GONE THROUGH THE MASADA RITUAL.

MASADA RITUAL?

WELL, THINK ABOUT IT. WE GO ON A PHYSICAL QUEST--THE DRAMATIC HIKE AT SUNRISE...

THEN WE'RE TOLD AN INSPIRING TALE DESIGNED TO GIVE US MORAL GUIDANCE...

YOU'RE LOOKING OUT ON THE DESERT, PHYSICALLY UNCHANGED SINCE THE SICARII'S TIME. FEELING THAT YOU ARE A PART OF THEIR HISTORY IS ALMOST EFFORTLESS.

AND ISRAEL HAS TONS OF ENEMIES WHO YOU CAN PUT IN PLACE OF THE ROMANS.

IF YOU SEE THEM AS ROLE MODELS, ONES THAT COULD EVEN BE YOUR OWN ANCESTORS, WHY WOULDN'T YOU BE INSPIRED TO DEFEND YOUR OWN COUNTRY AT ALL COSTS?

TRUE...

BUT WHAT IF GIL DOESN'T KNOW THAT HE LEFT STUFF OUT OR REPEATED MADE-UP STORIES? MAYBE HE'S JUST TELLING US WHAT HE'S BEEN TOLD?

HMM...

YEAH, YOU COULD BE RIGHT ABOUT THAT.

IT'S JUST AN INTERESTING STORY, THAT'S ALL.

LIKE ANY MAJOR TOURIST ATTRACTION, MASADA OFFERS A GIGANTIC GIFT SHOP AND VISITORS CENTER BUILT INTO ITS BASE, RIGHT NEXT TO AN AUTOMATED TRAM FOR THOSE NOT UP TO THE HIKE.

WHETHER YOU BELIEVE THE SICARII WERE HEROES OR NOT, THEY DID MEET A HORRIFYING END, AND THE FACT THAT YOU CAN BE PONDERING THAT IN ONE MOMENT AND THEN BROWSING DEAD SEA SKIN RENEWAL PRODUCTS IN THE NEXT IS A LITTLE DISTURBING.

MAYBE IN 1900 MORE YEARS, SOME 26-YEAR-OLD GIRL WILL BE ABSENTMINDEDLY REGARDING ILLEGAL SETTLEMENT SNOW GLOBES IN THE ISRAELI-PALESTINIAN CONFLICT REMEMBRANCE HALL GIFT SHOP, WONDERING HOW SUCH BRUTAL VIOLENCE COULD EVER HAVE EXISTED.

IT'S A COMFORTING THOUGHT.

AHAVA
ESSENTIAL DEAD SEA MUD

EVERYONE IS EXCITED FOR THE REQUISITE STOP AT THE DEAD SEA. I'M PRETTY SURE THAT PROGRAMMING WHICH INVOLVES SEMI-NUDITY IS PART OF BIRTHRIGHT'S SECRET MATCHMAKING AGENDA.

THERE'S ALREADY BEEN A FAIR AMOUNT OF CANOODLING WITHIN OUR GROUP.

DON'T THEY BOTH HAVE SIGNIFICANT OTHERS?

YEP!

NOW, I HAVE TO GIVE YOU SOME WARNINGS ABOUT THE DEAD SEA SO PLEASE LISTEN CAREFULLY...

THIS WATER IS FULL OF MINERALS. IT IS SAID TO HAVE POWERFUL HEALING EFFECTS BUT WILL BURN EYES, CUTS AND SCRAPES, EVEN TINY ONES. I HOPE NONE OF YOU HAVE SHAVED TODAY.

IN ADDITION, THE ROCKS AT THE BOTTOM OF THE SWIMMING AREA ARE COVERED WITH CRYSTALS FROM THESE SAME MINERALS, AND THEY ARE LIKE THOUSANDS OF LITTLE RAZORS, SO WEAR SHOES AND **DO NOT** TOUCH THEM.

THOUSANDS OF LITTLE RAZORS...THIS IS GOING TO BE FUN.

OH MY GOD...

THIS ISN'T FUN, THIS IS CARNAGE!

ARE WE GONNA DO THIS?

WELL, WE BOUGHT THESE WATER SHOES.

TO BE IN THIS WATER IS TO FEEL POWERLESS AND OUT OF CONTROL. PADDLING IS OUT OF THE QUESTION BECAUSE IT WOULD DISTURB THE WATER AND SEND IT FLYING INTO MY EYES. I TRY A KIND OF WRIGGLING MOTION.

IT FEELS ALL SLIMY!

YOU DON'T SWIM IN THE DEAD SEA, YOU SIT IN IT.

I FEEL LIKE THIS IS A METAPHOR FOR SOMETHING, BUT I'M NOT QUITE SURE WHAT.

I WONDER IF THE HEALING POWERS ARE WORKING.

HEY, CHECK IT OUT, YOU CAN STAND UP! LIKE A DOLPHIN!

I'VE GOT DISCO FEVER!

CAREFUL, BUDDY...

UH OH--

GIL WAS RIGHT, ONE TINY DROP AND MY EYE IS ON FIRE. MY HAND FLIES UP TO THE PAIN INSTINCTIVELY, WHICH PUTS EVEN MORE OF THE POISONOUS STUFF TO WORK.

AAAUGGGHH!

DON'T TOUCH IT! GO RINSE IT OUT!

OH MY GOD, DON'T GET THIS SHIT IN YOUR EYES!

I CAN CHECK THE DEAD SEA EXPERIENCE OFF MY LIST OF THINGS TO DO IN LIFE.

NOW I UNDERSTAND WHY ALL THE ISRAELIS IN OUR GROUP ARE SITTING ON THE SHORE INSTEAD OF SWIMMING.

HEY.

HEY.

I STILL HAVEN'T TALKED TO OUR ISRAELI SOLDIERS YET, BUT I DON'T KNOW HOW TO BREAK THE ICE. TOO BAD I MISSED THE NAME GAME. I'LL SKETCH THE PEOPLE ON THE BEACH INSTEAD.

HMMM...I WISH I HAD A RED PEN...

DEAD SEA

WHAT ARE YOU DRAWING? ARE YOU AN ARTIST OR SOMETHING?

YEAH...I'M JUST DRAWING PEOPLE.

WHY?

UM, FOR FUN? I GUESS?

CAN YOU DRAW ME?

SURE, WHY NOT?

TURN A LITTLE TO THE LEFT. NO, JUST YOUR HEAD. OKAY, GOOD, HOLD THAT. HEY, WHAT'S YOUR NAME ANYWAY?

TZACHI.

YEAH, I KIND OF, UH, MISSED THE GAME WHERE WE MET YOU GUYS THE OTHER DAY.

WHERE WERE YOU?

LONG STORY. OKAY...AND...DONE. YOU CAN STOP POSING NOW.

LET ME SEE.

HERE.

HM. THAT'S NOT BAD, I GUESS.

YOU CAN KEEP IT IF YOU WANT.

NO, THAT'S OKAY.

OH WELL. SO MUCH FOR MEETING NEW PEOPLE.

OKAY...WELL, I'LL SEE YOU LATER.

ALL THE ISRAELIS I'VE KNOWN HAVE BEEN PRETTY BLUNT CRITICS.

TZACHI

135

WHEN I WAS NINETEEN, I PARTICIPATED IN A SUMMER DRAWING PROGRAM AT THE NEW YORK STUDIO SCHOOL WHERE I MET DOV, A GRAD STUDENT THERE.

HMMMM...

HE NEVER HESITATED TO POINT OUT THINGS THAT WEREN'T WORKING IN MY DRAWINGS, AND HELPED ME DEVELOP A THICK SKIN.

THIS ISN'T VERY GOOD. LOOK HOW FLAT THE SPACE IS. THERE'S NO DEPTH AT ALL.

THIS MEANT THAT I ACTUALLY BELIEVED HIM WHEN HE COMPLIMENTED MY WORK, THOUGH. AS SOMEONE WARY OF EMPTY PRAISE, I APPRECIATED IT IMMENSELY.

THIS IS A BEAUTIFUL DRAWING. SEE HOW YOU CAN FEEL THE SPACE? YOU'RE REALLY GETTING BETTER.

MY GRATITUDE TOWARDS THIS ISRAELI HONESTY DID HAVE ITS LIMITS, THOUGH...

YOU'RE VERY PRETTY NOW...BUT WHEN YOU GET OLDER YOU'LL LOSE ALL OF YOUR CHARM.

TO ME, IT'S WORTH GETTING OFFENDED BY SOMEONE IF IT MEANS I CAN TRUST THAT EVERY WORD IS THEIR TRUE OPINION.

NO, THE RETURN OF THE PALESTINIAN REFUGEES WOULD BE IMPOSSIBLE.

BUT WHY?

YOU SHOULD GO TO ISRAEL. SEE IT FOR YOURSELF AND MAYBE YOU'LL UNDERSTAND.

MMM. MAYBE. DOV?

YES?

WHAT WAS IT LIKE BEING IN THE ARMY?

I'D RATHER NOT TALK ABOUT THAT TIME.

OUR GROUP GETS UNLOADED AT KIBBUTZ MASHABE SADE, A SUBURBAN OASIS IN THE MIDDLE OF THE DESERT.

JUST LIKE SOME OF OUR FIRST KIBBUTZ EXPERIENCES, THERE ARE NO PEOPLE WALKING AROUND AND NO ONE HAS COME OUT TO GREET US. THIS MAKES ME FEEL LIKE I'M PART OF AN INVADING FOREIGN ARMY ON A NIGHTTIME RAID.

IT'S A LONELY FEELING.

I BET THERE ARE BIRTHRIGHT GROUPS STAYING HERE ALL THE TIME AND THEY'RE JUST SICK OF US.

WE DO END UP TRACKING THE KIBBUTZNIKS DOWN.

HEY, THERE THEY ARE!

HEY GUYS! WHAT'S SHAKING?

I DON'T THINK THEY LIKE US VERY MUCH.

LOOKS LIKE WE INTERRUPTED THEIR DINNER.

FOR THE FIRST TIME IN DAYS I'M STARVING. USUALLY IT'S ONLY DURING BAD BREAKUPS THAT I CAN'T EAT OR SLEEP, BUT THE MENTAL AND EMOTIONAL STRESS OF BEING HERE HAS KEPT ME APPETITE-FREE...UNTIL NOW AS WE STAND IN LINE WAITING FOR THE KITCHEN KIBBUTZNIKS TO BRING OUT DINNER.

OH MAN, OH MAN! THAT CHICKEN SMELLS GOOOOOD.

HEY SARAH, LOOK WHO'S HERE...

IT'S THAT SAME RUSSIAN BIRTHRIGHT GROUP FROM THE BEDOUIN TENT.

YEAH! WAIT, WHERE ARE THEY GOING?

THEY'RE CUTTING!

UM, EXCUSE ME? WELL, SEE, THERE'S ACTUALLY A LINE?

HEY!

I'M PRETTY SURE THIS IS A VIOLATION OF SOME SORT OF RUSSO-U.S. TREATY. I KNOW RUSSIANS KNOW HOW TO STAND IN LINE!

SHHH... EASY NOW.

WE SIT DOWN WITH JULIA AND ONE OF THE SOLDIERS WHO I HAVEN'T MET YET.

RUSSIANS. I CAN'T BELIEVE HOW RUDE THEY ARE.

SORRY... HI, I'M SARAH, WHAT'S YOUR NAME?

I'M ALEKSEY.

ALEKSEY'S FAMILY MOVED HERE FROM RUSSIA TWO YEARS AGO.

I...I DIDN'T MEAN THAT ABOUT RUSSIANS BEING RUDE!

DON'T WORRY ABOUT IT!

WE DON'T SEE THE KIBBUTZNIKS OR THE RUSSIANS AGAIN AFTER DINNER. APPARENTLY EVERYONE IS HOUSED IN DIFFERENT NEIGHBORHOODS OF THE KIBBUTZ AND WE ARE LEFT TO ROAM THE GROUNDS WITHOUT SUPERVISION. I GIVE JAMIL A CALL.

YEAH, I MISS YOU, TOO!

I TRY TO KEEP THINGS LIGHT AND AVOID ANY TALK OF POLITICS, BUT SOMEHOW...

I DON'T THINK YOU SHOULD HOLD YOUR BREATH WAITING FOR ISRAEL TO CHANGE. IF THEY WERE REALLY INTERESTED IN PEACE--

BUT THEY *ARE.* WELL, SOME OF THEM ARE, ANYWAY. LIKE NADAN, HE'S LEFT WING. WE'VE BEEN TALKING A LOT ABOUT THE CONFLICT AND HE SAYS EVERYONE WANTS A STATE FOR THE PALESTINIANS.

WHO'S NADAN?

ALL I'M SAYING IS THAT IT'S MORE COMPLICATED THAN I THOUGHT. IT'S MORE COMPLICATED THAN *YOU* THINK.

YOU KNOW, YOU DON'T HAVE TO TRY AND CONVINCE ME. WE DON'T HAVE TO AGREE ON EVERYTHING.

IT'S REALLY NOT THAT IMPORTANT TO ME WHETHER YOU SUPPORT ISRAEL OR NOT. JUST DON'T COME HOME HATING MUSLIMS.

I... OKAY. FINE.

LOOK, I HAVE TO GO. WE'RE ABOUT TO EAT DINNER.

OKAY. CALL ME AGAIN SOON. AND DON'T WORRY SO MUCH ABOUT THIS STUFF.

HOW DID THAT GO?

NOT GREAT. THIS IS EXACTLY WHAT I WAS AFRAID OF.

HE THINKS I'M IN THE TANK FOR ISRAEL NOW, WHICH IS *TOTALLY* NOT TRUE. I'M JUST...TRYING TO SEE THE OTHER SIDE, THAT'S ALL.

THAT'S THE PROBLEM WITH DATING A NON-JEW. THEY'LL NEVER REALLY UNDERSTAND.

NO, NO...THAT'S NOT IT AT ALL.

HE'S PROBABLY JUST JEALOUS. IT *IS* PRETTY UNFAIR THAT WE GET TO GO ON A FREE VACATION JUST FOR BEING JEWISH.

AND A FREE TRIP TO THE MIDDLE EAST IS PRETTY GOOD FOR A FIRST TIME ABROAD, RIGHT, MELISSA?

YUP.

I'M GOING TO BED. YOU PEOPLE ARE EXHAUSTING.

NIGHT!

HEY, SARAH? I LOVE YOU, HONEY, BUT...

CAN YOU STOP TALKING ABOUT HOW THIS IS MY FIRST TIME OUT OF THE U.S.? I'M KIND OF SENSITIVE ABOUT IT.

OH, MAN, I'M SORRY. HAVE I BEEN SAYING THAT A LOT?

YEAH. A BIT.

I DIDN'T EVEN REALIZE...I'M JUST EXCITED FOR YOU IS ALL.

I KNOW. IT'S JUST THAT THIS TRIP IS KIND OF A BIG DEAL FOR ME. I'M IN THIS OTHER COUNTRY AND LEARNING ALL ABOUT THIS HERITAGE OF MINE THAT'S BEEN KEPT FROM ME FOR MY WHOLE LIFE.

IT'S NOT A BIG DEAL, I JUST WOULD RATHER KEEP SOME THINGS PRIVATE, YOU KNOW?

OF COURSE.

I'M GOING TO TURN IN TOO. YOU COMING?

YEAH... I'LL BE UP IN A BIT.

140

WOAHHH LOOK AT YOUR FACE IN THAT ONE! HAW HAW!

SIGHHH...

EXCUSE ME?

WILL YOU DRAW ANOTHER PICTURE OF ME?

WELL... SURE. PULL UP A CHAIR.

HE'LL PROBABLY HATE THIS ONE, TOO.

OKAY, HERE.

SO... WHAT DO YOU THINK?

I LOVE IT. THANK YOU.

THANK YOU.

YOU'RE WELCOME!

WHAT A WEIRD GUY. HE LOOKED LIKE HE WAS ABOUT TO CRY OR SOMETHING...

HEY... SARAH?

OH, HEY, ANNIE. WHAT'S UP?

WELL SO, SINCE YOU'RE THE ARTIST OF THE GROUP, WE WERE WONDERING IF WE COULD ASK YOU A BIG FAVOR.

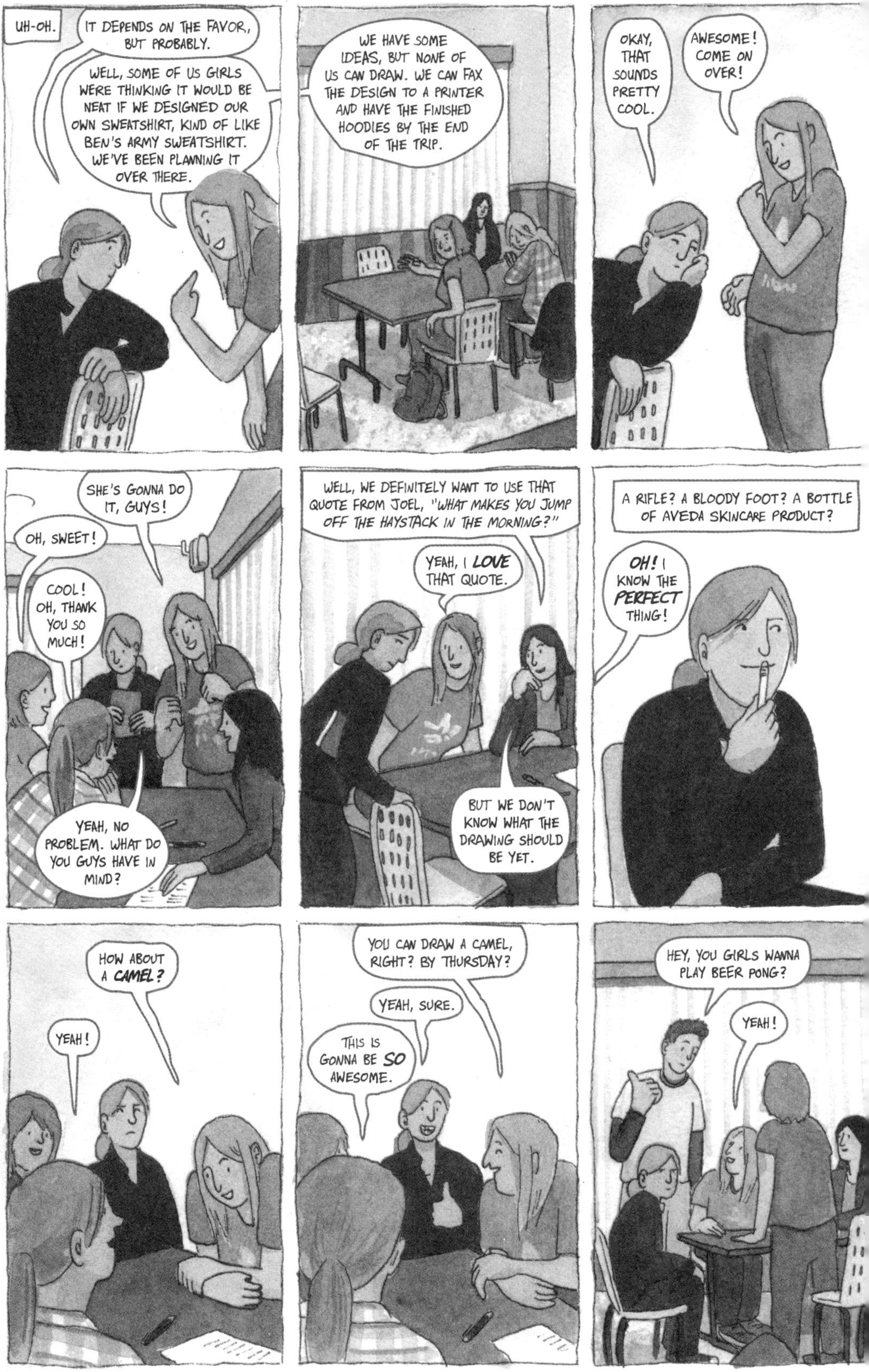
UH-OH.
IT DEPENDS ON THE FAVOR, BUT PROBABLY.
WELL, SOME OF US GIRLS WERE THINKING IT WOULD BE NEAT IF WE DESIGNED OUR OWN SWEATSHIRT, KIND OF LIKE BEN'S ARMY SWEATSHIRT. WE'VE BEEN PLANNING IT OVER THERE.
WE HAVE SOME IDEAS, BUT NONE OF US CAN DRAW. WE CAN FAX THE DESIGN TO A PRINTER AND HAVE THE FINISHED HOODIES BY THE END OF THE TRIP.
OKAY, THAT SOUNDS PRETTY COOL.
AWESOME! COME ON OVER!
SHE'S GONNA DO IT, GUYS!
OH, SWEET!
COOL! OH, THANK YOU SO MUCH!
YEAH, NO PROBLEM. WHAT DO YOU GUYS HAVE IN MIND?
WELL, WE DEFINITELY WANT TO USE THAT QUOTE FROM JOEL, "WHAT MAKES YOU JUMP OFF THE HAYSTACK IN THE MORNING?"
YEAH, I **LOVE** THAT QUOTE.
BUT WE DON'T KNOW WHAT THE DRAWING SHOULD BE YET.
A RIFLE? A BLOODY FOOT? A BOTTLE OF AVEDA SKINCARE PRODUCT?
OH! I KNOW THE **PERFECT** THING!
HOW ABOUT A **CAMEL?**
YEAH!
YOU CAN DRAW A CAMEL, RIGHT? BY THURSDAY?
YEAH, SURE.
THIS IS GONNA BE **SO** AWESOME.
HEY, YOU GIRLS WANNA PLAY BEER PONG?
YEAH!

THE NEXT DAY I TAKE AN EARLY MORNING WALK TO INSPECT THE IRRIGATION SYSTEM, WHICH FASCINATES ME.

I'VE SEEN THESE TUBES STICKING OUT OF BUSHES ALL OVER THE PLACE TO KEEP THINGS GREEN WHERE THERE USED TO BE DESERT. THERE MUST BE A STATE DEPARTMENT OF IRRIGATION, WITH LEGIONS OF ENGINEERS EMPLOYED TO MAINTAIN A VAST UNDERGROUND NETWORK OF GARDEN HOSE!

INTERESTING...

WE'RE MORE THAN HALFWAY THROUGH THE TRIP BY NOW, AND OUR GROUP HAS GROWN ACCUSTOMED TO THE RHYTHMS OF BIRTH-RIGHT TOURISM. WE ARE A TRAVELING CIRCUS.

AT THIS VERY MOMENT, HOW MANY OTHER BUSLOADS OF US ARE THERE LOADING AND UNLOADING ALL OVER THE COUNTRY? AND WHAT MUST ISRAELIS THINK OF US, PRIVILEGED YOUNG PEOPLE WHO NOT ONLY NEVER HAD TO JOIN THE ARMY BUT GET A FREE TRIP TO BOOT?

HEY, NADAN?

THAT'S MY NAME!

WHAT DO ISRAELIS THINK OF AMERICANS? AND BIRTHRIGHT?

WHAT DO WE THINK? WE LIKE AMERICANS. AND WE LIKE TAGLIT.

REALLY? YOU CAN TELL ME THE TRUTH, YOU KNOW.

NO, REALLY! AMERICA IS OUR FRIEND. OF COURSE WE LIKE YOU. IS THAT HARD TO BELIEVE?

KIND OF. WE'RE NOT REALLY USED TO HAVING FRIENDS THESE DAYS.

A SHORT DRIVE THROUGH THE DESERT LATER AND I'M SITTING UNDER AN UNLIKELY TREE IN ANOTHER MANMADE OASIS, THINKING ABOUT THE TWO DAVID BEN-GURIONS.

GIL IS TELLING US ABOUT ONE OF THEM.

HE WAS A SOCIALIST-ZIONIST, ORGANIZING LABOR UNIONS DURING THE '30S AND '40S. HE ESTABLISHED ISRAEL'S FIRST SELF-DEFENSE FORCES AS WELL AS SPECIAL UNITS TO FIGHT IN WORLD WAR TWO.

HE SAID:

WE MUST HELP THE BRITISH ARMY FIGHT THE NAZIS AS IF THERE WAS NO WHITE PAPER, AND THE WHITE PAPER AS IF THERE WAS NO WAR.

ON HIS URGING, ISRAEL DECLARED INDEPENDENCE IN 1948, AND HE LED THE JEWS TO VICTORY. HE WAS THE NATURAL CHOICE FOR ISRAEL'S FIRST PRIME MINISTER.

LATER, HE BEGAN A PUSH TO BUILD CITIES IN THE NEGEV DESERT, NECESSARY TO HOUSE ALL THE NEW IMMIGRANTS COMING TO ISRAEL. TO HIM, CULTIVATING THE BARREN LAND AND MASTERING NATURE WOULD MEAN CULTIVATING A NATION.

FOR THOSE WHO MAKE THE DESERT BLOOM THERE IS ROOM FOR HUNDREDS, THOUSANDS, AND EVEN MILLIONS!

BEN-GURION LOVED AND BELIEVED IN THE NEGEV SO MUCH THAT WHEN HE RETIRED FROM POLITICS HE MOVED TO KIBBUTZ SDE BOKER, NOT FAR FROM HERE, WHERE HE REMAINED FOR THE REST OF HIS LIFE. AND NOW HE'S BURIED HERE OVERLOOKING THE DESERT HE LOVED SO MUCH.

THIS IS THE BEN-GURION THAT IS EASIEST TO DIGEST, THE PATERNAL HERO OF ISRAEL. HE'S THE ONE WHO BELIEVED EARLY ON THAT ZIONISM, ESPECIALLY AFTER THE HOLOCAUST, WAS NECESSARY, BUT THAT IT DIDN'T HAVE TO MEAN WAR.

I AM UNWILLING TO FORGO EVEN ONE PERCENT OF ZIONISM FOR "PEACE"--YET I DO NOT WANT ZIONISM TO INFRINGE UPON EVEN ONE PERCENT OF LEGITIMATE ARAB RIGHTS.

BUT AS TENSIONS MOUNTED, THE REALITY OF THE SITUATION BEGAN TO SET IN. HE UNDERSTOOD THE ARAB RESISTANCE TO ISRAEL'S CREATION, BUT PUT HIS OWN PEOPLE FIRST. THIS IS WHERE THE SECOND BEN-GURION APPEARED.

WERE I AN ARAB...I WOULD RISE UP AGAINST AN IMMIGRATION LIABLE IN THE FUTURE TO HAND THE COUNTRY AND ALL OF ITS ARAB INHABITANTS OVER TO JEWISH RULE.

TO PALESTINIANS, BEN-GURION WAS A RACIST WHO EXPELLED THEM FROM THEIR OWN LAND. TO ME HE REPRESENTS WHAT I'VE BEEN COMING TO REALIZE ABOUT ISRAEL'S CREATION...

THAT MAYBE IT WASN'T PERSONAL, THE ARABS JUST GOT IN THE WAY. EVERYONE WAS JUST DOING WHAT THEY THOUGHT THEY NEEDED TO IN ORDER TO SURVIVE IN AN UNJUST WORLD.

WHY SHOULD THE ARABS MAKE PEACE? IF I WAS AN ARAB LEADER I WOULD NEVER MAKE TERMS WITH ISRAEL. THAT IS NATURAL: WE HAVE TAKEN THEIR COUNTRY. SURE GOD PROMISED IT TO US, BUT WHAT DOES THAT MATTER TO THEM?...THERE HAS BEEN ANTI-SEMITISM, THE NAZIS, HITLER, AUSCHWITZ, BUT WAS THAT THEIR FAULT?

THEY ONLY SEE ONE THING: WE HAVE COME HERE AND STOLEN THEIR COUNTRY. WHY SHOULD THEY ACCEPT THAT? THEY MAY PERHAPS FORGET IN ONE OR TWO GENERATIONS' TIME, BUT FOR THE MOMENT THERE IS NO CHANCE.

SO, IT'S SIMPLE: WE HAVE TO STAY STRONG AND MAINTAIN A POWERFUL ARMY. OUR WHOLE POLICY IS THERE. OTHERWISE THE ARABS WILL WIPE US OUT.

≥SIGH≤

I WONDER IF HE REGRETTED WHAT ISRAEL HAD TO DO TO SURVIVE. MAYBE THAT'S WHY HE WANTED TO ESCAPE TO THE DESERT, WHERE IT'S EASIER TO IGNORE THE LEGACY OF THE STRUGGLE.

BUT YOU CERTAINLY CAN'T IGNORE IT IN JERUSALEM, AND THAT'S WHERE WE'RE HEADED NEXT.

CHAPTER
SIX
JERUSALEM

HOTEL

THE SHUK

THE OL[D]
CITY

MT. HERZL
CEMETERY

YAD VASHEM

JERUSALEM
MALL

WE ARE DROPPING OFF THE SOLDIERS AT A BUS STATION SOMEWHERE BETWEEN THE DESERT AND JERUSALEM.

I FEEL LIKE I DIDN'T GET TO KNOW THEM VERY WELL.

OTHERS IN OUR GROUP DIDN'T HAVE AS MUCH TROUBLE.

I'M GONNA MISS YOU SO MUCH!

I WAS TOO BUSY BEING CONFUSED BY THEM.

I STILL DON'T GET IT, MELISSA.

AYA TO

LIKE, WHEN WE HEAR ABOUT THE I.D.F. SENDING TROOPS IN TO BULLDOZE A HOUSE OR TO CAPTURE A MILITANT, ARE THEY THESE KIDS? OR DO THEY HAVE CAREER SOLDIERS WHO DO THE DIRTIER WORK?

DO THEY DREAD GOING INTO THE ARMY OR JUST ACCEPT IT?

WHY DIDN'T YOU ASK THEM THAT WHILE THEY WERE WITH US?

I DUNNO.

I GUESS I COULDN'T FIGURE OUT THE RIGHT WAY TO PHRASE THE QUESTION.

BY THE TIME WE ARRIVE IN JERUSALEM IT'S DUSK, TOO LATE TO DO ANY SIGHT-SEEING IN THE CITY ITSELF. I CAN SEE IT IN THE DISTANCE FROM THE HIGHWAY.

OUR HOTEL IS BARELY EVEN IN JERUSALEM, CERTAINLY NOT CLOSE ENOUGH TO WALK ANYWHERE INTERESTING. I HAVE A SERIOUS URGE TO BREAK THE RULES AND THUMB A RIDE IN.

AWW! IT'S NOT FAIR!

I'VE BEEN LOOKING FORWARD TO BEING IN JERUSALEM MOST OF ALL. IT'S THE EPICENTER OF THE BIG MESS: ANCIENT, HOLY AND CONSTANTLY OSCILLATING BETWEEN NEGOTIABLE AND NON-NEGOTIABLE.

HMM, LET'S SEE WHAT'S GOING ON IN JERUSALEM'S NIGHTLIFE? ON FRIDAY NIGHT DJ MARKY-FUNK IS SPINNING AT HAOMAN 17. THAT LOOKS GOOD. OOH, ON SATURDAY IT'S ARMAGEDDON!

HA HA.

WE SHOULD START THINKING OF WHAT WE WANT TO DO AFTER THE BIRTH-RIGHT TRIP IS OVER. IT'S ONLY A FEW DAYS AWAY.

YEAH, I NEED TO CALL HUSSEIN AND SEE ABOUT GOING INTO THE WEST BANK.

YEAH, DO CALL HIM. AND YOU KNOW WHAT? I THINK I DO WANT TO GO TO THE WEST BANK AFTER ALL. YOU'RE RIGHT, IT IS IMPORTANT.

ALL RIGHT! I'LL CALL HIM RIGHT NOW!

...I'LL CALL HIM LATER..

AFTER A QUICK DINNER, WE ARE USHERED INTO A CONFERENCE ROOM TO LISTEN TO SOME GUEST SPEAKERS.

PLEASE FIND A SEAT QUICKLY, GUYS. THE SPEAKERS FROM THE BEREAVED FAMILY FORUM WILL BE HERE SHORTLY.

I'M TRYING TO THINK OF THE BEST WAY TO PREPARE MYSELF FOR SOMETHING SAD WHEN THEY COME IN...

MY NAME IS GUY AND WE ARE FROM THE BEREAVED FAMILY FORUM. WE HELP FAMILIES FROM BOTH SIDES WHO HAVE LOST LOVED ONES TALK TO EACH OTHER AND HELP EACH OTHER. AND TODAY AMIT AND MAHA ARE HERE TO SHARE WITH YOU.

AS AMIT STEPS FORWARD, THERE IS A WEIGHTY MOMENT IN WHICH THE GROUP SILENTLY WONDERS WHETHER TO CLAP OR NOT, THEN DECIDES AGAINST IT.

AMIT WILL SPEAK FIRST...

MY SISTER WAS KILLED IN A SUICIDE ATTACK IN JERUSALEM IN 1997. SHE WAS FOURTEEN YEARS OLD.

I WANTED TO USE THE ARMY TO AVENGE MY SISTER'S DEATH. IT WAS VERY EASY FOR ME TO SEE ALL ARABS AS ONE BIG FAMILY FROM WHICH THE BOMBER HAD COME.

OUR PLATOON WAS ABOUT TO GO TO LEBANON AND WE ALL WANTED TO KILL AS MANY TERRORISTS AS WE COULD. BUT THEN MY MOTHER FOUND A LOOPHOLE IN THE LAW THAT SAID BEREAVED PARENTS COULD KEEP THEIR CHILDREN FROM COMBAT DUTY.

I WAS TRANSFERRED TO A MECHANIC'S POST. FOR SIX MONTHS I DIDN'T SPEAK TO MY MOTHER BECAUSE I FELT THAT SHE HAD UPROOTED ME FROM MY COUNTRY, FROM MY CHANCE FOR WHAT I THOUGHT WAS REVENGE.

MEANWHILE MY PLATOON WENT TO LEBANON. ONE FRIEND WAS KILLED AND ANOTHER WAS SEVERELY BURNED. I HAD NEVER SEEN THE EFFECTS OF WAR LIKE THIS, AND BY THE END OF MY SERVICE I WAS SHOCKED BY THE WHOLE OF ISRAEL'S SOCIETY.

I WENT TO THE U.S. AND FOUND WORK UNDER THE TABLE AND IT WAS MY FIRST TIME EXPERIENCING WHAT IT IS TO HAVE NO RIGHTS. I REALIZED ALL THE BENEFITS I HAD AT HOME, AND HOW MANY PEOPLE WERE SUFFERING BECAUSE OF IT.

I WENT TO UNIVERSITY IN FRANCE WHERE THERE ARE MANY PEOPLE OF ARAB ORIGIN. THERE WAS A SYRIAN AND TWO PALESTINIANS IN MY CLASS AND AT FIRST IT WAS VERY DIFFICULT. THE IDEA OF THE PALESTINIAN STATE TO ME WAS OBVIOUS BUT I DIDN'T KNOW WHAT IT MEANT TO THEM.

WE BECAME FRIENDS AND I BEGAN LEARNING THEIR LANGUAGE AND ABOUT THEIR CULTURE. SO I CAME BACK AND NOW I AM IN A MIXED AREA TEACHING THEATER AT A BILINGUAL SCHOOL AND IT GIVES ME A NEW OPPORTUNITY TO HELP MAKE CHANGE.

BEYOND ALL POLITICAL VIEWS AND SOCIAL DISTINCTIONS, I THINK THAT THIS PLACE IS IMPORTANT TO THE WORLD AND NEEDS TO BE IN PEACE, AND I THANK YOU FOR LISTENING. THANK YOU.

HELLO, I AM MAHA. I COME FROM A VILLAGE NEAR HEBREW UNIVERSITY IN JERUSALEM.

IN MY FAMILY I WAS THE ONLY GIRL. I HAD SIX BROTHERS AND I SPENT ALL MY TIME WITH THE BOYS, BUT I HAD A SPECIAL CONNECTION WITH MY BROTHER FADI.

OUR BIRTHDAYS WERE ONLY SEPARATED BY ONE DAY AND WE ALWAYS HAD A PARTY TOGETHER.

WHEN I WAS TURNING FIFTEEN AND FADI WAS TURNING SIXTEEN WE TALKED A LOT ABOUT OUR PLANS FOR THE FUTURE: WHICH UNIVERSITY WE WOULD GO TO AND WHAT WE WOULD STUDY...WE WERE VERY EXCITED.

A FEW WEEKS LATER AN ISRAELI SETTLER ENTERED A MOSQUE AND KILLED FIVE PEOPLE. THE ISRAELI GOVERNMENT PUT A CHECKPOINT IN OUR VILLAGE AFTER THAT, BUT WE ARE USED TO THESE.

SO THAT FRIDAY FADI WOKE UP TO GO HELP OUR GRANDFATHER IN HIS FIELD. HE ASKED ME IF I WOULD COME, BUT I WANTED TO SLEEP IN BECAUSE IT WAS THE WEEKEND.

I DIDN'T KNOW IT WOULD BE THE LAST TIME I WOULD SEE HIS FACE OR HEAR HIS VOICE.

A FEW MINUTES LATER WE HEARD SHOOTING. THEN MY MOTHER SAID FADI WAS HURT. I WAS CONFUSED; I THOUGHT IT WAS A CAR ACCIDENT. I DIDN'T KNOW WHAT HAPPENED.

SUDDENLY THERE WERE SO MANY PEOPLE COMING INTO OUR HOME AND THEY WERE CRYING. MY AUNT WAS SCREAMING, "THEY KILLED HIM!" AND I DIDN'T KNOW IT WAS MY BROTHER THEY WERE TALKING ABOUT AT FIRST.

WE STILL DON'T KNOW WHAT HAPPENED. MY MOTHER HAD A NERVOUS BREAKDOWN AND MY FATHER HAD A HEART ATTACK. AT THE HOSPITAL, WHEN I FOUND OUT IT WAS A SOLDIER WHO KILLED FADI, I NEVER WANTED TO GO TO MY HOME AGAIN.

ONE DAY WE GOT A CALL FROM THE LEADER OF FAMILY FORUM. HE ASKED IF HE COULD COME SPEAK TO US AT OUR HOME. FOR US IT WAS NEW TO HEAR FROM AN ISRAELI MAN.

WHEN HE CAME IT WAS SHOCKING BECAUSE HE WAS RELIGIOUS BUT WHEN HE STARTED TALKING ABOUT HOW HIS SON WAS KILLED IT DIDN'T MATTER THAT HE WAS JEWISH AND WE WERE ARAB. WE JUST SAW THAT HE WAS HUMAN AND HAD OUR SAME PAIN.

NOW THROUGH ACTIVITIES WITH THE FAMILY FORUM IN PALESTINE WE SPREAD OUR MESSAGES OF PEACE AND RECONCILIATION. WE HAVE TO REHUMANIZE THE OTHERS. THE MAIN IDEA IS THAT YOU HAVE TO TALK TO SOMEONE ON THE OTHER SIDE.

WE ASK ONLY ONE THING OF YOU AND THAT IS NOT TO BE PRO-ISRAEL OR PRO-PALESTINE, BUT TO BE PRO-PEACE. AND WHEN YOU GO BACK TO YOUR COUNTRY EXPLAIN TO YOUR FRIENDS ABOUT WHAT WE DO HERE AND HELP THEM BE PRO-PEACE, TOO.

THANK YOU.

WE WOULD BE GLAD TO TAKE ANY QUESTIONS YOU MAY HAVE.

YES, YOU IN THE FRONT?

WHAT KEEPS YOU IN ISRAEL TRYING TO SOLVE THE PROBLEM INSTEAD OF GOING SOMEWHERE ELSE?

I AM IN AWE OF THESE PEOPLE.

I LOST A BROTHER TOO, BUT TO A BUS ACCIDENT. IF THERE HAD BEEN SOMEONE TO BLAME FOR IT, A WHOLE GROUP OF PEOPLE TO BLAME FOR IT, I DON'T KNOW IF I COULD BE WHERE THESE PEOPLE ARE TODAY.

THEY LOST THEIR FAMILY MEMBERS YEARS AGO, BUT THEY ARE WEARING THE GRIEF OF A MONTH. I KNOW THE FEELING; EVERY TIME YOU TALK ABOUT A LOSS IT FEELS LIKE IT JUST HAPPENED.

THE MEDIA IS A BUSINESS AND WE ARE PRODUCTS...THEY NEED THE WAR TO KEEP GOING.

YET THEY ALLOW THEMSELVES TO GO THROUGH THAT PAIN OVER AND OVER AGAIN, TALKING TO GROUPS OF PRIVILEGED FOREIGNERS ON FREE TRIPS IN HOTEL CONFERENCE ROOMS, HOPING SOMETHING WILL STICK.

I WANT TO ASK THEM HOW THEY CAN DO THIS.

AND I KNOW THEIR ANSWER WOULD PROBABLY BE "WE MAKE OURSELVES DO IT BECAUSE WE WANT THIS TO END SO BADLY."

I WISH I COULD DO THAT. I DON'T KNOW IF I COULD.

I AM TRYING TO FIND A WAY TO TELL THEM WHAT I THINK ABOUT THEM.

HI, UM, I JUST WANT TO SAY... THANK YOU.

I WONDER IF I HAVE JERUSALEM SYNDROME.

IT'S A REAL CONDITION THAT STRIKES FOREIGN VISITORS TO THE CITY. ITS MANIFESTATION HAS VARIATIONS, THE MOST DRAMATIC ONE BEING WHEN NORMAL TOURISTS SUDDENLY GO PSYCHOTIC.

THEY BELIEVE THEY ARE ON A MISSION FROM GOD AND BEGIN TRAIPSING TO HOLY SITES AND RECITING SCRIPTURE. THEY START PERFORMING ABLUTIONS AND DRESSING IN MAKESHIFT TOGAS.

AREA HOTELS REPORTEDLY LOSE A LOT OF BEDSHEETS THIS WAY.

BUT THERE ARE MILDER FORMS OF IT, WHERE PEOPLE BECOME OBSESSED WITH JERUSALEM AND ITS SIGNIFICANCE IN THE WORLD AND FEEL THE URGE TO DO SOMETHING.

SHoo

I GUESS I CAN'T HAVE JERUSALEM SYNDROME, BECAUSE WE HAVEN'T REALLY EVEN SEEN THE CITY YET. BUT THE SPEAKERS LAST NIGHT INSPIRED ME. WHAT CAN I DO?

CAN I DO **ANYTHING?**

OHHH, MAN. WHAT TIME IS IT?

I THINK MAYBE I SHOULD STAY LONGER... YOU THINK MY BOSS WOULD LET ME USE MY SICK DAYS?

GOOD MORNING TO YOU TOO, BUDDY.

WE'RE ON OUR WAY TO YAD VASHEM, ISRAEL'S HOLOCAUST MUSEUM.

IT'S THE KIND OF PLACE THAT I THINK SECRETLY, NO ONE WANTS TO GO TO, THEY JUST KNOW THEY **SHOULD**. WE DON'T HAVE A CHOICE; IT'S A BIRTHRIGHT REQUIREMENT.

IF I HAD AN EMOTIONAL FREAK-OUT AT MODEST OLD INDEPENDENCE HALL, HOW AM I GOING TO REACT TO THIS?

GIL IS REPLACED FOR OUR VISIT WITH AN OFFICIAL YAD VASHEM GUIDE.

GOOD MORNING. BEFORE WE ENTER THE MUSEUM PLEASE MAKE SURE YOUR PHONES ARE TUNED OFF. THERE IS NO PHOTOGRAPHY AND NO GUM CHEWING IN THE MUSEUM.

IN ORDER TO KEEP TOURS QUIET, YAD VASHEM CONNECTS VISITORS TO THEIR GUIDES VIA WIRELESS HEADSETS.

WOW, HIGH TECH!

WE MOVE INTO THE MUSEUM'S MAIN HALL, STARK AND ANGULAR YET BEAUTIFULLY DESIGNED. I'M MESMERIZED BY A TRIANGULAR VIDEO SHOWING LIFE ON THE SHTETLS BACK BEFORE THE NAZIS TOOK POWER.

OKAY, CAN EVERYONE HEAR ME?

IT IS VERY IMPORTANT TO LEARN ABOUT THE SHOAH SO WE MAY NEVER LET IT HAPPEN AGAIN. THIS DARK TIME BEGAN WHEN GERMANY WAS HUMILIATED AFTER THE FIRST WORLD WAR...

I BEGIN TO DISLIKE OUR GUIDE ALMOST IMMEDIATELY.

YOU SEE HERE SOME OF THE TYPES OF BOOKS THAT THE NAZIS BURNED. NOW PLEASE WALK THIS WAY.

I'VE HEARD SUBWAY SERVICE ANNOUNCEMENTS MORE EMOTIONAL THAN THE WAY HE'S RECITING THE HOLOCAUST NARRATIVE. I FEEL LIKE WE'VE BURDENED HIM BY MAKING HIM LEAD YET ANOTHER TOUR.

...AND NAZI PROPAGANDA PUSHED ON THE PEOPLE...

HIS ROBOTIC DELIVERY COMBINED WITH THE FACT THAT I CAN SEE THE OTHER GROUPS AHEAD OF US MAKES ME FEEL LIKE I'M ON A CONVEYOR BELT, MECHANICALLY MOVING THROUGH THE DARKEST MOMENT IN 20TH CENTURY HISTORY.

I ALMOST CONSIDER TAKING OFF MY HEADSET AND LOOKING AROUND ON MY OWN.

...THE WARSAW GHETTO WAS THE LARGEST. IT WAS BASICALLY A GIANT PRISON. JEWISH COMMUNITY LEADERS WERE FORCED TO RUN DAY-TO-DAY LIFE AND RATION THE SMALL AMOUNT OF FOOD GIVEN TO THEM BY THE GERMANS.

THEY WERE ALSO FORCED TO ARRANGE THE DEPORTATION OF OTHER JEWS TO AUSCHWITZ. LET US LOOK AT THESE PHOTOS OF THE UPRISING AT THE WARSAW GHETTO FOR A MOMENT.

WHICH ONE AFFECTS YOU THE MOST?

UMM... THAT ONE?

HM. THAT'S VERY INTERESTING. A MAN JUMPING FROM A BURNING BUILDING.

I THINK IT STRIKES YOU BECAUSE IT REMINDS YOU OF WHEN THE TOWERS FELL AND THEY SHOWED THE PHOTOS OF PEOPLE JUMPING OUT OF THE BUILDINGS ON THE NEWS.

THIS WAY, PLEASE.

WHAT THE FUCK IS WRONG WITH THIS GUY?

...AND THE TRAIN ENDED HERE AT AUSCHWITZ. YES, A QUESTION?

WHY DIDN'T THE ALLIES BOMB AUSCHWITZ?

I DON'T HAVE AN ANSWER FOR THAT. SOME SAY IT WAS TO SPARE THE LIVES OF THE PRISONERS.

OR WHY DIDN'T THEY JUST BOMB THE TRAIN TRACKS, AT LEAST?

I CAN'T TELL YOU WHY.

AUSCHWITZ WAS THE LARGEST OF THE CONCENTRATION CAMPS. PEOPLE REMOVED FROM THE TRAIN CARS WERE SPLIT UP...

WE'VE BEEN MOVING SO FAST THAT WE'VE CAUGHT UP WITH ANOTHER BIRTHRIGHT GROUP AHEAD OF US. IT'S THE ISRAEL OUTDOORS GROUP THAT WAS WITH US AT THE NEWARK AIRPORT.

...AND THE DOORS WERE CLOSED AND THE ZYKLON B DROPPED DOWN, KILLING THEM ALL WITHIN TWENTY MINUTES...

...AND WHEN THE ALLIES APPROACHED THEY WERE SENT ON DEATH MARCHES TO BERGEN-BELSEN AND OTHER CAMPS AND 100,000 DIED IN THESE MARCHES ALONE....

...BUT THE LIBERATION WAS TOO LATE FOR THOSE SIX MILLION. THOSE WHO SURVIVED SAW HORRORS THAT SCARRED THEM FOREVER.

DO YOU THINK THE PRISONERS WHO WERE LIBERATED WERE HAPPY? LOOK AT THIS PHOTO TAKEN WHEN THE ALLIES ARRIVED.

HE DOESN'T LOOK VERY HAPPY, DOES HE?

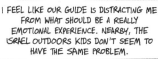

I FEEL LIKE OUR GUIDE IS DISTRACTING ME FROM WHAT SHOULD BE A REALLY EMOTIONAL EXPERIENCE. NEARBY, THE ISRAEL OUTDOORS KIDS DON'T SEEM TO HAVE THE SAME PROBLEM.

I WISH I WAS THEM RIGHT NOW.

THIS CONCLUDES OUR TOUR. PLEASE MAKE SURE TO RETURN YOUR HEADSETS.

SO, GUYS, WE HAVE ABOUT FIFTEEN MINUTES TO SPEND IN THE MUSEUM HOW YOU PLEASE, THEN MEET BACK OUTSIDE, OKAY?

FINALLY, SOME TIME TO MYSELF.

The Hall of Names at Yad Vashem is the Jewish People's memorial to each and every Jew who perished in the Holocaust - a place where they may be commemorated for generations to come.

The main circular hall houses the extensive collection of "Pages of Testimony" - short biographies of each Holocaust victim. Over two million Pages are stored in the circular repository around the outer edge of the Hall, with room for six million in all.

The ceiling of the Hall is composed of a ten-meter high cone reaching skywards, displaying 600 photographs and fragments of Pages of Testimony. This exhibit represents a fraction of the murdered six million men, women and children from the diverse Jewish world destroyed by the Nazis and their accomplices.

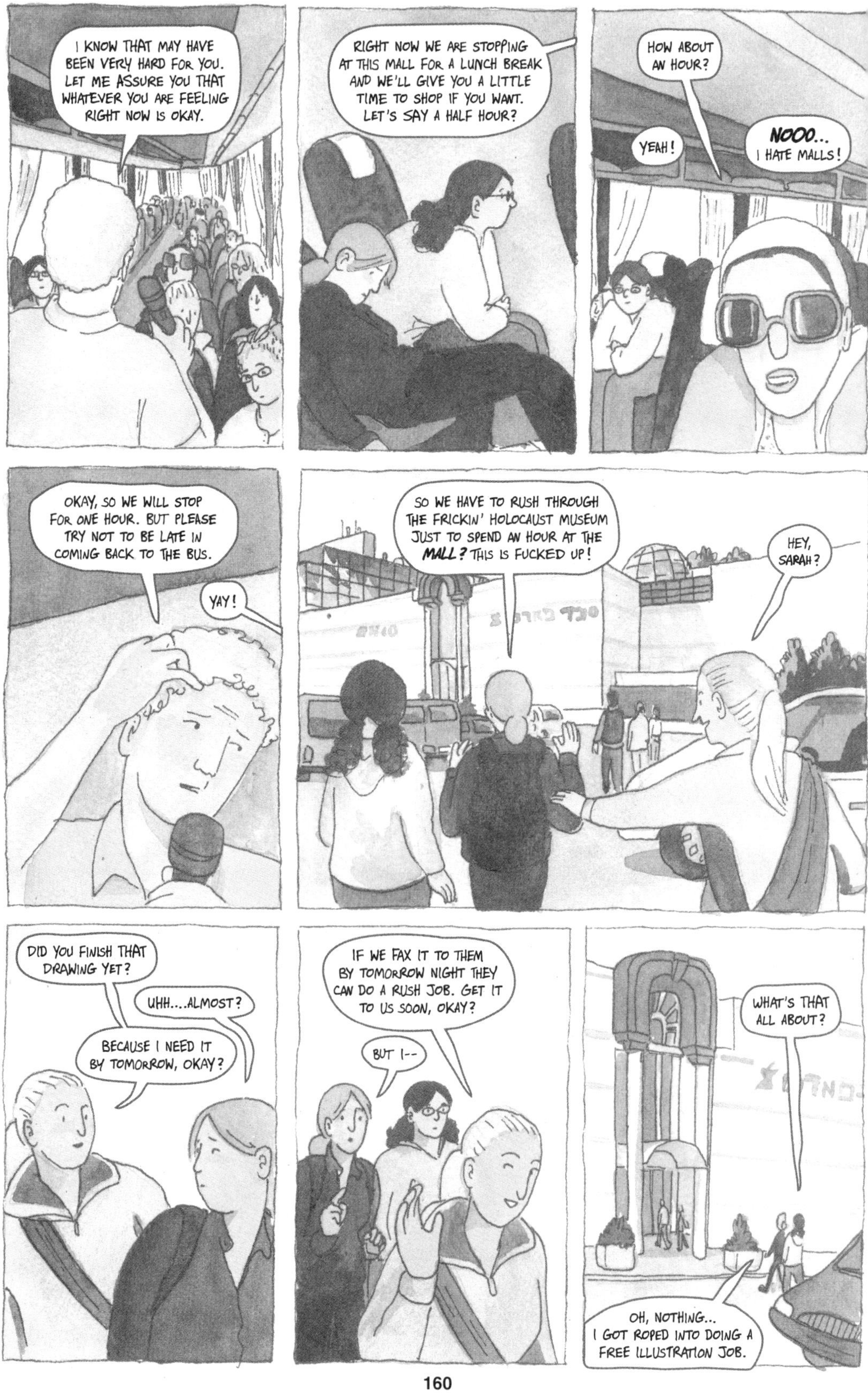
I KNOW THAT MAY HAVE BEEN VERY HARD FOR YOU. LET ME ASSURE YOU THAT WHATEVER YOU ARE FEELING RIGHT NOW IS OKAY.
RIGHT NOW WE ARE STOPPING AT THIS MALL FOR A LUNCH BREAK AND WE'LL GIVE YOU A LITTLE TIME TO SHOP IF YOU WANT. LET'S SAY A HALF HOUR?
HOW ABOUT AN HOUR?
YEAH!
NOOO... I HATE MALLS!
OKAY, SO WE WILL STOP FOR ONE HOUR. BUT PLEASE TRY NOT TO BE LATE IN COMING BACK TO THE BUS.
YAY!
SO WE HAVE TO RUSH THROUGH THE FRICKIN' HOLOCAUST MUSEUM JUST TO SPEND AN HOUR AT THE MALL? THIS IS FUCKED UP!
HEY, SARAH?
DID YOU FINISH THAT DRAWING YET?
UHH....ALMOST?
BECAUSE I NEED IT BY TOMORROW, OKAY?
IF WE FAX IT TO THEM BY TOMORROW NIGHT THEY CAN DO A RUSH JOB. GET IT TO US SOON, OKAY?
BUT I--
WHAT'S THAT ALL ABOUT?
OH, NOTHING... I GOT ROPED INTO DOING A FREE ILLUSTRATION JOB.

MY APPETITE HAS DISAPPEARED AGAIN.

I'M, UH, GOING TO GO FIND A PLACE TO WORK ON THIS CAMEL DRAWING. SEE YOU GUYS BACK ON THE BUS.

WHEN I WENT TO CHINA, WE HAD AN OFFICIAL STATE GUIDE.

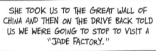

SHE TOOK US TO THE GREAT WALL OF CHINA AND THEN ON THE DRIVE BACK TOLD US WE WERE GOING TO STOP TO VISIT A "JADE FACTORY."

I HAD BEEN KIND OF EXCITED TO SEE WHAT A JADE CARVING FACTORY WOULD LOOK LIKE, BUT IT TURNED OUT TO BE LITTLE MORE THAN A GIGANTIC GIFT SHOP OF JADE TRINKETS WITH ONE PERSON IN THE CORNER GIVING A CARVING DEMONSTRATION.

IF THEY WANTED US TO GIVE BACK TO THE ISRAELI ECONOMY, THEY JUST COULD HAVE ASKED FOR TWENTY BUCKS OR SOMETHING.

MY STOMACH HURTS.

FROM THE MALL WE DRIVE A SHORT DISTANCE TO MOUNT HERZL, NAMED FOR THE FATHER OF THE ZIONIST MOVEMENT THAT BEGAN ISRAEL'S NEW HISTORY.

THEODORE HERZL DIED IN 1904, BUT HE STATED IN HIS WILL THAT HE WANTED TO BE BURIED IN THE CAPITAL OF THE JEWISH STATE WHICH WAS HIS LIFE'S DREAM. HE WAS TRANSFERRED HERE AFTER THE WAR OF INDEPENDENCE.

THIS SITE WAS CHOSEN AS A SPECIAL CEMETERY BOTH FOR HIM AND OTHER LEADERS OF THE JEWISH STATE. ALONG WITH SOLDIERS WHO FELL IN BATTLE, ALMOST ALL THE PRIME MINISTERS AND PRESIDENTS ARE HERE...

MORE TUBES!

...AND THESE ARE THE GRAVES OF YITZHAK RABIN AND HIS WIFE LEAH...

NOW THAT YOU HAVE HEARD THE STORY OF ISRAEL'S LEADERS, I WOULD LIKE TO TELL YOU A STORY OF MY OWN.

I GREW UP IN A NEIGHBORHOOD NOT FAR FROM HERE, A PRETTY AVERAGE SECULAR NEIGHBORHOOD LIKE ANY OTHER.

I WAS THIRTEEN IN 1982 WHEN THE WAR WITH LEBANON STARTED. THERE WERE MANY CASUALTIES IN THE FIRST MONTHS OF FIGHTING, AND EVERY AFTERNOON MY FRIENDS AND I WOULD SIT OUTSIDE AND COUNT THE FUNERALS BY THE NUMBER OF GUN SALUTES.

ONE DAY THERE WOULD BE 16 FUNERALS, THEN THE NEXT DAY, 24 FUNERALS. EVERY DAY WE WOULD LISTEN AND HAVE THE SAME DISCUSSION: WHAT WOULD WE DO WHEN WE WERE EIGHTEEN AND STARTED OUR OWN ARMY SERVICE?

EVER SINCE I HAD BEEN FIVE YEARS OLD I HAD TOLD MY FATHER TWO THINGS: THAT I WOULD BE A PARATROOPER AND THAT I WOULD BE TALLER THAN HIM. WELL, BY 1987 BOTH OF THOSE THINGS BECAME TRUE.

THIS WAS THE TIME OF THE FIRST INTIFADA. I WAS STATIONED IN BETHLEHEM WHICH I NOW KNOW BETTER THAN EVEN DEGANYA. UDI, MY FRIEND FROM HOME, WAS THERE TOO, AS A MEDIC.

WE WERE PLANNING ON GOING ON A TRIP AROUND THE WORLD AFTER OUR TWO YEARS WITH OUR FRIEND MIKEY, BUT JUST AS HIS SERVICE ENDED, UDI WAS CALLED BACK TO BETHLEHEM FOR TWO WEEKS TO FILL IN FOR SOMEONE WHO WAS LATE.

ONE MORNING HE WENT OUT TO GET SOME FOOD FOR THE OTHER SOLDIERS AND WAS SHOT IN THE STREET.

NOT LONG AFTERWARDS, MIKEY WAS KILLED TOO.

SO WE NEVER DID GO ON OUR TRIP. OUT OF THE FIVE OF US WHO WOULD ARGUE ABOUT WHAT WE WOULD BE WHEN WE GREW UP, THERE ARE ONLY THREE OF US LEFT.

HERE IS UDI. MIKEY IS OVER THERE.

Panel 1:

IT'S OUR LAST DAY OF THE TRIP. THIS MORNING WE'RE FINALLY GOING TO THE OLD CITY.

MELISSA, LISTEN TO THIS...

Panel 2:

"AS THE NAVEL IS SET IN THE HUMAN BODY, SO IS THE LAND OF ISRAEL THE NAVEL OF THE WORLD...AND JERUSALEM IS IN THE CENTER."

Panel 3:

WHAT'S THAT FROM?

THE MIDRASH. IT'S OLD. BUT IT'S TRUE EVEN NOW, DON'T YOU THINK? HOW MANY TIMES A DAY DO YOU SEE THE WORD "JERUSALEM" IN THE NEWSPAPER?

WELL, NOT AS MUCH AS YOU, BUT YOU GO LOOKING FOR IT.

Panel 4:

WHAT COUNTRY DO YOU THINK THEY'RE FROM?

I DON'T KNOW. HOW COME **WE** DIDN'T GET MATCHING HATS?

Panel 5:

THAT BRIGHT YELLOW BIBLE GROUP REMINDS ME OF SOMETHING I HAD FORGOTTEN: THAT ISRAEL, JERUSALEM SPECIFICALLY, IS ALSO THE HOLY LAND FOR THAT **OTHER** MAJOR RELIGION.

Panel 6:

THE CHRISTIAN CONNECTION TO JERUSALEM ONLY SEEMS TO EXIST IN THE PAST AND THE FUTURE WHILE THE OTHER TWO ABRAHAMIC FAITHS ARGUE LOUDLY OVER PRESENT DAY OWNERSHIP.

THE CRUSADES

Panel 7:

THIS DOESN'T MEAN THAT CHRISTIANITY IS NOT INVOLVED IN THE SITUATION. FUNDAMENTALIST CHRISTIAN GROUPS ARE MAJOR DONORS TO ZIONIST ORGANIZATIONS AND AMERICAN JEWISH LOBBIES.

Panel 8:

THE SOONER ALL THE JEWS RETURN TO JERUSALEM, THE STORY GOES, THE SOONER THE CHRISTIANS CAN GET RAPTURED INTO ETERNITY.

Panel 9:

SO KNOWING HOW MUCH WEIGHT SO MANY MILLIONS OF PEOPLE GIVE THIS ONE LITTLE OLD CITY AND STANDING JUST A FEW FEET AWAY FROM IT...HOW COULD ANYONE EVER AVOID JERUSALEM SYNDROME?

EVEN THE CITY WALLS, WITH THEIR TIME-WORN SMOOTHNESS AND BULLET HOLES, JUST SCREAM, "I AM IMPORTANT. GO NUTS BEFORE ME."

THIS IS THE ZION GATE TO THE OLD CITY, WHICH LEADS INTO THE ARMENIAN QUARTER. WE WILL JUST WALK IN, BUT THERE WAS A TIME WHEN IT WASN'T SO EASY FOR A JEW TO ENTER JERUSALEM.

AFTER THE ROMANS EXPELLED THE JEWS IN 70 C.E., THE REVOLT THAT ENDED WITH MASADA, WE WERE FORBIDDEN TO RETURN FOR 700 YEARS.

THIS LOSS CHANGED JUDAISM FOREVER. THE RELIGION FOCUSED ON THE YEARNING TO COME HOME. FOR HUNDREDS OF PASSOVERS OUR ANCESTORS HAVE SAID, "NEXT YEAR IN JERUSALEM!"

FOR A LONG TIME IT SEEMED THAT ONLY WITH THE COMING OF THE MESSIAH WOULD WE BE ALLOWED BACK INTO THE CITY. THIS TURNED OUT NOT TO BE TRUE, BUT WE WERE AGAIN EXILED AFTER 1948.

THOUGH THIS MOST RECENT EXILE WAS SHORT, ITS EFFECTS WERE POWERFUL.

EVERY TIME I WALK THROUGH THIS GATE I FEEL THANKFUL.

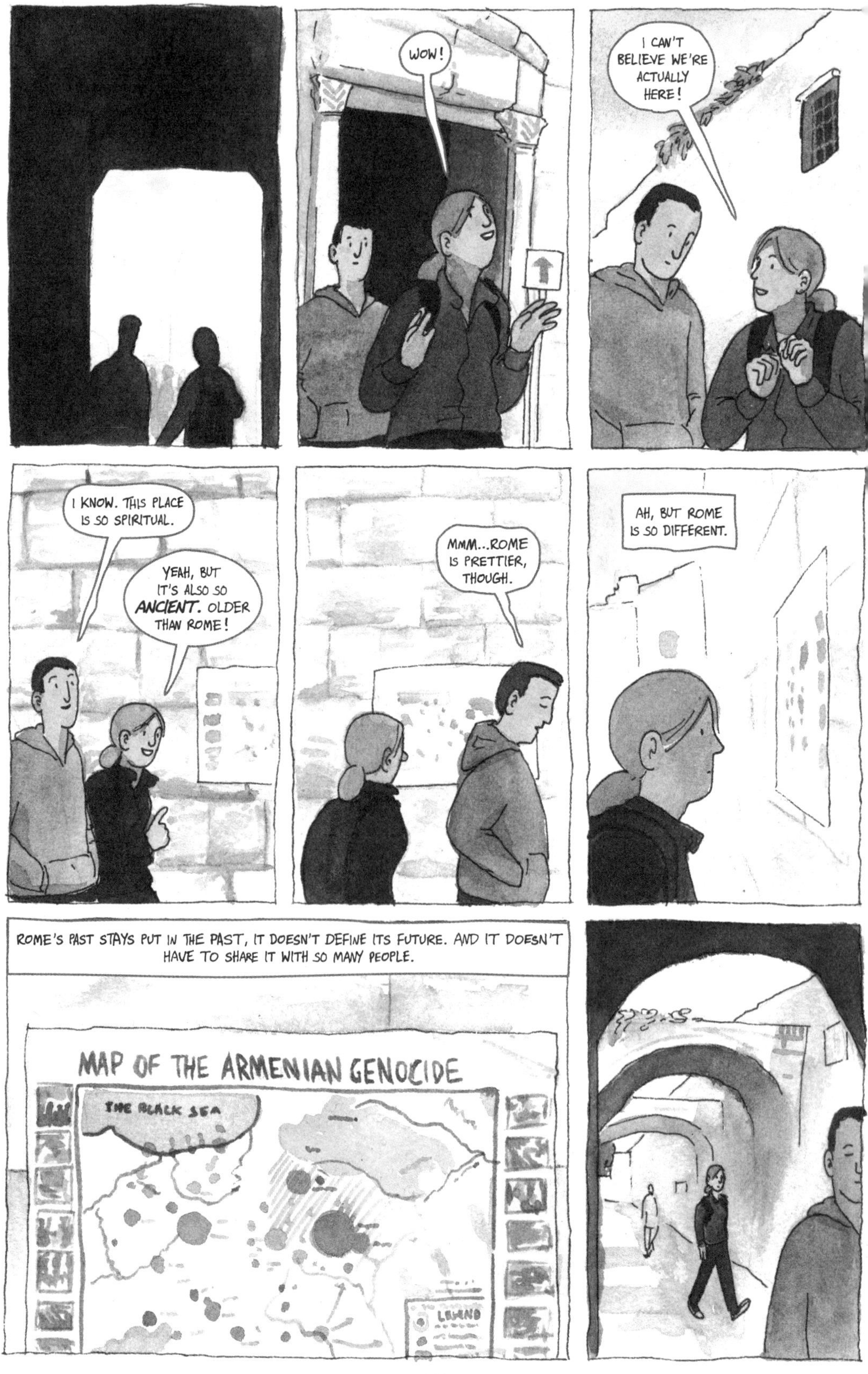
WOW!
I CAN'T BELIEVE WE'RE ACTUALLY HERE!
I KNOW. THIS PLACE IS SO SPIRITUAL.
YEAH, BUT IT'S ALSO SO ANCIENT. OLDER THAN ROME!
MMM...ROME IS PRETTIER, THOUGH.
AH, BUT ROME IS SO DIFFERENT.
ROME'S PAST STAYS PUT IN THE PAST, IT DOESN'T DEFINE ITS FUTURE. AND IT DOESN'T HAVE TO SHARE IT WITH SO MANY PEOPLE.
MAP OF THE ARMENIAN GENOCIDE
THE BLACK SEA
LEGEND

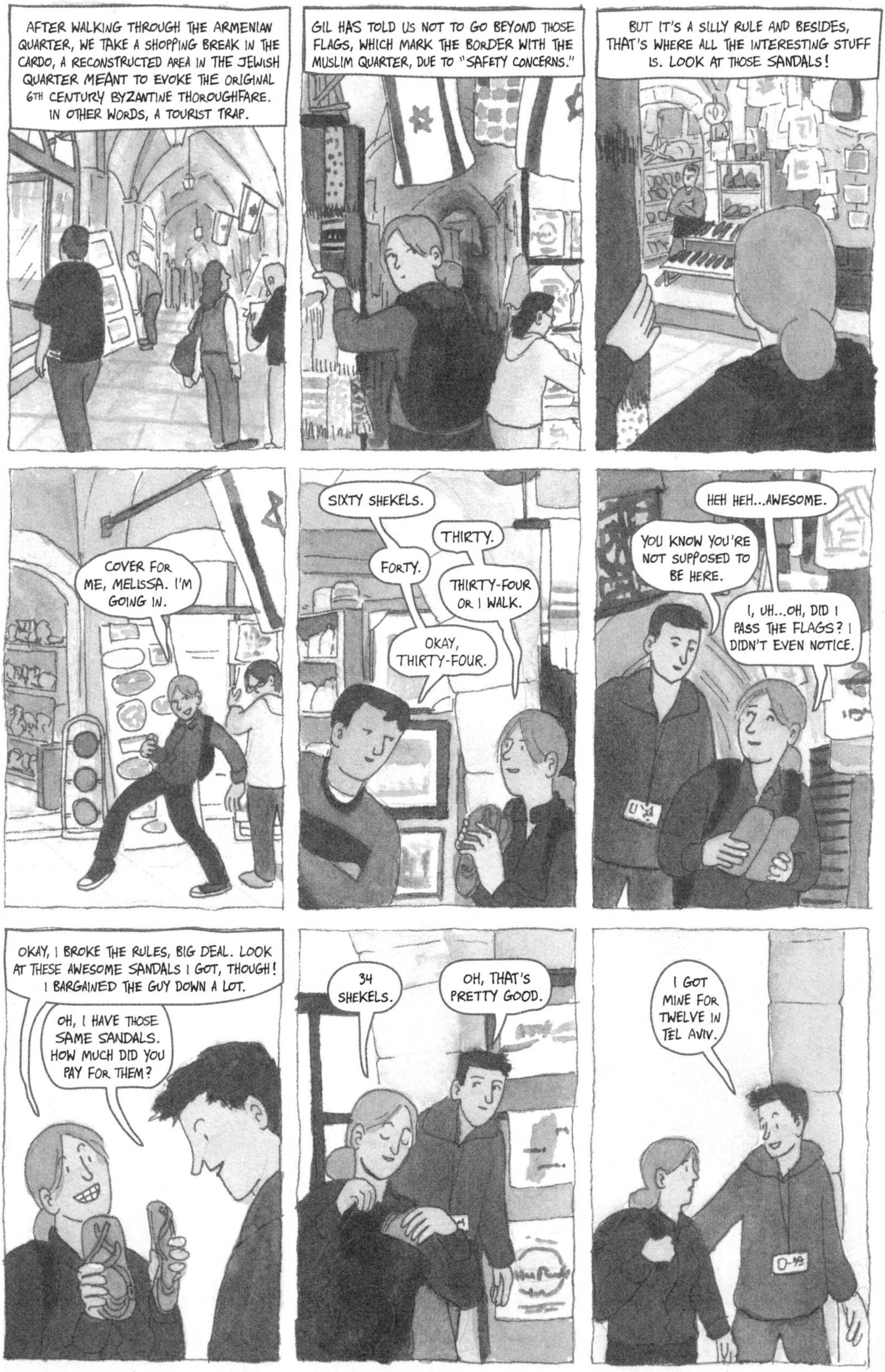
AFTER WALKING THROUGH THE ARMENIAN QUARTER, WE TAKE A SHOPPING BREAK IN THE CARDO, A RECONSTRUCTED AREA IN THE JEWISH QUARTER MEANT TO EVOKE THE ORIGINAL 6TH CENTURY BYZANTINE THOROUGHFARE. IN OTHER WORDS, A TOURIST TRAP.
GIL HAS TOLD US NOT TO GO BEYOND THOSE FLAGS, WHICH MARK THE BORDER WITH THE MUSLIM QUARTER, DUE TO "SAFETY CONCERNS."
BUT IT'S A SILLY RULE AND BESIDES, THAT'S WHERE ALL THE INTERESTING STUFF IS. LOOK AT THOSE SANDALS!
COVER FOR ME, MELISSA. I'M GOING IN.
SIXTY SHEKELS.
FORTY.
THIRTY.
THIRTY-FOUR OR I WALK.
OKAY, THIRTY-FOUR.
HEH HEH...AWESOME.
YOU KNOW YOU'RE NOT SUPPOSED TO BE HERE.
I, UH...OH, DID I PASS THE FLAGS? I DIDN'T EVEN NOTICE.
OKAY, I BROKE THE RULES, BIG DEAL. LOOK AT THESE AWESOME SANDALS I GOT, THOUGH! I BARGAINED THE GUY DOWN A LOT.
OH, I HAVE THOSE SAME SANDALS. HOW MUCH DID YOU PAY FOR THEM?
34 SHEKELS.
OH, THAT'S PRETTY GOOD.
I GOT MINE FOR TWELVE IN TEL AVIV.

OKAY, SO WE HAVE TALKED A BIT ABOUT THE PERIOD LEADING UP TO 1948. THE NATIVE ARABS FELT THREATENED BY SO MANY NEW JEWISH IMMIGRANTS AND PERSUADED THE BRITISH TO ISSUE THE "WHITE PAPER" WHICH VIRTUALLY PROHIBITED MORE JEWS FROM ENTERING THE TERRITORY.

THIS UNFORTUNATELY COINCIDED WITH HITLER'S RISE TO POWER. THOUSANDS OF REFUGEES WERE TURNED AWAY FROM PALESTINE AND SENT BACK TO EUROPE TO BE SLAUGHTERED.

THE FIGHTING BEGAN...JEWS TARGETED ARABS, ARABS ATTACKED JEWS, AND BOTH GROUPS RESENTED THE BRITISH AND FOUGHT THEM AS WELL.

THE PARTITION PLAN THAT THE UNITED NATIONS SUGGESTED WAS REJECTED BY THE ARABS, WHO DID NOT FEEL THAT THEY SHOULD HAVE TO GIVE UP ANY OF THEIR OWN LAND. THE FAILURE OF THIS RESOLUTION ONLY SWELLED THE FIGHTING.

OVERWHELMED BY THE TURMOIL IN PALESTINE, THE BRITISH DECIDED TO END THEIR MANDATE AND WITHDRAW ALL THEIR TROOPS FROM THE REGION.

JERUSALEM WAS ONE OF THE FIRST AREAS TO BE EVACUATED.

THE MORNING THEY LEFT, THE FIGHTING PAUSED. PEOPLE WATCHED THROUGH THEIR WINDOWS AS THE BRITISH ARMY MARCHED IN FORMATION THROUGH THE STREETS OF THE OLD CITY PLAYING BAGPIPES.

THEY STOPPED AT THE HOME OF JERUSALEM'S HEAD RABBI IN THE JEWISH QUARTER. THE BRITISH COMMANDER KNOCKED ON THE DOOR HOLDING A PIECE OF RUSTY SCRAP METAL.

"JERUSALEM IS THE CAPITAL OF THE JEWISH PEOPLE," HE SAID, "AND NOW WE ARE LEAVING THE CITY. WHY AREN'T YOU OUT IN THE STREETS CELEBRATING?"

"SO MANY CONQUERING ARMIES HAVE COME AND LEFT THIS LAND," THE OLD RABBI SAID. "THE BABYLONIANS, THE ROMANS, THE TURKS AND NOW YOU."

"THIS IS JUST ANOTHER DAY IN JERUSALEM."

THE COMMANDER WISHED THE RABBI LUCK AND HELD OUT THE PIECE OF METAL. "HERE IS THE KEY TO THE ZION GATE BECAUSE I CAN'T GIVE YOU THE WHOLE CITY."

THE RABBI ACCEPTED THE "KEY" AND WENT BACK INSIDE. AS SOON AS THE BRITISH WERE OUT OF THE GATE, THE FIGHTING RESUMED.

THE JORDANIAN ARMY EVENTUALLY WON THE BATTLE OVER JERUSALEM AND EXPELLED THE JEWISH RESIDENTS. BUT THE KING OF JORDAN NEVER ALLOWED ANYONE TO MOVE INTO THE EVACUATED BUILDINGS THERE. THEY SAT VACANT UNTIL, YEARS LATER, HE ORDERED THEM TO BE BULLDOZED.

OF COURSE, THE ISRAELIS "LIBERATED" THE OLD CITY FROM THE JORDANIANS IN 1967.

I'VE SEEN THE PHOTOGRAPHS OF THAT DAY: ISRAELI SOLDIERS EMBRACING AND CRYING IN FRONT OF THE WESTERN WALL, JERUSALEM'S RELIGIOUS CENTERPIECE.

FOR SOME THE WALL IS A BITTERSWEET REMINDER OF A LOST KINGDOM ONLY PARTIALLY, YET MIRACULOUSLY REGAINED.

WOW...

WOULD YOU LOOK AT THAT!

IT CAN ALSO SERVE AS PROOF OF A DIVINE PROMISE FULFILLED, A REWARD FOR CENTURIES OF PATIENCE AND PRAYER.

FOR ME, IT MIGHT BE THE CLUE I'VE BEEN WAITING FOR THIS WHOLE TIME. IT'S THE LINCHPIN OF THE SITUATION, AFTER ALL.

IF THIS WALL, AND THE MUSLIM HOLY SITE SITTING ABOVE IT, IS CENTRAL TO THIS STRUGGLE, I WANT TO DISCOVER WHY EVERYONE CARES ABOUT IT SO MUCH. MAYBE HEARING ABOUT IT IN CONTEXT WILL MAKE THINGS CLEARER.

SO, LET'S TALK ABOUT THE WESTERN WALL.

LET ME START AT THE BEGINNING...

IN THE BEGINNING...
(ACCORDING TO RELIGIOUS TEXTS)

GOD PLUCKED A STONE FROM HIS THRONE AND CREATED THE HEAVENS AND THE EARTH OUT OF IT. THE TIP OF THIS STONE BECAME THE HIGHEST PEAK IN JERUSALEM.

THE FOUNDATION STONE

WHERE ABRAHAM ALMOST KILLED HIS OWN SON!

WHERE JACOB DREAMED OF ANGELS!

A

B

KING DAVID

I SHOULD BUILD THE TEMPLE HERE!

THE PAST
(THE 2ND TEMPLE)

SO KING DAVID AND HIS SON SOLOMON BUILT THE FIRST TEMPLE THERE, BUT IT WAS DESTROYED BY THE BABYLONIANS, WHO EXPELLED THE JEWS FROM JERUSALEM.

BUT THEY CAME BACK AND REBUILT IT AND LATER HEROD EXPANDED IT, ADDING A LARGE PLATFORM TO ACCOMMODATE ALL THE PILGRIMS.

THEN THE ROMANS DESTROYED THE 2ND TEMPLE.

THE FOUNDATION STONE BECAME THE CENTRAL CHAMBER OF THE TEMPLE: THE HOLY OF HOLIES ONLY THE HIGH PRIEST WAS ALLOWED INSIDE.

BURNT OFFERING

ESSENCE OF GOD

THEY TIED A ROPE TO HIS ANKLE SO IF HE DIED INSIDE THEY COULD PULL HIM OUT WITHOUT SETTING FOOT IN THE HOLY OF HOLIES.

THE PRESENT
(THE DOME OF THE ROCK AND AL-AQSA MOSQUE)

WHEN THE MUSLIMS TOOK JERUSALEM FROM THE BYZANTINES IN 638 CE, THE TEMPLE MOUNT HAD BECOME A GARBAGE DUMP TO SPITE THE JEWS. CALIPH UMAR CLEANED IT UP AND BUILT WHAT LATER BECAME AL-AQSA MOSQUE.

CALIPH ABD AL-MALIK BUILT THE DOME OF THE ROCK IN 691 TO HOUSE THE FOUNDATION STONE.

MOHAMMED ASCENDED TO HEAVEN FROM THE FOUNDATION STONE. IT'S THE 3RD HOLIEST SITE IN ISLAM.

MUSLIM QUARTER ENTRANCE

MUSLIM QUARTER

JEWISH QUARTER ENTRANCE

AL-AQSA

WESTERN WALL

CONTROVERSIAL RAMP NOW UNDER CONSTRUCTION

SO WHY DON'T THE JEWS WANT TO REBUILD THE TEMPLE?

WELL, EVEN THOUGH THE DOME OF THE ROCK IS SUPPOSEDLY BUILT OVER THE FOUNDATION STONE, THERE IS NO WAY TO BE CERTAIN OF ITS LOCATION ACCORDING TO JEWISH LAW.

SO IF A JEW WENT UP ON THE TEMPLE MOUNT, THERE IS A CHANCE THEY COULD STEP IN THE AREA WHICH WAS ONCE THE HOLY OF HOLIES, AND THAT IS FORBIDDEN.

Q: WHY NOT REBUILD THE TEMPLE?

A: BECAUSE THE HOLY OF HOLIES WILL MELT YOUR FACE OFF JUST LIKE IN INDIANA JONES

THEREFORE, WHILE THERE ARE SOME FANATICS WHO ARE TRYING TO SPEED ALONG THE PROCESS, MOST RELIGIOUS JEWS ARE WAITING FOR THE MESSIAH TO COME BEFORE THEY CAN REBUILD THE TEMPLE.

AT THE WESTERN WALL, WE ARE NOT PRAYING TO HEROD'S STONES. WE PRAY BECAUSE THAT IS THE CLOSEST WE CAN GET TO GOD UNTIL THAT NEW MESSIANIC AGE.

SOME PEOPLE CRY THERE BECAUSE IT WAS SUCH A LONG TIME UNTIL WE COULD EVEN GET THAT CLOSE.

BY THE WAY, THAT SONG YOU HEAR NOW IS THE MUSLIM CALL TO PRAYER.

LOOK AT ALL THAT BELIEF IN ONE SPOT! HOW MUCH PRAYER AND CHANTING HAS GONE ON HERE FOR SO MANY YEARS? THOSE ANCIENT STONES! THAT GLITTERING GOLD DOME...

UGH! WHY DON'T THEY JUST GO AWAY?

DANIA!

OH MY GOD!

172

WHAT? I MEAN, WE WERE HERE FIRST, RIGHT?

JUST IGNORE HER.

NOW LISTEN, WE NEED TO BE RESPECTFUL OF EVERYONE'S RELIGIONS HERE. COMMENTS LIKE THAT ARE NOT HELPFUL.

OKAY, WE'RE RUNNING LATE. LET'S GO DOWN TO THE WALL.

WHAT ARE YOU LOOKING AT? YOU DON'T THINK THEY SAY THE SAME THING ABOUT US?

BUT A PALESTINIAN WHO WOULD SAY SOMETHING LIKE THAT PROBABLY GREW UP IN SQUALOR. YOU'RE FROM *ORANGE COUNTY!*

WHAT-EVER.

HOW ARE YOU SUPPOSED TO DO THIS?

DON'T ASK ME. I JUST WASHED MY HANDS IN THE BATHROOM ANYWAY.

I THINK IT'S A SPIRITUAL THING, SARAH.

OKAY, HERE I GO.

THE ROCK THAT STARTED IT ALL IS SOMEWHERE UP THERE? THE ROCK WITH GOD'S NAME WRITTEN ON IT WHICH EXPANDED INTO THE WHOLE UNIVERSE?

I SUPPOSE IF I BELIEVED IN GOD, I WOULD BE CRYING AND PRAYING FOR IT, TOO.

BUT THIS PLACE THAT MAKES PILGRIMS CRY IS ALSO THE FULCRUM TO THE WHOLE CONFLICT. ALL THAT BLOOD...

IT'S SO POWERFUL.

IT'S AMAZING.

BUT WHO AM I TO JUDGE SOMEONE ELSE'S HOLY SITE? IT FEELS ALMOST LIKE AN ACT OF VIOLENCE TO BECOME ANGRY AT A PLACE CONSIDERED INSPIRING AND DIVINE TO MILLIONS OF PEOPLE.

I'D BETTER WRITE A LITTLE PRAYER AND STICK IT IN THE CRACKS IN THE WALL LIKE EVERYONE ELSE AND STOP INTRUDING ON SACRED AIRSPACE.

OF ALL THE TIMES AND PLACES TO WISH FOR PEACE, THIS ONE SEEMS LIKE THE MOST APPROPRIATE.

NOW JUST TO TEAR IT OUT AND--

SHIT.

LET THERE BE PEACE BETWEEN THE ISRAELIS AND PALESTINIANS

JUST WONDERFUL. NOW I'VE CURSED PEACE IN THE MIDDLE EAST.

AS I START TO CRY, I'M CONFUSED.

I TRY NOT TO GIVE IN TO MAGICAL THINKING, BUT THIS SEEMS LIKE SOME SORT OF SIGN THAT ALL MY HOPES THAT THIS CONFLICT WILL EVER END ARE NAIVE.

"IT'S JUST ANOTHER DAY IN JERUSALEM." DO I REALLY THINK THAT THE COMPROMISE OF THE MILLENNIUM WILL JUST FALL OUT OF THE SKY?

FOLD

OR SPRING OUT OF A HOLY ROCK?

THE RETURN OF THE MESSIAH IS JUST AS LIKELY. MAYBE THESE PEOPLE AND I ARE ALL WAITING FOR THE SAME THING...

...JUST UNDER DIFFERENT NAMES.

YEAH...I GUESS I COULD DO THAT. IS IT SAFE TO DO THAT?

SHABBAT IS COMING IN A FEW HOURS, SO WE'RE AT THE *SHUK* TO WITNESS THE HOLY CITY PREPARE.

UH HUH. NO, I MEAN I'M FINE WITH THAT, IT'S JUST...UH HUH?

...YEAH, NO PROBLEM...

MEANWHILE, MY VISIT TO THE WEST BANK IS NOT TURNING OUT TO BE AS EASY AS I THOUGHT IT WAS GOING TO BE.

OKAY. YEAH, LET ME CHECK ON A FEW THINGS AND I'LL CALL YOU BACK IN A FEW DAYS. THANKS SO MUCH, HUSSEIN. OKAY, TALK TO YOU SOON!

MELISSA?

SARAH?

SORRY I LOST YA, HON. I JUST HAD TO TALK TO THIS GUY WHO WAS SELLING THESE CRAZY FLAG CANDLES.

WHAT'S WRONG?

I JUST CALLED HUSSEIN AND HE'S HAD HIS MOVEMENT WITHIN ISRAEL RESTRICTED RECENTLY AND NOW HE CAN'T COME MEET ME IN JERUSALEM.

HE SAYS I CAN JUST TAKE A TAXI INTO RAMALLAH AND MEET HIM THERE. DO YOU THINK THAT'S SAFE?

I DON'T KNOW. WHAT IF I COME WITH YOU?

HE'S NOT FREE UNTIL WEDNESDAY AND YOUR FLIGHT IS ON TUESDAY.

HMM...I DON'T KNOW, BUDDY. MAYBE YOU SHOULD ASK NADAN ABOUT THAT. WHAT DOES HUSSEIN SAY?

WELL, *HE* SAYS IT'S SAFE.

WHAT DOES YOUR GUT SAY?

I DON'T KNOW.

WELL, THINK IT OVER, TALK TO NADAN. HEY, BY THE WAY...WHERE ARE WE GOING TO STAY TOMORROW NIGHT ONCE THE TRIP IS OVER?

IT'S OUR LAST NIGHT TOGETHER, AND AT A LITTLE PARTY IN TAL AND DAVID'S HOTEL ROOM, THE GROUP VIBE IS OVERWHELMINGLY PLEASANT.

IT'S LIKE THAT LAST PARTY BEFORE THE END OF HIGH SCHOOL THAT IS ALWAYS REPRESENTED IN TEEN MOVIES BUT WHICH I NEVER GOT TO EXPERIENCE MYSELF...

OH MY GAWD! IT'S GREAT! THANK YOU!

...WHEN YOU TOLERATE THINGS THAT ANNOY YOU ABOUT PEOPLE BECAUSE YOU'RE NEVER GOING TO SEE THEM AGAIN...

NOW CAN YOU JUST WRITE ALL OUR HEBREW NAMES ON IT REAL QUICK? HERE'S THE LIST.

...WHILE OTHERS MAKE PLANS TO STAY IN TOUCH DESPITE PESKY OBSTACLES LIKE DISTANCE.

WELL, TO ANSWER YOUR FIRST QUESTION, OF **COURSE** YOU GUYS CAN STAY AT MY PLACE. I HAVE SCHOOL DURING THE DAY, BUT MY PLACE IS WALKING DISTANCE TO PRETTY MUCH EVERYTHING.

AWESOME!

BUT REALLY, SARAH, YOU SHOULD NOT GO TO THE WEST BANK. NO WAY, NUH-UH.

YOU REALLY THINK IT'S THAT BIG OF A DEAL? HUSSEIN SAID IT WAS SAFE.

PLEASE. YOU ARE JEWISH AND A WOMAN, IT'S DANGEROUS! HAVE HIM COME HERE.

FOR YOUR INFORMATION, HE CAN'T COME HERE BECAUSE ISRAEL HAS TAKEN AWAY HIS TRAVEL PERMIT.

WELL, IF THIS GUY IS A SECURITY THREAT THEN MAYBE IT'S BETTER YOU DON'T SEE HIM AT ALL.

WHAT THE-- HE'S A **PEACE** ACTIVIST!

MAYBE WE'LL FIND ANOTHER WAY.

I DON'T SEE WHY YOU GUYS WANT TO GO THERE SO BADLY IN THE FIRST PLACE.

WELL, WE FIGURE WE'RE HERE...WE WANT TO PEEK BEHIND THE CURTAIN, YOU KNOW?

HA! PEEK BEHIND THE CURTAIN.

YOU DON'T EVEN KNOW ANYTHING ABOUT THE CURTAIN ITSELF.

NADAN'S
APARTMENT

DAVID

INDEPENDENCE
GARDEN

HEROD'S
GATE

DAMASCUS
GATE

MUSLIM
QUARTER

CHURCH OF THE
HOLY SEPULCHRE

NEW
GATE

CHRISTIAN
QUARTER

DOME
OF THE
ROCK

LION
GATE

TEMPLE
MOUNT

OLD CITY

JAFFA
GATE

ARMENIAN
QUARTER

WESTERN
WALL

JEWISH
QUARTER

DUNG
GATE

ZION GATE

CITY
OF
DAVID

SILWAN

KHAN THEATER

SHALOM HARTMAN
INSTITUTE

EVERY MOMENT SINCE THE MAYA TOURS BUS PULLS AWAY IS BEING LOGGED IN SOME NEW FOLDER IN MY MIND LABELED "REAL ISRAEL."

GOODBYE, TAGLIT!

FOR THE FIRST TIME SINCE WE ARRIVED, WE'LL BE ABLE TO EXPERIENCE THE COUNTRY WITHOUT A FILTER.

WELP, THAT WAS FUN. NOW WHAT?

TAXI!

THIS IS A REAL ISRAELI TAXI!

1·4·4·2·

WITH REAL ISRAELI RADIO!

WE'RE STAYING IN A REAL ISRAELI RESIDENTIAL NEIGHBORHOOD!

IN A REAL ISRAELI APARTMENT!

ONE OF YOU CAN TAKE THE COUCH. I'LL GO GET OUR AIR MATTRESS. MAKE YOURSELVES AT HOME!

AND THIS IS A REAL ISRAELI ROOMMATE!

HI, I'M MATTI.

MELISSA, NICE TO MEET YOU.

ACTUALLY, MATTI IS A REAL AMERICAN ROOMMATE WHO MOVED TO ISRAEL TO GO TO REAL ISRAELI RABBINICAL SCHOOL.

NADAN'S DISHES ARE IN THAT CUPBOARD. YOU CAN USE THOSE, BUT DON'T USE MINE BECAUSE I KEEP KOSHER. AND DON'T WASH ANY OF HIS DISHES IN THE DAIRY SINK, OKAY?

OKAY, BUT I DON'T THINK WE'RE GOING TO BE COOKING VERY MUCH.

WELL, IT'S JUST BETTER THAT YOU KNOW, ANYWAY.

WE'RE ALL EXHAUSTED, SO WE END THE NIGHT WATCHING SOME REAL ISRAELI TV.

HEY, SEINFELD IS ON! DO YOU LIKE SEINFELD?

ARE YOU KIDDING? SEINFELD IS LIKE MY RELIGION!

WE CAN GO TO THE OLD CITY AGAIN... AND THEN WE CAN LOOK INTO GIL'S WEST BANK CONTACTS, RIGHT?

YEAH, SOUNDS GOOD! I'LL CALL THEM FIRST THING TOMORROW MORNING.

I'D HAD A FEELING THAT NADAN WAS EXAGGERATING THE DANGER OF GOING INTO THE WEST BANK, BUT I WANTED A SECOND OPINION FROM SOMEONE PRACTICAL BEFORE WE PARTED WAYS WITH ISRAEL EXPERTS.

I HAVE SMALLS HERE! WHO ORDERED A SMALL?

NICE JOB ON THE CAMEL, BUDDY. WHERE'S YOURS?

I DIDN'T ORDER ONE. HAVE YOU SEEN GIL? I WANT TO ASK HIM A QUESTION.

YOU DIDN'T ORDER ONE? WHY NOT?

MEH. I'D NEVER WEAR IT. OH, THERE'S GIL. BE RIGHT BACK.

HMMM...WHO IS THIS GUY YOU KNOW IN THE WEST BANK?

HE'S A FRIEND OF SOME JOURNALIST FRIENDS OF MINE. HE DOESN'T THINK IT'S DANGEROUS TO TAKE A CAB, BUT NADAN MAKES IT SOUND LIKE I'LL BE INSTANTLY SHOT OR SOMETHING. WHAT DO YOU THINK?

HONESTLY? YOU WOULD PROBABLY BE FINE. EVEN MILITANT GROUPS KNOW BETTER THAN TO TARGET AMERICANS, AND RAMALLAH IS PRETTY SAFE. IT WOULD STILL BE BETTER IF YOU COULD GET SOMEONE TO GO WITH YOU THOUGH, ESPECIALLY SINCE YOU'RE NOT FAMILIAR WITH THE AREA.

BUT I DON'T HAVE ANYONE TO GO WITH ME!

IF YOU REALLY WANT TO GO INTO THE WEST BANK, YOU MAY BE BETTER OFF GOING WITH AN N.G.O. I HAVE A FEW FRIENDS INVOLVED IN PRO-PEACE GROUPS WHO I'M SURE WOULD BE HAPPY TO HELP YOU OUT.

THAT WOULD BE GREAT! THANKS!

182

SO I CALLED THE "ALL NATIONS CAFE" AND THEY SAID THEY CAN PICK US UP IN THEIR SHUTTLE VAN. WE'RE SUPPOSED TO CALL TO MAKE ARRANGEMENTS WITH THEM TOMORROW AFTERNOON.

GREAT, SO THAT'S A START. OH, I NEED TO STOP AT THIS ATM.

EXCUSE ME, ARE YOU IN LINE?

OH NO, GO AHEAD.

YOU'RE AMERICAN...ARE YOU HERE AFTER YOUR BIRTHRIGHT TRIP TOO?

ME? NO. WELL, I DID GO ON A BIRTHRIGHT TRIP A YEAR AGO. BUT I LIVE HERE NOW. I'M VISITING JERUSALEM FROM BE'ERSHEVA IN THE SOUTH.

IT TURNS OUT THAT OUR NEW FRIEND, WHOSE NAME IS DAVID, JUST MADE ALIYAH THREE MONTHS AGO AND IS ON HIS WAY TO BECOMING AN ISRAELI CITIZEN. WE INVITE HIM TO BREAKFAST.

...AND NOW I'M LIVING AT A KIBBUTZ UNTIL MY ARMY SERVICE STARTS.

WHAT MADE YOU DECIDE TO MOVE HERE? WAS IT BECAUSE OF YOUR BIRTHRIGHT TRIP?

NAH. ACTUALLY, I HAD A TERRIBLE GUIDE. BUT JUST BEING HERE...I CAN'T EXPLAIN IT. MY BEST FRIEND USED TO GO ON AND ON ABOUT HOW IMPORTANT ISRAEL WAS TO THE WORLD, BUT I NEVER LISTENED TO HIM. FROM WITHIN THE U.S., YOU CAN'T IMAGINE HOW ANYWHERE COULD BE BETTER FOR THE JEWS.

BUT THEN I CAME HERE AND SAW ALL THESE PEOPLE WHO WORK SO HARD FOR THEIR COUNTRY. I WAS IN SCHOOL TO BE A DENTIST AND HAD A COMFORTABLE LIFE AHEAD OF ME, BUT I STARTED THINKING THAT MAYBE THAT'S NOT WHAT I'M ON EARTH FOR...

AMERICA MAY BE THE BEST COUNTRY IN THE WORLD, BUT I'M NOT GOING BACK. THE GOAL THERE IS JUST TO SAVE UP MONEY AND BUY MORE THINGS, BUT HERE THERE ARE DIFFERENT VALUES.

IT'S JUST THAT...OUR GENERATION IS GOING TO FACE A LOT OF PROBLEMS THAT THE OLDER GENERATION IS RESPONSIBLE FOR. THEY MADE THIS HUGE MESS BUT THEY STILL DON'T WANT TO HAND OVER THE REINS TO US. IN THE STATES, YOUNG PEOPLE HAVE ALMOST NO POWER.

BUT WHEN ALMOST EVERY YOUNG PERSON HERE IS WORKING TOGETHER IN THE ARMY, THE WHOLE COUNTRY IS IN THEIR HANDS. ISRAEL RESPECTS ITS SOLDIERS, ITS YOUNGER GENERATION. AND BECAUSE THEY'RE IN THE ARMY, THEY ARE MORE CONNECTED TO WHAT'S GOING ON IN THEIR OWN COUNTRY.

BACK IN THE STATES, IT'S EASY TO IGNORE ALL THE PROBLEMS OUR COUNTRY HAS. THE ONLY REASON WE HAVE SUCH GREAT LIVES BACK THERE IS BECAUSE THERE ARE "HAVE-NOTS" AND WE'RE THE "HAVES."

SOMETIMES I THINK WE JUST LIKE COMPLAINING ABOUT ISRAEL'S MORE OBVIOUS PROBLEMS BECAUSE IT'S EASIER THAN LOOKING IN THE MIRROR.

DAVID DOESN'T FIT MY OWN STEREOTYPE OF THE KIND OF PERSON WHO MAKES ALIYAH. I NEVER IMAGINED THEM BEING SO SELF-AWARE.

THERE'S SOMETHING A LITTLE SNOBBY ABOUT BEING A ZIONIST. FOR ME TO LEAVE ALL OF MY FAMILY AND FRIENDS TO COME HERE, IT'S LIKE I'M TELLING THEM THAT I'M BETTER THAN THEM OR SOMETHING.

I HAD ALWAYS FIGURED THAT PEOPLE MADE ALIYAH BECAUSE THEY WERE BOTH RUNNING AWAY FROM THEIR OLD LIVES AND RUNNING TOWARDS AN IDEALIZED VISION OF WHAT LIFE IN ISRAEL IS LIKE.

I JUST WANT TO DO MY PART, YOU KNOW?

I DABBLED IN THAT KIND OF EXPATRIATION WHEN BUSH GOT RE-ELECTED IN 2004, THINKING THAT LIFE IN SOCIALIST-DEMOCRATIC SPAIN WOULD BE BETTER.

GUERRA NUNCA MAS

MATA BUSH

BUT IN BARCELONA, I JUST ENDED UP SPENDING A YEAR FEELING POWERLESS IN ANOTHER LANGUAGE. I ENVY DAVID'S FEELING OF PARTICIPATION IN A GREATER GOOD. MAYBE I WOULDN'T HAVE MOVED TO SPAIN IF I HADN'T LOST FAITH IN THE IDEA THAT I COULD MAKE A DIFFERENCE IN AMERICA.

...ANYWAY, I'M GOING THAT WAY. IT WAS REALLY NICE MEETING YOU GUYS. GOOD LUCK WITH THE REST OF YOUR JOURNEY!

THIS IS OUR SECOND TIME IN THE OLD CITY.

WITHOUT GIL'S DRAMATIC COMMENTARY, THIS PLACE FEELS BOTH MORE FAMILIAR AND LESS SO AT THE SAME TIME.

MMM! GIANT BAGELS!

HELLO! YOU NEED A GUIDE? WHAT WOULD YOU LIKE TO SEE?

WE DON'T NEED A GUIDE. BUT CAN YOU TELL US HOW TO GET TO THE MUSLIM QUARTER?

MUSLIM QUARTER? WHY WOULD YOU WANT TO GO THERE? BETTER NOT TO GO. THE JEWISH QUARTER, CHRISTIAN QUARTER, THEY ARE SAFER.

I THINK WE'LL BE OKAY. WHICH WAY IS IT?

WE EVENTUALLY GET DIRECTIONS FROM OUR WOULD-BE GUIDE, BUT NOT BEFORE HE TRIES SEVERAL MORE TIMES TO CONVINCE US THAT A TOUR OF THE JEWISH QUARTER WITH HIM WOULD BE A MUCH BETTER IDEA THAN WHAT WE HAVE PLANNED FOR OUR DAY.

DANGEROUS MY ASS. I DON'T KNOW WHAT THAT GUY WAS TALKING ABOUT. THIS PLACE IS FULL OF TOURISTS!

AH, IT'S PROBABLY JUST FEAR. I'M SURE THE TENSION HERE JUST ISN'T VISIBLE TO US AS MUCH.

HMMM... THESE EARRINGS ARE NICE...

DO YOU NEED ANY HELP, MISS?

MAYBE... HOW MUCH ARE THESE?

I START CHATTING WITH THE SHOPKEEPER, WHOSE NAME IS SAMI, AND TELL HIM ABOUT HOW THE STREET GUIDE HAD WARNED US AGAINST COMING HERE.

HAHA! MAYBE HE'S AFRAID OF LOSING BUSINESS TO US. BUT YOU FEEL THE DIFFERENCE, YES?

IN THE JEWISH QUARTER IT IS ONLY JEWS. BUT IN THE OTHER QUARTERS IT'S MIXED. YOU HAVE TOURISTS, ARABS, CHRISTIANS. AND JEWS TOO! YOU CAN FEEL THE DIFFERENCE.

WHAT PART OF AMERICA ARE YOU FROM?

OH, WE BOTH LIVE IN NEW YORK.

NEW YORK! I LIVED THERE SEVEN YEARS WITH MY COUSIN, IN QUEENS. I MISS MY BASEBALL TEAM STILL.

YOUR BASEBALL TEAM? METS OR YANKEES?

THE YANKEES, OF COURSE!

THE YANKEES! I DON'T KNOW IF I CAN BUY THESE EARRINGS AFTER ALL.

YOU'RE A METS FAN?

NO, I'M A **RED SOX** FAN.

RED SOX! WELL THEN I DON'T KNOW IF I CAN SELL YOU THESE EARRINGS! GET OUT OF MY SHOP! HAHA.

FOR A SECOND I FORGET THAT I'M NOT BACK IN NEW YORK.

GOODBYE! SAY HELLO TO THE BIG APPLE FOR ME!

I THINK THE EASIEST WAY TO GET TO THE TEMPLE MOUNT IS TO JUST GO BACK TO THE RAMP AT THE WESTERN WALL.

WHICH WAY IS THAT?

HMM...THIS WAY?

ARE YOU SURE WE CAN JUST GO UP THERE?

YEAH, I THINK SO.

I'M PRETTY SURE ANYONE IS ALLOWED TO GO UP THERE, JUST NOT BY RELIGIOUS LAW IF YOU'RE A RELIGIOUS JEW.

AND WE'RE NOT RELIGIOUS, SO IT'S OKAY.

AT LEAST... I *THINK* IT'S OKAY.

WELL, LOOK AT THAT!

THERE'S A PARK UP HERE? THAT FAMILY IS HAVING A PICNIC!

I GUESS PEOPLE JUST COME HERE TO HANG OUT.

CAN WE GO INSIDE?

I DON'T THINK SO.

REMEMBER IN 2000 WHEN ARIEL SHARON CAME UP HERE AND IT WAS SUCH A BIG DEAL? THEY SAY IT SPARKED THE SECOND INTIFADA.

BECAUSE OF THAT I ALWAYS THOUGHT IT WOULD BE SUPER QUIET UP HERE WITH ALL KINDS OF RULES... LIKE HOW DOWN AT THE WESTERN WALL YOU'RE NOT EVER SUPPOSED TO TURN YOUR BACK TO THE WALL.

IT'S SO MUCH MORE LAID BACK THAN I THOUGHT IT WOULD BE!

WHAT THE...? HOW DID THEY GET THOSE CAP GUNS THROUGH SECURITY?

SNAP
SNAP SNAP!

OH. NO METAL DETECTORS OR BULLETPROOF-VESTED GUARDS AT THIS ENTRANCE, I GUESS!

NOW THAT WE'VE SEEN THE MUSLIM HOLY SITE OF JERUSALEM, ITS TIME TO CHECK OUT THE CHRISTIAN ONE. WE EXIT THE TEMPLE MOUNT THROUGH THE MUSLIM SECTION AND TRY TO ORIENT OURSELVES.

THIS MAP IS KIND OF HARD TO READ.

EXCUSE ME, HI. WE'RE LOOKING FOR THE STATIONS OF THE CROSS. APPARENTLY THE FIRST ONE IS SUPPOSED TO BE NEAR HERE. DO YOU KNOW WHERE IT IS?

YOU JUST PASSED IT. IT'S BACK THERE.

REALLY?

THE LACK OF FANFARE WE ARE FINDING IN THE STATIONS OF THE CROSS IS SURPRISING, TO SAY THE LEAST.

I EXPECTED ALL THE THINGS DESIGNED TO MAKE PILGRIMAGE EASY: ARROWS, PLAQUES, MAPS OF THE AREA TO TELL YOU THAT "YOU ARE HERE."

HEY, THERE'S ANOTHER ONE HERE.

WHAT HAPPENED HERE?

UM...MARY COMES TO SEE JESUS OR SOMETHING?

OKAY, WHAT'S NEXT?

THE NEXT FOUR STATIONS ARE IN THE CHURCH OF THE HOLY SEPULCHRE. IT SHOULD BE RIGHT UP HERE.

THE MORE TIME WE SPEND OUTSIDE OF "ISRAEL PROPER" AND THE CONFINES OF JUDAISM, THE MORE I FEEL A CERTAIN CREEPING ANXIETY.

WE'RE SUDDENLY IN THE LAND OF "I DON'T KNOW."

IS THIS THE ENTRANCE?

I DON'T KNOW WHERE TO STAND, HOW MUCH TO PAY OR WHETHER I'M WEARING THE RIGHT THING

THAT'S JESUS' TOMB.

SHOULD WE GO INSIDE?

UM...THE LINE IS KIND OF LONG. LET'S GET OUT OF HERE.

YOU OKAY, BUDDY? YOU SEEM KIND OF ON EDGE.

OH, I...IT'S JUST THAT ESPRESSO I HAD WITH LUNCH IS MAKING ME JITTERY. THAT'S ALL.

MELISSA WANTS TO SEE THE ARCHEOLOGICAL REMAINS OF THE CITY OF DAVID, WHICH SHE SAYS IS FEATURED IN SOLOMON'S "SONG OF SONGS."

IT'S SITUATED IN EAST JERUSALEM, IN SILWAN, A PALESTINIAN NEIGHBORHOOD WHICH WE WALK BACK THROUGH.

BUT THERE WERE NEW BUILDINGS BACK THERE WITH ISRAELI FLAGS. IS THIS ONE OF THOSE PLACES IN EAST JERUSALEM FROM THE NEWS? WHERE SETTLEMENTS ARE BEING BUILT UP ILLEGALLY? I DIDN'T READ ABOUT THIS PLACE BEFORE I GOT HERE.

WHAT HAPPENED TO THAT HOUSE? WHERE'S THE PLAQUE EXPLAINING WHAT'S GOING ON HERE? WHERE IS GIL?

ARE THOSE PALESTINIAN BOYS YELLING AT US OR JUST PLAYING?

I SUDDENLY WANT TO BE BACK INSIDE A HOMEY JERUSALEM CAFE TALKING ABOUT THE CITY'S CULTURE CLASH INSTEAD OF WANDERING AROUND INSIDE IT.

NADAN HAS MISSED MORE THAN A WEEK OF CLASS AT HEBREW UNIVERSITY AND IS BUSY CATCHING UP, BUT HE WAS ABLE TO USE HIS STUDENT UNION CONNECTIONS TO GET MELISSA AND ME FREE FRONT-ROW TICKETS TO "LIFE IS A DREAM," A PLAY BY SPANISH PLAYWRIGHT PEDRO CALDERON.

I'M IMPRESSED BY THE ART DIRECTION AND COSTUME DESIGN.

BUT THE PLAY IS IN HEBREW AND MY VOCABULARY IN THE LANGUAGE IS LIMITED TO THE HANDFUL OF WORDS I CAN REMEMBER FROM SUNDAY SCHOOL.

I THINK HE JUST SAID "WATER."

I TRY TO FOLLOW ALONG WITH THE STORY AS BEST I CAN. THERE IS A KING, A JAILED MAN, A REBEL ARMY.

I FEEL RELAXED. THE SEATS ARE COMFORTABLE; IT'S DRY AND WARM IN HERE AGAINST THE COLD RAIN OUTSIDE. BUT MY EASE IN HERE GOES BEYOND THAT.

ALMOST EVERYONE IN THIS ROOM IS JEWISH. MANY OF THEM ARE YOUNG. THEY LIKE INTELLECTUAL THEATER WHICH MEANS THEY PROBABLY LIKE CONTEMPORARY ART AND TRANSLATED NOVELS.

THEY LIVE IN ISRAEL, I DON'T. THEY UNDERSTAND WHAT IS HAPPENING IN THIS PLAY, I DON'T. BUT WE PROBABLY HAVE SO MUCH IN COMMON. I'M ASHAMED TO ADMIT TO MYSELF THAT I LIKE THIS FEELING OF BEING IN THIS ROOM. I'M EVEN MORE ASHAMED AT HOW MUCH I DIDN'T LIKE BEING OUTSIDE OF IT.

I LET THE SHAME AND COMFORT WASH OVER ME AND TRY TO PICK OUT THE HEBREW WORDS THAT I KNOW.

IT'S MELISSA'S LAST DAY HERE SO WE SPENT THE MORNING CHECKING OUT SOME MUSEUMS AND WALKING AROUND THE CITY. BACK AT NADAN'S APARTMENT, MELISSA IS GETTING THE DETAILS ON WHERE TO MEET UP WITH THE N.G.O. GIL RECOMMENDED WHICH WILL TAKE US INTO THE WEST BANK.

I STILL NEED TO MAKE A DECISION ABOUT GOING INTO RAMALLAH ALONE. I NEED TO CALL HUSSEIN BACK.

GREAT...THANK YOU *SO* MUCH, ANDREW. WE'RE REALLY LOOKING FORWARD TO IT. OKAY, SEE YOU THEN.

SO WHAT DID HE SAY? ARE WE GOING?

YUP, HE TOLD ME WHERE THE MEETING SPOT IS AND SAID THAT HE'LL PICK US UP THERE AT FOUR. WE BETTER GET A MOVE ON IF WE'RE GONNA MAKE IT IN TIME.

ARE WE LATE YET?

WE STILL HAVE ABOUT FIVE MINUTES. SHIT, HE SAID TO MEET AT THE ENTRANCE OF THE PARK BUT HE DIDN'T SAY WHICH ENTRANCE.

MAYBE WE SHOULD HAVE TAKEN THE BUS INSTEAD OF WALKED! WHAT IF THEY LEAVE WITHOUT US?

DON'T WORRY, I'M CALLING ANDREW NOW TO FIND OUT WHERE EXACTLY WE'RE SUPPOSED TO WAIT.

YEAH, WE'RE CROSSING THE PARK NOW. WHERE? AHH, I SEE IT NOW, OKAY.

I GUESS THIS IS THE SPOT. HE SAID HE WAS RUNNING A FEW MINUTES BEHIND. KEEP AN EYE OUT FOR A GREY MINIVAN.

OKAY.

WHAT TIME IS IT NOW?

TEN AFTER FOUR.

HE'S PROBABLY PICKING UP OTHER PEOPLE FIRST.

THE N.G.O. WE'RE WAITING FOR IS CALLED THE ALL NATIONS CAFÉ. THEIR ORGANIZATION BRINGS ISRAELIS, PALESTINIANS, LEBANESE AND OTHERS TOGETHER TO GET TO KNOW EACH OTHER IN A PLEASANT OUTDOOR SETTING JUST OUTSIDE THE GREEN LINE.

IT'S NOT A VISIT TO RAMALLAH, BUT IT SHOULD BE ENLIGHTENING.

WHAT TIME IS IT NOW?

FOUR THIRTY.

MAYBE HE'S GETTING GAS OR SOMETHING.

HEY LOOK, SOMEONE'S COMING OVER HERE.

HI! I MEAN... SHALOM?

SHALOM.

ARE YOU GIRLS WAITING FOR ANDREW?

YEAH, HE'S RUNNING A BIT LATE IT SEEMS.

WELL, THAT'S A GOOD THING FOR ME AT LEAST. I WAS RUNNING LATE TOO.

ARE YOU FROM THE STATES?

I WAS. MADE ALIYAH ABOUT TWENTY YEARS AGO. MY LIFE IS HERE NOW.

HAVE YOU DONE ANYTHING WITH ALL NATIONS BEFORE?

OH YES, I GO ALL THE TIME.

WHAT'S IT LIKE?

IT'S WHAT YOU WOULD EXPECT. WE TALK, DISCUSS THINGS. WE DON'T ALWAYS AGREE BUT IT'S VERY OPEN.

IT SOUNDS GREAT...IF THIS DUDE EVER SHOWS UP TO BRING US THERE.

MAYBE I SHOULD CALL HIM ONE MORE TIME.

WHILE MELISSA CALLS ANDREW AGAIN, I TRY TO GET TO KNOW OUR FELLOW ALL NATIONS PARTICIPANT. I'M SURPRISED THAT SOME OF HIS VIEWS ARE NOT WHAT I CONSIDER TO BE PROGRESSIVE.

BUT DON'T YOU THINK THAT IF ISRAEL GIVES THEM BACK THE TERRITORIES THERE WILL BE *LESS* VIOLENCE?

COULD BE. BUT WE DON'T HAVE ANY PROOF OF THAT. THEY CAN'T BE TRUSTED WITH A STATE OF THEIR OWN. AT LEAST NOT NOW.

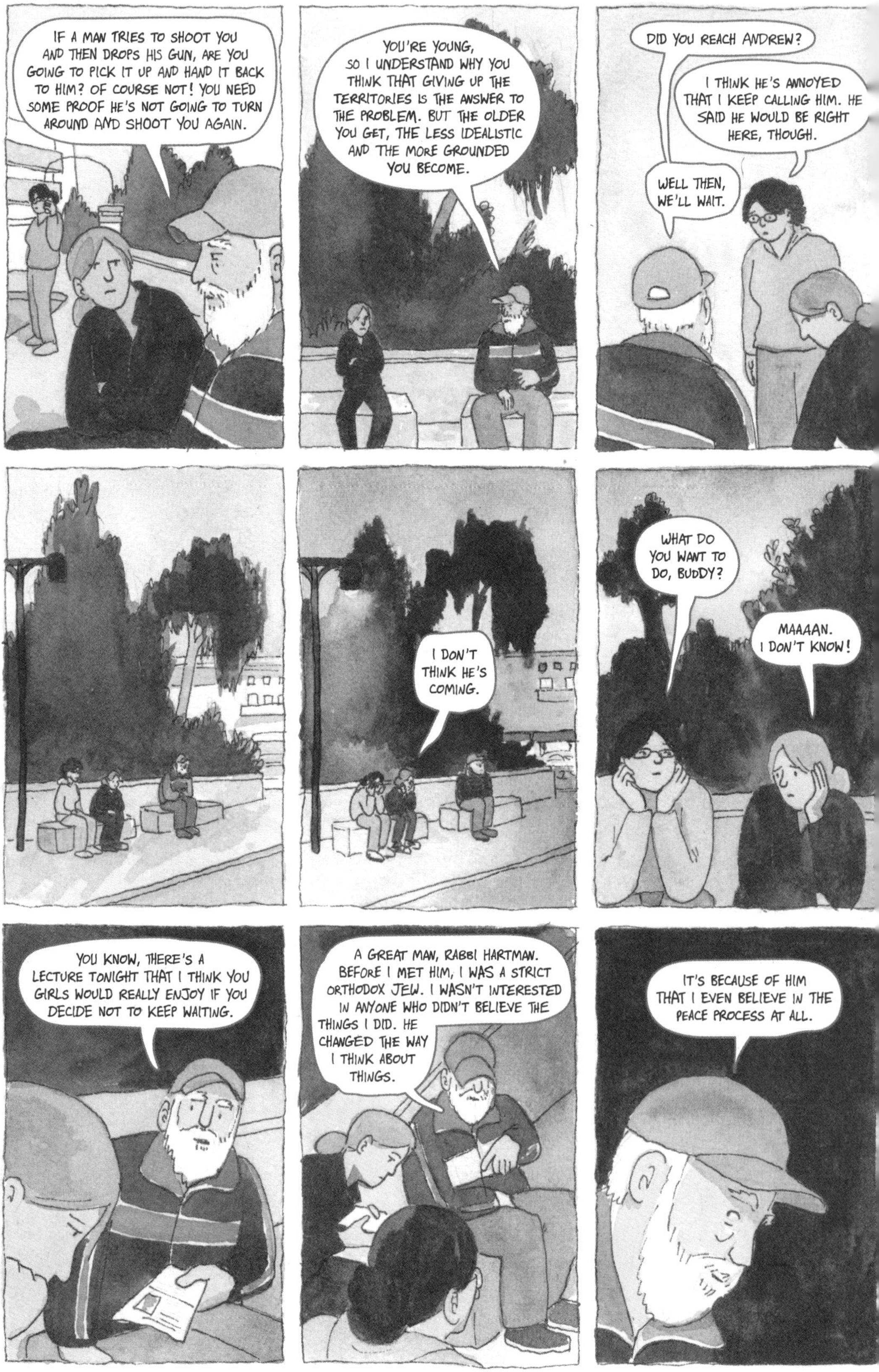
IF A MAN TRIES TO SHOOT YOU AND THEN DROPS HIS GUN, ARE YOU GOING TO PICK IT UP AND HAND IT BACK TO HIM? OF COURSE NOT! YOU NEED SOME PROOF HE'S NOT GOING TO TURN AROUND AND SHOOT YOU AGAIN.
YOU'RE YOUNG, SO I UNDERSTAND WHY YOU THINK THAT GIVING UP THE TERRITORIES IS THE ANSWER TO THE PROBLEM. BUT THE OLDER YOU GET, THE LESS IDEALISTIC AND THE MORE GROUNDED YOU BECOME.
DID YOU REACH ANDREW?
I THINK HE'S ANNOYED THAT I KEEP CALLING HIM. HE SAID HE WOULD BE RIGHT HERE, THOUGH.
WELL THEN, WE'LL WAIT.
I DON'T THINK HE'S COMING.
WHAT DO YOU WANT TO DO, BUDDY?
MAAAAN. I DON'T KNOW!
YOU KNOW, THERE'S A LECTURE TONIGHT THAT I THINK YOU GIRLS WOULD REALLY ENJOY IF YOU DECIDE NOT TO KEEP WAITING.
A GREAT MAN, RABBI HARTMAN. BEFORE I MET HIM, I WAS A STRICT ORTHODOX JEW. I WASN'T INTERESTED IN ANYONE WHO DIDN'T BELIEVE THE THINGS I DID. HE CHANGED THE WAY I THINK ABOUT THINGS.
IT'S BECAUSE OF HIM THAT I EVEN BELIEVE IN THE PEACE PROCESS AT ALL.

WITH OUR LUCK, ANDREW'S VAN WILL SHOW UP AS SOON AS WE'RE OUT OF EYE-SHOT.

NO...I DON'T THINK HE'S COMING.

BUT I JUST DON'T GET IT! *WHY* DIDN'T HE COME GET US? AND HE KEPT SAYING HE WAS ON HIS WAY. WHAT A LIAR!

ARGHH! THIS STUPID COUNTRY!

AT LEAST YOU CAN STILL GO TAKE THAT TAXI TO RAMALLAH TOMORROW TO VISIT HUSSEIN. THIS WAS MY ONLY CHANCE.

YEAH ABOUT THAT...

OKAY, WE'RE ON GEDALYAHU ALON STREET...WE'RE LOOKING FOR NUMBER 11.

THE SHALOM HARTMAN INSTITUTE. THIS IS IT.

SHALOM HARTMAN INSTITUTE

HOW DID I LET MELISSA TALK ME INTO THIS? A LECTURE FROM A RABBI ABOUT JEWISH LAW IS THE EXACT OPPOSITE OF WHAT WE'RE SUPPOSED TO BE DOING TONIGHT. WELL, SHE WANTS TO LEARN MORE ABOUT BEING JEWISH, SO I GUESS HER WISH IS ABOUT TO BE GRANTED.

THERE'S TWO SEATS HERE!

GOOD EVENING EVERYONE, AND THANK YOU FOR COMING...

HEY, YOU THINK HE'S FROM BROOKLYN?

MUST BE. THAT ACCENT IS UNMISTAKABLE!

MANY JEWS ARE MISTAKEN ABOUT WHAT IT MEANS TO BE OBSERVANT. I WANT TO CLARIFY TONIGHT THAT A RULE-BASED RELIGIOUS LIFE IS NOTHING COMPARED TO A TRUE WORSHIP OF GOD. REAL SPIRITUALITY CAN NEVER BE ACHIEVED SIMPLY BY FOLLOWING A SET OF LAWS.

מכון שלום הרטמן
SHALOM HARTMAN INSTIT

WAIT A MINUTE...IS HE GOING TO ARGUE **AGAINST** FOLLOWING RELIGIOUS LAWS BLINDLY? MAYBE THIS WON'T BE A WASTE OF TIME AFTER ALL?

SOMEONE ONCE TOLD ME THAT THE KEY TO A HAPPY MARRIAGE IS TO BRING YOUR WIFE FLOWERS EVERY MONTH. BUT ISN'T IT MORE IMPORTANT TO BE A PERSON CAPABLE OF LOVING MARRIED LIFE? AND SO IT IS THE SAME WITH *HALACHAH*, THE JEWISH LAW.

IT'S NOT ENOUGH JUST TO READ THE RIGHT PRAYERS AT THE RIGHT TIME. ARE YOU RECITING THE HAGGADAH TO LET GOD KNOW WHAT'S WRITTEN IN THERE? OR ARE YOU UNDERSTANDING WHAT IT MEANS TO BE FREE?

THE TORAH SPEAKS OF HOW THE ENSLAVED JEWISH PEOPLE ESCAPED THE OPPRESSION OF THE EGYPTIANS. AMAZING. BUT HOW DO WE JUSTIFY THAT THE TORAH ALSO TELLS US THAT THIS KIND OF TREATMENT IS ACCEPTABLE FOR NON-JEWS, THAT YOU MAY TREAT A MISBEHAVING ARAB SLAVE WITH RIGOR?

THESE ARE ANCIENT LAWS WRITTEN BY MEN. BUT THOSE WHO ARE TRULY PIOUS, WHO TRULY LOVE GOD WILL SURPASS THIS WITH WISDOM AND SENSITIVITY. THE LAW ALLOWS IT, BUT YOU MUST GO BEYOND THE LAW TO FIND GOD. IF YOU REMAIN WITHIN THE LAW, YOU ARE A PAGAN!

THESE ARE LAWS THAT MUST BE STRICKEN FROM THE TALMUD, LAWS MADE DURING WARTIME TO JUSTIFY ACTS AGAINST THEIR ENEMIES. UNLESS WE HAVE THE COURAGE TO CHANGE THESE UGLY LAWS, WE ARE DESTROYING OUR OWN FAITH.

SHALOM HARTMA

THE DIFFERENCE BETWEEN JEW AND NON-JEW DOES NOT EXIST. WE ARE ALL MEMBERS OF THE HUMAN CONDITION.

IF YOU ARE A RELIGIOUS JEW, A DOCTOR, ON SEEING A PALESTINIAN INJURED ON THE SIDE OF THE ROAD, YOU SHOULD NOT HAVE TO THINK ABOUT WHETHER OR NOT TO HELP HIM. HE IS THE SAME AS YOU.

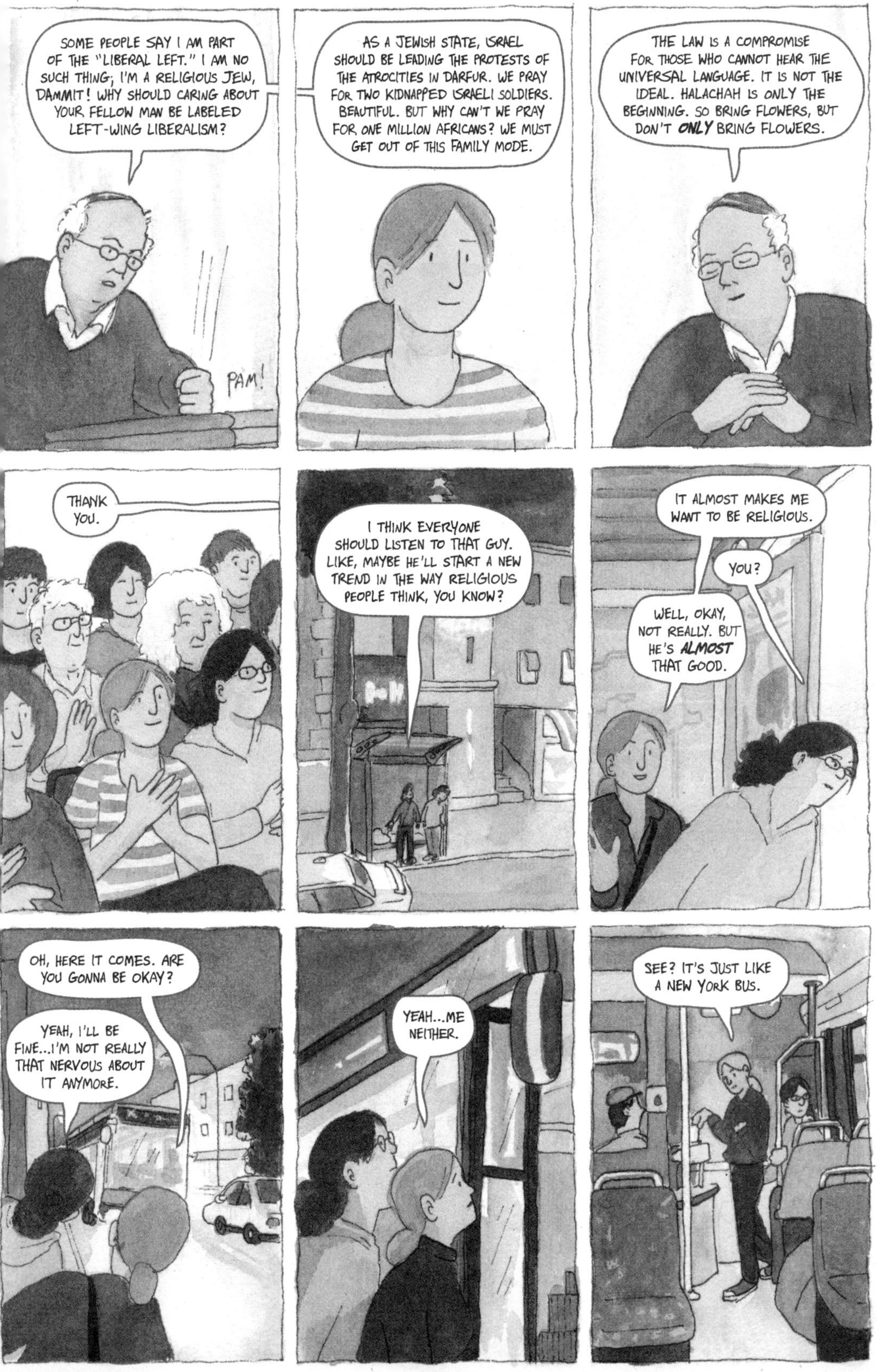
SOME PEOPLE SAY I AM PART OF THE "LIBERAL LEFT." I AM NO SUCH THING; I'M A RELIGIOUS JEW, DAMMIT! WHY SHOULD CARING ABOUT YOUR FELLOW MAN BE LABELED LEFT-WING LIBERALISM?
PAM!
AS A JEWISH STATE, ISRAEL SHOULD BE LEADING THE PROTESTS OF THE ATROCITIES IN DARFUR. WE PRAY FOR TWO KIDNAPPED ISRAELI SOLDIERS. BEAUTIFUL. BUT WHY CAN'T WE PRAY FOR ONE MILLION AFRICANS? WE MUST GET OUT OF THIS FAMILY MODE.
THE LAW IS A COMPROMISE FOR THOSE WHO CANNOT HEAR THE UNIVERSAL LANGUAGE. IT IS NOT THE IDEAL. HALACHAH IS ONLY THE BEGINNING. SO BRING FLOWERS, BUT DON'T **ONLY** BRING FLOWERS.
THANK YOU.
I THINK EVERYONE SHOULD LISTEN TO THAT GUY. LIKE, MAYBE HE'LL START A NEW TREND IN THE WAY RELIGIOUS PEOPLE THINK, YOU KNOW?
IT ALMOST MAKES ME WANT TO BE RELIGIOUS.
YOU?
WELL, OKAY, NOT REALLY. BUT HE'S **ALMOST** THAT GOOD.
OH, HERE IT COMES. ARE YOU GONNA BE OKAY?
YEAH, I'LL BE FINE...I'M NOT REALLY THAT NERVOUS ABOUT IT ANYMORE.
YEAH...ME NEITHER.
SEE? IT'S JUST LIKE A NEW YORK BUS.

I GUESS IT WAS PRETTY SILLY OF ME TO INSIST WE WALK EVERYWHERE UNTIL NOW...I'M SURE ISRAELIS TAKE THE BUS EVERY DAY WITHOUT EVEN THINKING ABOUT IT.

YEAH, LIKE I SAID BEFORE: WE'RE PERFECTLY SAFE!

DING DING!

STEP STEP STEP

CHHI-CHK!

SO...YOU'RE NOT GOING TO TAKE THAT CAB INTO RAMALLAH, ARE YOU?

NO. I DON'T THINK SO.

WHAT CAN I SAY? I'M A BIG HYPOCRITE, TALKING ABOUT HOW PEOPLE NEED TO MOVE PAST THEIR PREJUDICES AND FEARS BUT THEN I CAN'T TAKE A FIFTEEN-MINUTE TAXI TRIP WITHOUT SOMEONE HOLDING MY HAND.

WELL, IT'S UNDERSTANDABLE. I DON'T KNOW IF I WOULD DO IT EITHER. BUT WOULD IT REALLY HAVE CHANGED ANYTHING FOR YOU? IT'S NOT LIKE YOU'RE NOT ALREADY SYMPATHETIC TO THE PALESTINIANS.

I KNOW. IT PROBABLY WOULDN'T HAVE CHANGED ANYTHING.

I BET JAMIL'S GONNA BE DISAPPOINTED IN ME, THOUGH. HE'S GOING TO THINK THAT I DECIDED NOT TO GO BECAUSE THE BIRTHRIGHT TRIP CHANGED THE WAY I THINK ABOUT THE "SITUATION."

SARAH, THIS ISN'T ABOUT WHAT JAMIL THINKS. DO YOU THINK THE TRIP CHANGED THE WAY YOU THINK ABOUT IT?

I REALLY DON'T KNOW YET.

MAYBE IT DID.

200

MELISSA'S FLIGHT LEAVES TODAY, SO SHE'S CATCHING THE EARLY SHUTTLE BUS TO BEN GURION AIRPORT. NADAN AND I ACCOMPANY HER AS FAR AS THE SECURITY STATION.

NADAN! COME TO NEW YORK ANY-TIME! THANK YOU FOR EVERYTHING!

OF COURSE! YOU'RE ALWAYS WELCOME!

SO YOU'RE GOING TO GO TO TEL AVIV LATER TODAY?

YEAH, I GUESS I'LL JUST SPEND THE AFTERNOON WANDERING AROUND AND THEN I'LL CRASH AT MY COUSIN'S PLACE.

THEN MY FLIGHT TO ISTANBUL LEAVES AT 5 A.M. TOMORROW MORNING. YIKES!

HEY, I HAVE A GOOD IDEA...

MY FRIEND DANI LIVES IN TEL AVIV AND HE HAS A CAR. WHY DON'T WE GO OUT TONIGHT AND THEN WE CAN GIVE YOU A RIDE TO THE AIRPORT?

YEAH, SURE. I CAN SEE SOME OF TEL AVIV'S "FAMOUS NIGHTLIFE." I CAN JUST SLEEP ON THE PLANE.

I DON'T KNOW HOW MUCH SLEEP YOU'LL GET. ISN'T IT ONLY A TWO-HOUR FLIGHT?

AH, SOMETHING LIKE THAT. I'LL SLEEP WHEN I'M DEAD.

SO WHY ARE YOU GOING TO ISTANBUL? I THOUGHT YOU WERE GOING HOME.

WELL, I HAD TO BOOK MY TICKET BACK WITH TURKISH AIRLINES AND THERE'S AN OPTION TO STAY OVER FOR 24 HOURS AT NO EXTRA CHARGE, SO I DECIDED TO TAKE IT. I THOUGHT IT MIGHT BE NICE TO DECOMPRESS FOR A DAY.

ISRAEL MUST BE REALLY STRESSFUL TO YOU IF YOU CONSIDER ISTANBUL A PLACE TO DECOMPRESS!

BEFORE I CATCH MY BUS TO TEL AVIV, NADAN AND I GRAB SOME LUNCH AND I ASK HIM SOME MORE QUESTIONS ABOUT LIFE IN ISRAEL.

...SO I WORKED ON HER CAMPAIGN AND NOW I'M AN INTERN FOR HER AT THE KNESSET ONCE A WEEK.

I LIKE NADAN. HE CARES ABOUT PEOPLE AND HE AND I SEEM TO SHARE A SIMILAR WORLDVIEW...THAT IS, UNTIL WE START TALKING ABOUT "THE SITUATION" AGAIN.

PLEASE. ISRAEL IS NOT RACIST.

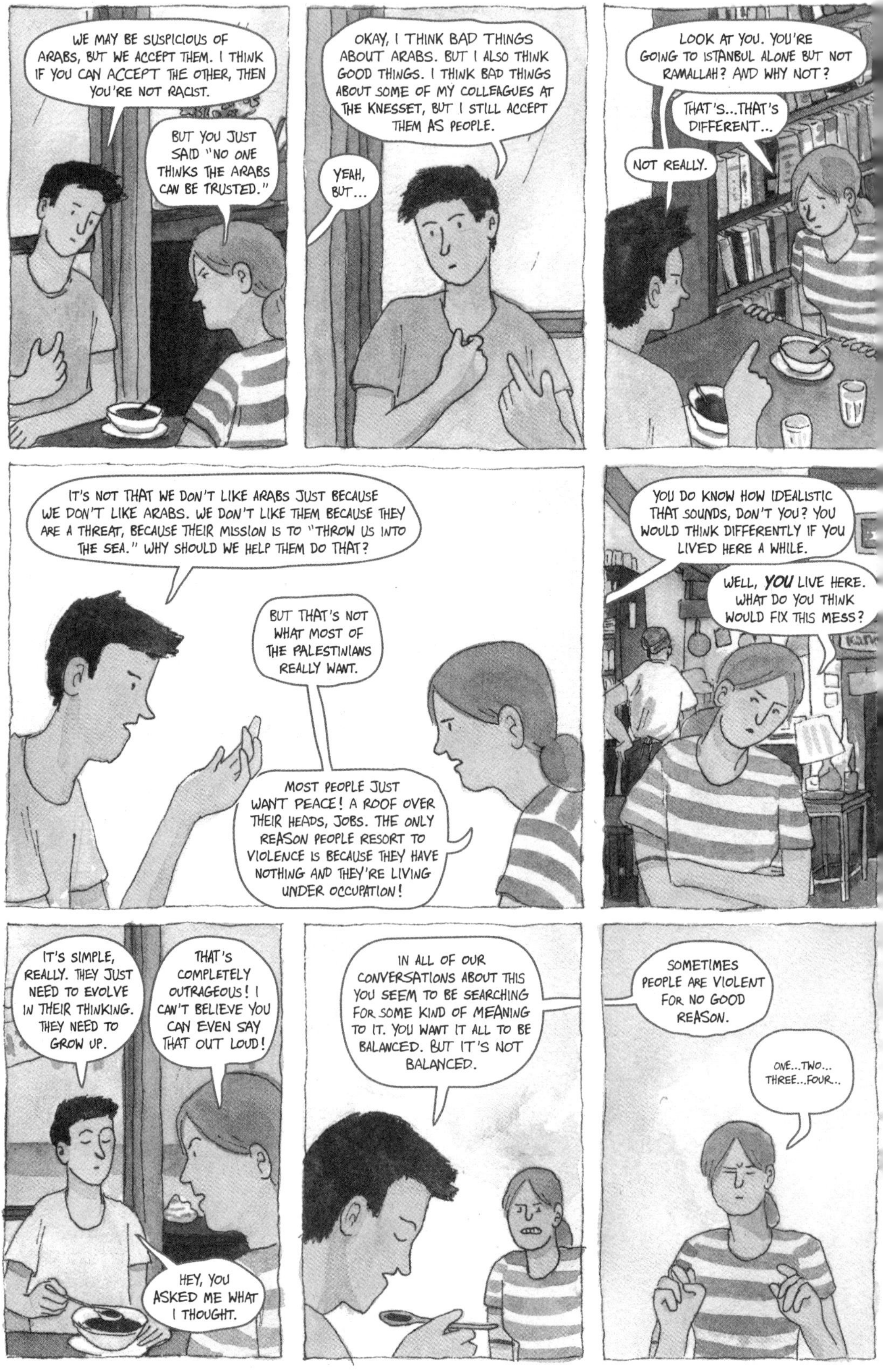
WE MAY BE SUSPICIOUS OF ARABS, BUT WE ACCEPT THEM. I THINK IF YOU CAN ACCEPT THE OTHER, THEN YOU'RE NOT RACIST.
BUT YOU JUST SAID "NO ONE THINKS THE ARABS CAN BE TRUSTED."
OKAY, I THINK BAD THINGS ABOUT ARABS. BUT I ALSO THINK GOOD THINGS. I THINK BAD THINGS ABOUT SOME OF MY COLLEAGUES AT THE KNESSET, BUT I STILL ACCEPT THEM AS PEOPLE.
YEAH, BUT...
LOOK AT YOU. YOU'RE GOING TO ISTANBUL ALONE BUT NOT RAMALLAH? AND WHY NOT?
THAT'S...THAT'S DIFFERENT...
NOT REALLY.
IT'S NOT THAT WE DON'T LIKE ARABS JUST BECAUSE WE DON'T LIKE ARABS. WE DON'T LIKE THEM BECAUSE THEY ARE A THREAT, BECAUSE THEIR MISSION IS TO "THROW US INTO THE SEA." WHY SHOULD WE HELP THEM DO THAT?
BUT THAT'S NOT WHAT MOST OF THE PALESTINIANS REALLY WANT.
MOST PEOPLE JUST WANT PEACE! A ROOF OVER THEIR HEADS, JOBS. THE ONLY REASON PEOPLE RESORT TO VIOLENCE IS BECAUSE THEY HAVE NOTHING AND THEY'RE LIVING UNDER OCCUPATION!
YOU DO KNOW HOW IDEALISTIC THAT SOUNDS, DON'T YOU? YOU WOULD THINK DIFFERENTLY IF YOU LIVED HERE A WHILE.
WELL, **YOU** LIVE HERE. WHAT DO YOU THINK WOULD FIX THIS MESS?
IT'S SIMPLE, REALLY. THEY JUST NEED TO EVOLVE IN THEIR THINKING. THEY NEED TO GROW UP.
THAT'S COMPLETELY OUTRAGEOUS! I CAN'T BELIEVE YOU CAN EVEN SAY THAT OUT LOUD!
HEY, YOU ASKED ME WHAT I THOUGHT.
IN ALL OF OUR CONVERSATIONS ABOUT THIS YOU SEEM TO BE SEARCHING FOR SOME KIND OF MEANING TO IT. YOU WANT IT ALL TO BE BALANCED. BUT IT'S NOT BALANCED.
SOMETIMES PEOPLE ARE VIOLENT FOR NO GOOD REASON.
ONE...TWO... THREE...FOUR..

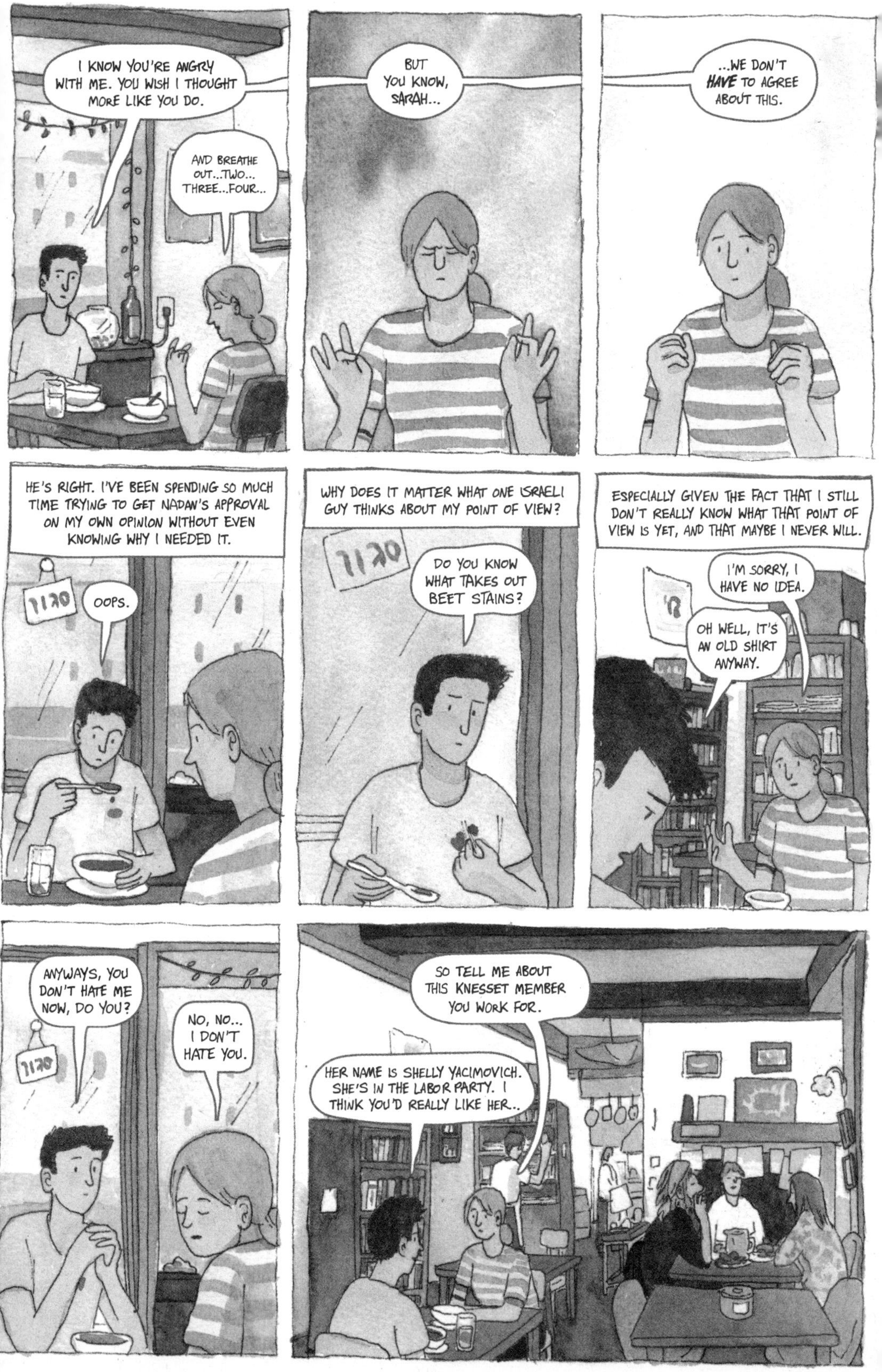
I KNOW YOU'RE ANGRY WITH ME. YOU WISH I THOUGHT MORE LIKE YOU DO.
AND BREATHE OUT...TWO... THREE...FOUR...
BUT YOU KNOW, SARAH...
...WE DON'T HAVE TO AGREE ABOUT THIS.
HE'S RIGHT. I'VE BEEN SPENDING SO MUCH TIME TRYING TO GET NADAN'S APPROVAL ON MY OWN OPINION WITHOUT EVEN KNOWING WHY I NEEDED IT.
OOPS.
WHY DOES IT MATTER WHAT ONE ISRAELI GUY THINKS ABOUT MY POINT OF VIEW?
DO YOU KNOW WHAT TAKES OUT BEET STAINS?
ESPECIALLY GIVEN THE FACT THAT I STILL DON'T REALLY KNOW WHAT THAT POINT OF VIEW IS YET, AND THAT MAYBE I NEVER WILL.
I'M SORRY, I HAVE NO IDEA.
OH WELL, IT'S AN OLD SHIRT ANYWAY.
ANYWAYS, YOU DON'T HATE ME NOW, DO YOU?
NO, NO... I DON'T HATE YOU.
SO TELL ME ABOUT THIS KNESSET MEMBER YOU WORK FOR.
HER NAME IS SHELLY YACIMOVICH. SHE'S IN THE LABOR PARTY. I THINK YOU'D REALLY LIKE HER..

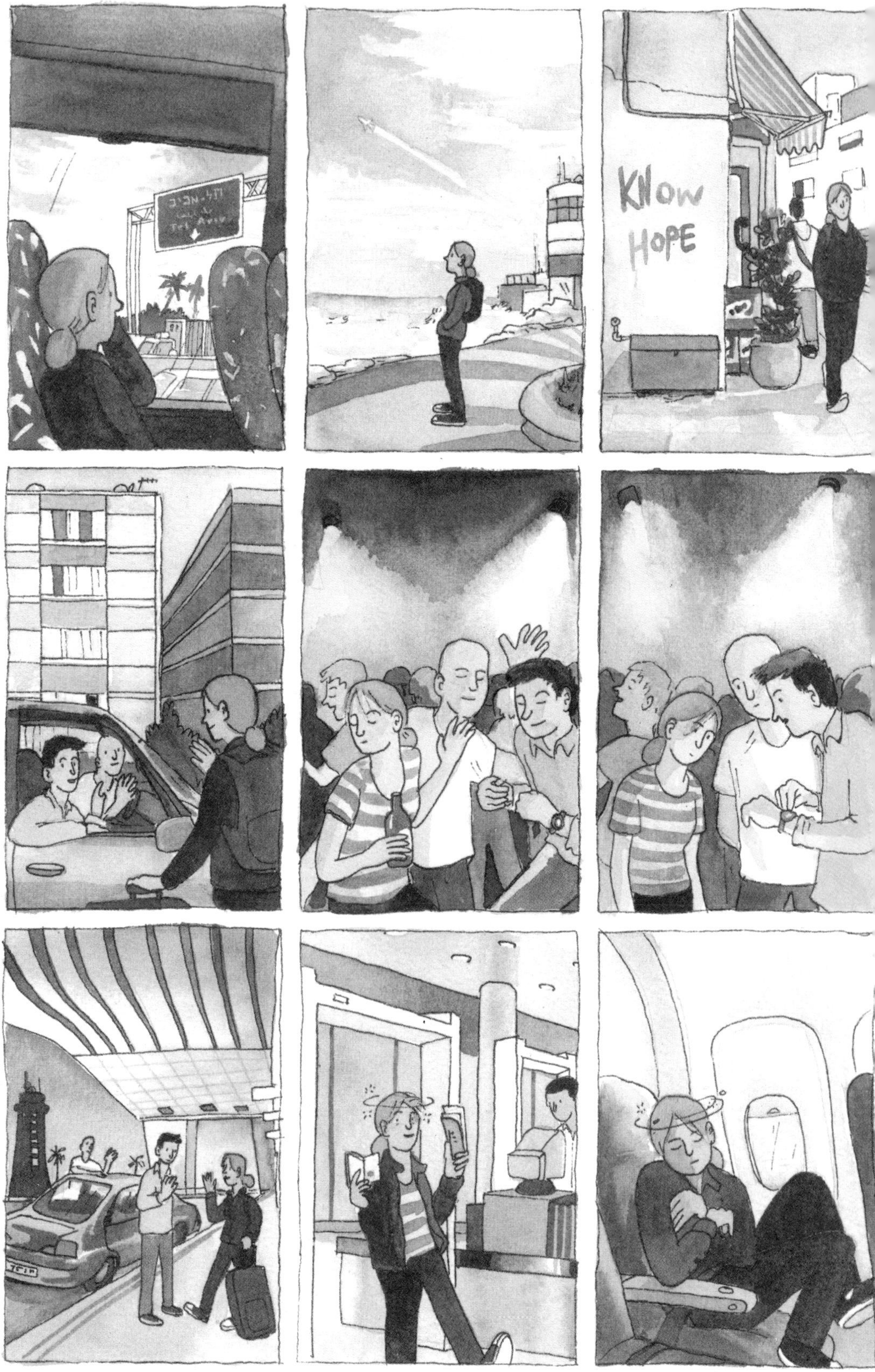
KNOW
HOPE

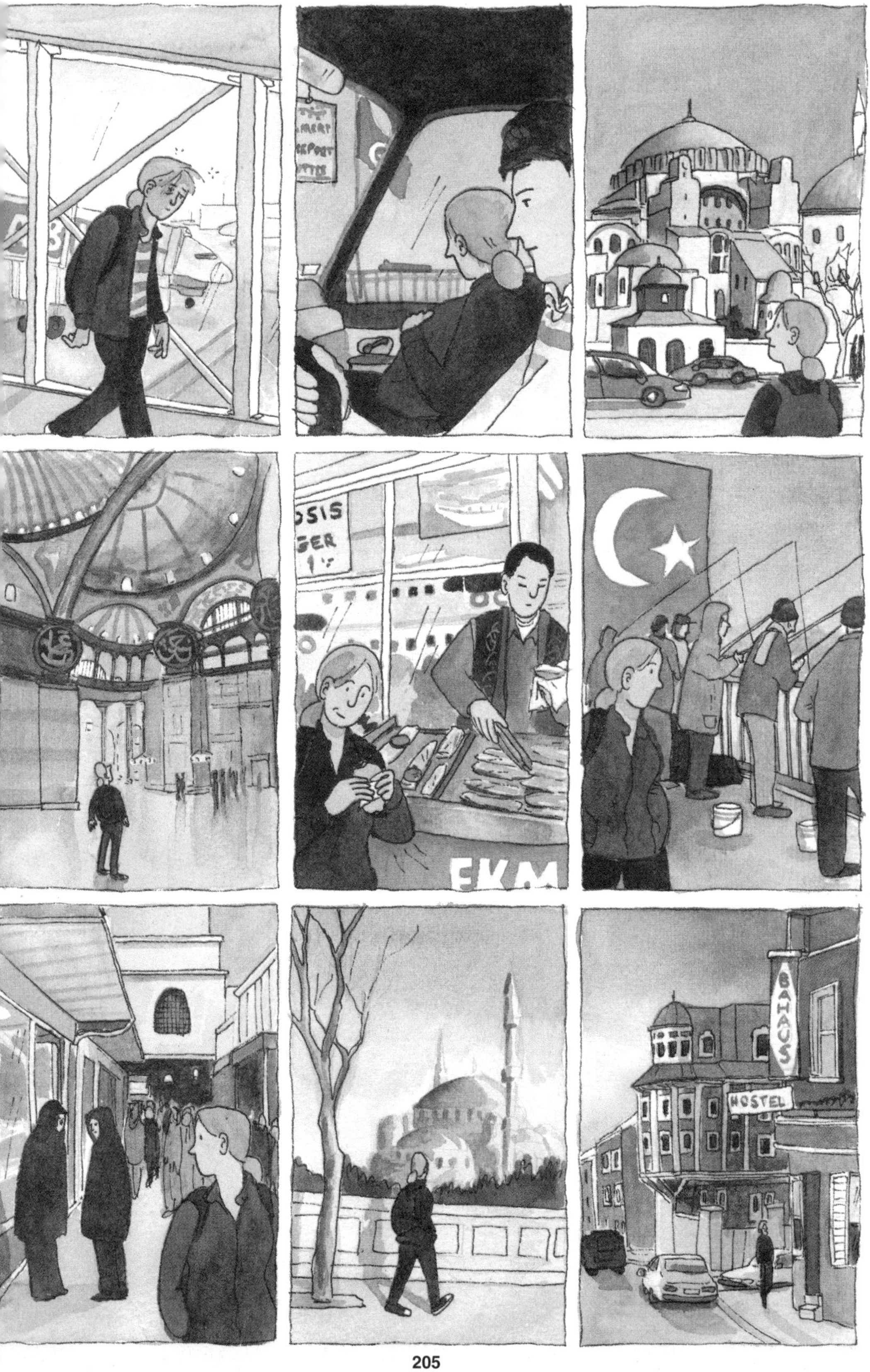
BAHAUS
HOSTEL

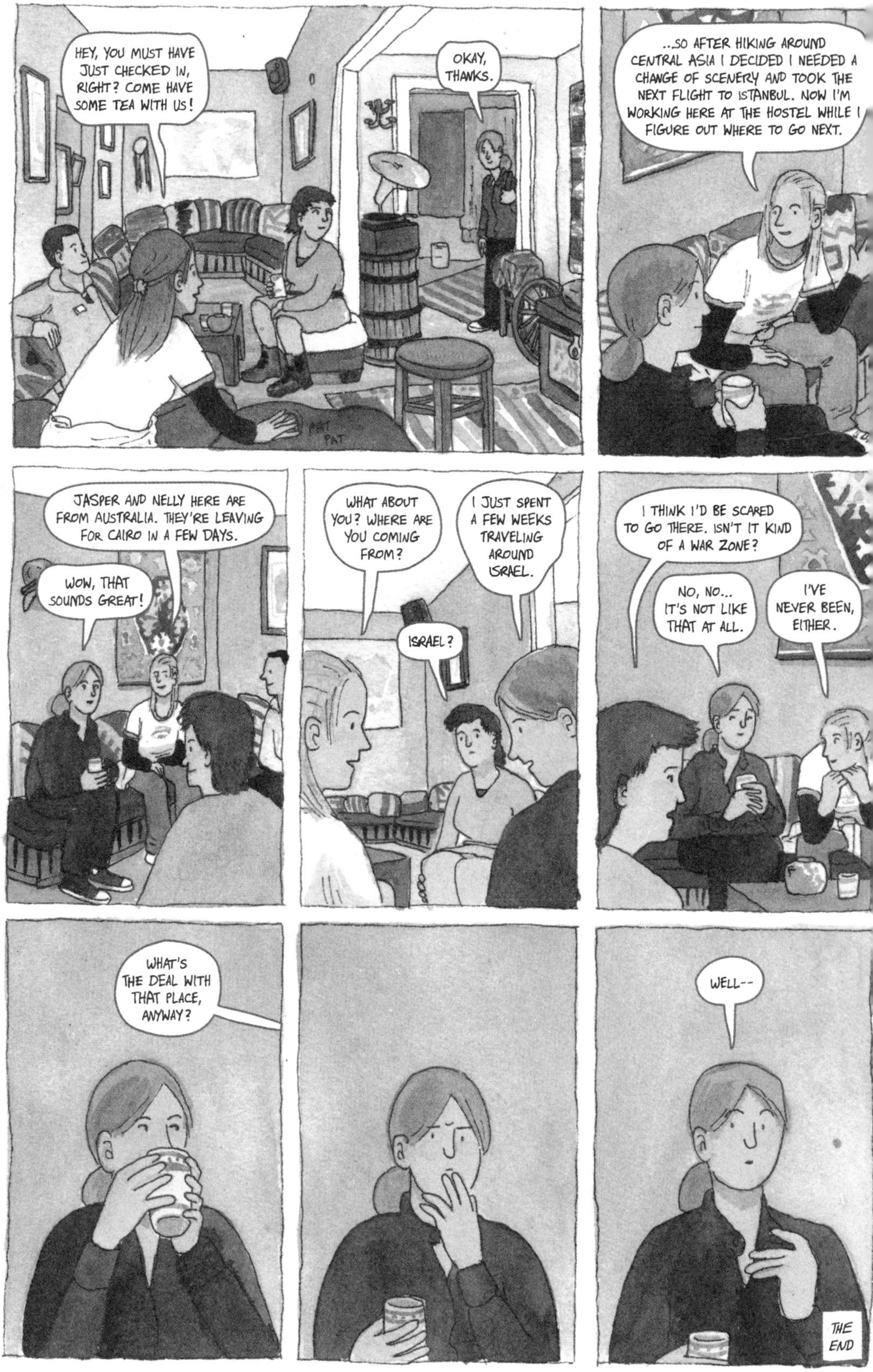
HEY, YOU MUST HAVE JUST CHECKED IN, RIGHT? COME HAVE SOME TEA WITH US!
OKAY, THANKS.
PAT PAT
...SO AFTER HIKING AROUND CENTRAL ASIA I DECIDED I NEEDED A CHANGE OF SCENERY AND TOOK THE NEXT FLIGHT TO ISTANBUL. NOW I'M WORKING HERE AT THE HOSTEL WHILE I FIGURE OUT WHERE TO GO NEXT.
JASPER AND NELLY HERE ARE FROM AUSTRALIA. THEY'RE LEAVING FOR CAIRO IN A FEW DAYS.
WOW, THAT SOUNDS GREAT!
WHAT ABOUT YOU? WHERE ARE YOU COMING FROM?
I JUST SPENT A FEW WEEKS TRAVELING AROUND ISRAEL.
ISRAEL?
I THINK I'D BE SCARED TO GO THERE. ISN'T IT KIND OF A WAR ZONE?
NO, NO... IT'S NOT LIKE THAT AT ALL.
I'VE NEVER BEEN, EITHER.
WHAT'S THE DEAL WITH THAT PLACE, ANYWAY?
WELL--
THE END

GLOSSARY

Aliyah: A Hebrew word which translates to "going up" or "ascent" and refers to the emigration of a Jew to Israel. Israel's "Law of Return" states that any Jew may be granted Israeli citizenship. Aliyah also refers to several waves of emigration to Israel, the first Aliyah taking place at the tail end of the 19th century.

British Mandated Palestine: After the first world war the Ottoman Empire was dissolved and its territories split up by the Allied European forces. Britain took control over the areas then known as Palestine and Transjordan (now Jordan) and remained in control until 1947.

Dreyfus Affair: A political scandal that took place at the end of the 19th century in which a young French-Jewish military officer was accused of spying even after evidence of his innocence surfaced. This signaled to many Western European Jews that they were not as accepted by the rest of society as they had previously believed.

Green Line: The armistice line agreed upon by Israel, Syria, Jordan and Egypt after the war of 1948 in which Israel gained its independence. This line separates Israel from the Gaza Strip, the Golan Heights the West Bank and the Sinai Penninsula, territory that Israel later captured in the war of 1967.

Hamas: Palestinian Islamist group and political party which now governs the Gaza Strip. The original Hamas charter called for eradicating Israel as a Jewish state, and encourages suicide bombings and other means of violent action. Although Hamas still refuses to recognize Israel as a Jewish state, in 2009 a spokesman for the group announced that it would be willing to work towards a two-state peace agreement.

Hasidic Judaism: An Ultra-Orthodox sect of Judaism with origins in the shtetls of Eastern Europe.

Hezbollah: Shi'a Islamist organization based in Lebanon classified by many Western countries, the United States and Israel as a terrorist organization. Hezbollah's mission statement includes the erasure of the state of Israel through violent means.

Intifada: An Arabic word which translates to "uprising" and refers to a mass uprising of the Palestinian population against Israeli occupation. The second Intifada, much more violent than the first, occurred from 2000 to 2005 with a death toll of 5,500 Palestinians and 1,100 Israelis, as estimated by B'TSELEM: The Israeli Information Center for Human Rights in the Occupied Territories.

Kibbutz: A collective community started in Israel in the early 20th century with roots in Zionism and Socialism. A kibbutznik is a member of a kibbutz.

Koenig Memorandum: An internal Israeli report which was leaked to an Israeli newspaper in 1976 and sparked outrage among the Palestinian population. The report suggested ways to reduce the influence of Arab citizens of Israel.

Knesset: Israeli legislative body which operates out of Jerusalem.

T.E. Lawrence: (Made famous by the film *Lawrence of Arabia*) British officer who acted as a liaison and fought alongside those involved in the Arab Revolt against the Ottoman Empire in the years 1916-1918.

Moshe Dayan: Israeli military figure who played a large role in the 1948 war and went on to become Defense Minister during the wars in 1967 and 1973.

Palestinian Authority (PA): Administrative body responsible for the West Bank and, until 2006 the Gaza Strip. Hamas has controlled Gaza since 2006.

Purim: This Jewish holiday commemorates a biblical event in which the Jews living in Persia were saved from an extermination plot by Esther, wife of the King of Persia, who kept her identity as a Jew a secret, and her cousin Mordecai. Purim is celebrated in a carnivalesque fashion which includes costumes. For this reason Americans consider Purim to be "Jewish Halloween."

Yitzhak Rabin: Israeli military commander during the 1948 war who went on to serve two nonconsecutive terms as Prime Minister. He was awarded the Nobel Peace Prize along with Yasser Arafat and Shimon Peres for his role in the signing of the Oslo Accords, and was assassinated in 1995 by Yigal Amir, an Orthodox Jew who was opposed to the peace process.

Rachel the Poet: Also known as Rachel Bluwstein Sela, one of Israel's most famous poets. She was born in Russia and was part of the first wave of Zionist immigrants in the early 20th century.

Shabbat: A weekly ritual practiced by all sects of Judaism which welcomes a day of rest, beginning at sundown on Friday night. Work is forbidden, and this includes driving and the lighting of fire, which means cooking is forbidden. Many Israelis are secular, but hotels and other businesses often keep Shabbat in deference to religious law.

Shiva: A Hebrew word which translates to "seven" and refers to the seven-day mourning ritual. When the family of the deceased is "sitting shiva," they stay at home and follow a variety of bereavement rituals. Friends and relatives visit and bring food to the grieving family.

The White Paper: British policy instituted in 1939 which put limits on how many Jewish immigrants were allowed into British-mandated Palestine.

Compiled by Sarah Glidden.

Bibliography

Agule, Rebecca. "Israel's Bedouin villages struggle for existence." Harvard Law Record Web. 19 Nov 2009. http://www.hlrecord.org/news/israel-s-bedouin-villages-struggle-for-existence-1.937787

Armstrong, Karen. *A Short History of Myth.* Canongate U.S., 2006.

Ben-Yehuda, Nachman. *The Masada Myth.* Univ. of Wisconsin Press, 1995.

Human Rights Watch. *Off The Map: Land and Housing Rights Violations in Israel's Unrecognized Bedouin Villages.* March, 2008. http://www.hrw.org/reports/2008/iopt0308/

Josephus, Flavius, Geoffrey Williamson, and E. Smallwood. *The Jewish War.* Penguin Classics, 1981.

Kushner, Tony and Solomon, Alisa (editors). *Wrestling with Zion: Progressive Jewish-American Responses to the Israeli-Palestinian Conflict.* Grove Press, 2003. (Melanie Kaye essay referenced from this book, Kaye anecdote attributed to Larry Bush.)

McGreal, Chris. "Bedouin feel the squeeze as Israel resettles the Negev desert." Guardian UK 27 Feb, 2003: Web. http://www.guardian.co.uk/world/2003/feb/27/israel.

Tessler, Mark. *A History of the Israeli-Palestinian Conflict.* Indiana University Press, 1994.

Ben Gurion quotations can be found at http://www.palestineremembered.com/Acre/Famous-Zionist-Quotes/Story638.html

A VERY INCOMPLETE TIMELINE OF THE HISTORY OF ISRAEL:

1880s: Over 200 anti-Jewish pogroms take place in Russia and Ukraine.

1894: Dreyfus Affair.

1897: First Zionist National Conference held in Switzerland, led by Theodore Herzl, and states goal to return Jews to Palestine or "Eretz Yisrael" (Land of Israel).

1882-1903: First Aliyah. About 35,000 Jews immigrate to Palestine.

1904-1914: Second Aliyah: about 40,000 Jews immigrate to Palestine.

1917: Balfour Declaration states British government's support for an "establishment of a national home for the Jewish people in Palestine."

1923: British Mandate of Palestine begins after post-WWI breakup of the Ottoman Empire. The British will remain in control of Palestine until 1948.

1936-1939: Arabs in Palestine revolt against British rulers and Jewish immigrants.

1939: British White Paper restricts Jewish immigrants to 75,000 over the following five years.

1939-1945: World War II. During this time approximately 100,000 Jewish refugees secretly entered Palestine to escape Nazis in Europe.

1947: After decades of friction between Jews and Arabs in Palestine, the British announce that they will end their mandate. The UN agrees on a partition plan splitting the land into Jewish and Palestinian states, but this is rejected by Arab leaders. Fighting intensifies between the groups.

1948: Israel declares its independence on the night before the British are set to end their mandate.

1948-1949: War between the Jews and Arabs, called the War of Independence by the Jews and the Nakba (Arabic for "catastrophe") by the Arabs. According to a United Nations estimate, 750,000 Arabs became refugees as a result of the war.

1967: Six Day War in which Israel captures territory now known as the Gaza Strip, the Golan Heights, the Sinai Peninsula and the West Bank, including East Jerusalem.

1973: Yom Kippur War in which Syria and Egypt launch attack on Israel.

1974: Israel begins withdrawal from Sinai Peninsula.

1979: Israel and Egypt sign peace treaty.

1982: Lebanon War in which Israel invades Lebanon to expel the Palestine Liberation Organization. Most Israeli troops are withdrawn by 1985 with Israel Defense Forces troops remaining in the south until the year 2000.

1987: First Intifada begins.

1991: Peace process begins with Madrid Conference in October.

1993: Palestine Liberation Organization Chairman Yasser Arafat and Israel Prime Minister Yitzhak Rabin agree to Declaration of Principles on Interim Self-Government, also known as Oslo Accords.

1994: Israel and Jordan sign peace treaty.

1995: Assassination of Yitzhak Rabin.

2000-2003: Second Intifada.

2005: Israel withdraws unilaterally from Gaza Strip.

2006: Hamas wins in first democratic Palestinian election and assumes poltical control of Gaza. Hamas not recognized as legitimate government by Israel, United States or European Union.

2006: Second Lebanon war, sparked when Hezbollah kills three IDF soldiers and kidnaps two others.

This book takes place in March of 2007.

Compiled by Sarah Glidden.